One Step Further

*Those whose gallantry was rewarded with the
George Cross*

Book L & M

Marion Hebblethwaite

Chameleon HH Publishing

First published in 2006

ISBN-10 0-9546917-7-6
ISBN-13 978-0-9546917-7-6

British Library Cataloguing in Publication Data.
A catalogue record for this book is available from the British Library.

I am most grateful to the copyright holders of all the pictures used on the covers of this book.
They have been designed by Sally Lace.

Chameleon HH Publishing Ltd
The Quarry House, East End, Witney, OX29 6QA
info@gc-database.co.uk
www.gc-database.co.uk

Produced on behalf of the publishers by Robert Boyd Printing and Publishing Services.

CONTENTS

For Julia,

With much love,
In memory of your dad.

Mother

Christmas 2006

See P. 81

for Harriet. She has brought love and fun to our family.

Dedicated to all those who lost their lives in their GC action. This book is also for the families of so many GCs whose names and actions are all but forgotten. May it remind us all.

But the bravest are surely those who have the clearest vision of what is before them, glory and danger alike, and yet notwithstanding go out to meet it.

Thucydides

Now go, write it before them in a table, and note it in a book, that it may be for the time to come for ever and ever.

Isaiah, 30:8

Introduction

Once again I am happy to be writing about another 40 or so men whose bravery was acknowledged to be of the highest order. There are both direct and indirect George Cross recipients in this book but again no women. There are stories that are long forgotten and some that are almost impossible to research, usually due to the wartime restrictions on information. But children and grandchildren who delve into their lofts and drawers as well as old photograph albums and their deepest memories have told me stories which I have endeavoured to relate honestly and accurately. Not all the men who were honoured with the GC were perfect fathers, husbands or colleagues. Indeed few probably were — they were ordinary men and women who did something once or perhaps more than once that makes us feel humble and also proud.

Some notes

Gazette dates. I have often included two dates — the first, if you are looking for a citation on the web, is the date you need to look for even though it may be a Supplement to another edition.
Citations. These are included as published. Spelling mistakes and the rather archaic language are not changed in any way.
Place of death. Although some people died in hospital, perhaps after only a short time there, family members may prefer to have it noted that their GC member died from his/her own home. Thus it may be that there will be some discrepancy in the place of death, giving a home address instead of the actual place of death.
Cause of death. Again, in deference to the families, I have not mentioned the cause of death unless it is a direct result of the GC action, such as drowning, as in the case of **T Kelly GC**, or in exceptional circumstances such as **JGM Turner GC** who died in the Hither Green rail crash in 1967.
Location of medals. This is only mentioned when they are on public display.
Prices fetched for GCs. I do not mention any prices on purpose. From time to time a medal or a group of medals comes up for sale and those who wish to know the price fetched will be able to find this out on the web. However, readers are welcome to phone me for recent information.
GC statistics. As mentioned in a previous book you will not find any rankings of GCs in this series; who was the first police GC, oldest recipient, longest held, etc. This information is on the website and there are many anomalies which would need clarification and much more research to verify absolutely, for instance why was the first awarded not the first gazetted, or who was the first recommended?
Reference to GCs. GC names in other books are in **bold**. Also in bold are contributors to actual entries, sometimes friends, sometimes family, where they have sent in significant information.
Sources. Specific sources for each GC are listed at the end of each entry. A complete set of references will appear in the final volume.
Exchanges. An explanation of these appears in Volume 1.
Index. In this Volume there is only an Index to this book. A complete Index will appear in the final Volume.

Acknowledgements

Due to the constraint of 160 pages may it suffice for me to say that without the help and enormous support of all the people listed within Sources this book would still not be written. Thank you to all those who entertained me to tea or lunch while reminiscing. To Alf Lowe, Bill Moxey, Robin Maxwell-Hyslop, Jocelyne Collis, Mary French and Margaret Liebert a big thank you for all your efforts on my behalf. To the families of John McCabe, Alfred Miles, Dudley Mason, William McCarthy, Joe Lungley, Lionel Matthews, Tommy McTeague, Bill McAloney, Raymond Lewin, Neil McKechnie, Joe Lynch, Walter Lee and Reginald Maltby I extend my warmest feelings of gratitude for I am so glad to have found you all through friends, through newspapers and through a bit of luck. I wish to thank Tom Johnson for proof-reading and checking on all the numbers for me and three special researchers Richard Yielding, Ivor Smith and Sydney Cauveren.

Some notes on truama

Many people are affected by just one traumatic event. The actions for which men and women received the George Cross were almost always traumatic. I thought it would be useful to include a small section on the effects of these experiences on three specific groups of people. There is a particularly good summary of all the different elements at *www.betterhealth.vic.gov.au*.

- The rescuer — who became a George Cross recipient
- The rescued — though of course many died
- The GC's family

GCs fall into two main groups — though there are a few who are outside both such as those who were in PoW camps.

1. Those whose actions took place while at work such as the bomb and mine disposal men, the miners and lifeboatmen. While a number of these GCs died in the action or suffered serious injury many, while facing extreme danger, did not in fact ever become physically or mentally wounded.

2. Those whose actions were quite apart from their normal work such as diving into the sea to save someone, going to the rescue of a pilot in a burning aircraft often with no training or prior experience. These actions usually resulted in grave injury which often lasted a life-time.

   Because of these differences the trauma for the second group appears to have had a more long-lasting effect on the men themselves and on their families. Does it come down to training, personality, counselling?

The rescuer

The following quotes express the emotions of survivors.

"It is those who passed through the horror and the terror and yet lived who have suffered the most". Maria Bath, mother of Capt Bath of HMS *Devonshire* in a letter to Albert Streams — see Maxwell-Hyslop GC.

When **Ernest Kent GC** returned from his awful experience down a pipe trying to save a man's life he went to lie down and when his wife asked him what had happened he said "nothing much".

Joe Lungley was to say, 50 years after the Quetta earthquake, that he was still haunted by the memories and seldom talked about the events that cost thousands of lives.
"I never take a room at the top of a hotel" he said remembering the devastation caused by the earthquake to even quite small buildings.

The two **Farr** brothers were awarded the GC and the GM respectively. Whereas one continued in his job the other left to join the Army. There is speculation that the wrong brother received the GC but neither ever wished to discuss it preferring just to go their separate ways.

Hamish Hay wrote about his father **David Hay GC**
"At one stage, and I think it was after the North African Landings, he was sent home to recuperate from shell shock. For some reason he ended up staying with his Uncle Gif at Yester, the ancestral home in East Lothian which was probably not a good thing at the time. He showed all the classical symptoms of what we now know is PTSD (post-traumatic stress disorder), he was tense, hyper-vigilant, startled by loud noises. I remember someone slamming a car door and he nearly jumped out of his skin. I think that he was expected to join in dinner parties with polite Border society, which was not his thing anyway and especially not at a time like that. He outraged his uncle by going down to the village pub and downing beers with other servicemen, whose experiences he could no doubt identify with. From a psychological point of view this was not only understandable but positively to be encouraged. Sadly, according to my brother Charles, this behaviour cost him his inheritance."

There was often a sense of guilt particularly amongst miners who were used to working as a team and knew also that the work the miners did, day in and day out, was in itself worthy of more recognition. Read **Allsop's** story.

Some reactions are short-lived while others may last a life-time. They could include any one or some of these.

Fear of darkness, water, loud noises
Guilt
Inability to sleep with nightmares
Anger and irritation with others
Anxiety with physical signs such as trembling
Emotional outbursts

Insecurity and difficulty in making decisions
Depression, sadness, tearfulness and withdrawal from conversations
Feeling overwhelmed
These *may* then result in a change of occupation, break-up of relationships, over-strict parenting.

Then there was what happens when the person received the medal. He or she was fêted, written about, perhaps even be offered a contract to write a book, or a film was made of the story. It may have been the first time that there was a little more money coming in — for soldiers, sailors and miners were/are not well paid. The medal itself had a value — some sold their medals early on especially during the Depression when money was short. (For some families of course the medal was all that remained of a son or husband and the photos of **Blaney** and **Fasson's** parents are a reminder of the suffering of the families.) All these changes in a person's life came at a time when he or she was still recovering physically as well as psychologically. We should bear this in mind.

HM The Queen told Johnson Beharry VC that it would be the inner wounds that would take the longest to heal. From all I have heard many never do, completely.

The rescued
The best example of this is Father Arbuthnott in **E Heming GC**'s entry. He wrote about the effects of being buried alive and being rescued in *A Priest's life.*

W Witchell's life was saved by **Pte JH Silk GC** whose action he has described as "sublime heroism".
"He saved me from a peppering of shrapnel by the supreme act he took to sacrifice his own life. Thus to date, he gave me some 62 years of life". Witchell has not only never forgotten, he has lived with the memory ever since in gratitude mixed with sadness.

I would liked to have spoken to **Doreen Ashburnham-Ruffner GC** as her story is somewhat different to most, for she and her cousin, in effect, both saved each other and themselves.

The families
Sheena d'Anvers Willis, sister of **Anthony Fasson GC**, who not only lost a brother but whose other brother, Jim, was captured by the Japanese and taken to the notorious Kinkaseki Camp in Formosa, explained the effect this had on her family and on Jim when he returned.

"My father insisted that we did not talk to my brother about the life endured and events seen by the Eastern PoWs. I think if my brother had talked a bit about it all to put it out of his head he might have felt much better and been able to cope with the terrible nightmares. We only ever talked about our happy past before the war."

During the war there was hardly time to grieve and this may be why so many families years later need to know more.

In one family the recipient took to drink, in another he left his wife, in yet another he sat with his head in his hands remembering the horrors of the fire or bomb damage where he was unable to save a person's life. All these are/were difficult for families to cope with.
Most significant of all is that almost to a man/woman they never talked about the event to their families. Medals were hidden away or just left in a drawer. Only one person I have come across told his work-mates how proud he was to be the wearer of a GC.

Simmon LATUTIN, GC

Self-sacrifice, 29th December 1944, Mogadishu, Somaliland

©*Janet Snowman*
Courtesy Somerset Military Museum

Simmon, Margaret and Anne in 1943.
©*M Liebert*

©*Charles Szlapak*

Status: 242974 Captain, The Somerset Light Infantry (Prince Albert's), seconded to the Somalia Gendarmerie
Life dates: 25th July 1916, St Pancras, London – 30th December 1944, Mogadishu, Somaliland. (There have been quite erroneous mentions in other books that Simmon was cremated.) Simmon was buried in Mogadishu and later moved to Nairobi without any discussion with his wife. In Nairobi War Cemetery the Grave Reference is Plot 1. Grave 3. The War Cemetery is on the south-western outskirts of Nairobi, about 10 kilometres west of the city centre on Ngong Road, which is the main road to the Government Forest Reserve.

Simmon had no obituary. Margaret, his pregnant young wife, was not told of his death for 4 or 5 days. His death symbolises death during conflict. One death is just "one soldier killed" to the public and barely rates a mention in any news bulletin — but to the family it is all. A wife becomes a widow, a single mother, and is left to find work, child-care and, almost inevitably experienced financial hardship. There was the added stress, to use a current expression, of not really knowing what had happened. There was disinformation, there were cover-ups, there were downright lies. Reports were lost and witnesses disappeared.

Biography: Simmon was the only child of Morris and Freda (Krafchig) Latutin. Morris, who had come from Latvia, and whose name at that time was spelt with a V, emigrated to England. In London he married Freda who had herself come from Poland. Simmon grew up in London attending the London Polytechnic from where he won a scholarship to the Royal Academy of Music. He played the violin and later the viola and by 1936 was a member of the London Symphony Orchestra which he entered through an audition in the normal way. In March 1940 he married Margaret Jacob whom he met at the Academy. He was "quite delightful" she remembers. In the Marriage Register his name is incorrectly spelt as Latukin. The couple had two daughters Anne and Elisabeth.

Simmon became a member of the Pioneer Corps and was commissioned as Cadet Simmon Latutin No 242974, 2/Lt, the Somerset Light Infantry on 21st August 1942. He served in Northern Ireland before being posted to East Africa where he commanded an Infantry Training School of Swahili troops from Kenya and taught infantry work to the Somaliland troops.

Despite the intense tropical heat, diseases and general discomfort Simmon, through strength of character and physical fitness, was able to overcome these. His extraordinary mental stamina, honed by hours of practice in music rooms, stood him in good stead for the difficulties of life in East Africa.

Citation: *10th September 1946*

The KING has been graciously pleased to approve the posthumous award of the GEORGE CROSS in recognition of most conspicuous gallantry in carrying out hazardous work in a very brave manner to:-

No 12788 Havildar Abdul Rehman 3/9th The Jat Regiment Indian Army

Captain Simmon Latutin (242974) Somalia Gendarmerie (Harrow, Middlesex).

The Citation as it appeared in *The Times* but not in *The London Gazette.*

On 29th December 1944 a fire occurred at the training school store, Somalia Gendarmerie, Mogadishu, while some Italian rockets and explosives were being taken out destined for another unit about to hold a New Year's entertainment. Captain Latutin, together with one officer, a company sergeant-major, and a personal boy were in this store selecting the explosives, the first-named standing in the main doorway; for some unexplained cause a fire commenced and almost simultaneously a great number of rockets commenced to explode and burn — there were some 170 cases in the store; with the force of the explosion and the fire the store became an inferno of danger. Captain Latutin, regardless of the detonating rockets, the intense heat generated by the fire, and the choking clouds of smoke, plunged into the store-room and succeeded in dragging out the officer, who was almost unconscious owing to his burning injuries. By this time Captain Latutin was himself alight, but without an instant's hesitation he again rushed into this seething holocaust of flames and rescued the company sergeant major, who by this time, owning to the fierce nature of the fire, was quite naked. The body of the boy was later recovered, but was not recognizable owning to the charred condition of his corpse.

The heroism of Captain Latutin was superb as he fully realized the acute danger which he must incur in entering the building, ablaze with explosives and flames; his unquenchable determination to succour the injured is evinced by his second entry into the store, though himself and his clothes already alight. His action was illustrative of the finest degree of British courage and a magnificent example of undaunted selflessness. Captain Latutin died as a result of his injuries on the following day.

Other awards: Defence Medal and War Medal 1939–45, Captain Simmon Latutin's George Cross is currently held, along with that of **JH Silk GC**, in the Somerset Military Museum, Taunton Castle.

©*Somerset Military Museum*

CAPTAIN SIMMON LATUTIN GC
Somerset Light Infantry attached Somalie Gendarmerie
29th December 1944   Mogadishu, Somaliland
A fire broke out in the explosives store of the Gendarmerie Training School and simultaneously a great number of rockets from the 170 cases in the store started to explode and burn. The building quickly became an inferno of danger, trapping its three occupants. Regardless of the detonating rockets, the intense heat and choking smoke, Captain Latutin ran into the building and dragged out an unconscious injured officer. Notwithstanding the fact that his own clothes were now burning, Captain Latutin re-entered the store and rescued a Warrant Officer whose clothes had now been completely burnt off by the intense heat. The body of the third person was recovered later.
Captain Latutin died of his injuries the following day.

The write-up accompanying the photograph and the medals in the Somerset Military Museum ©.

The story

Ministry of Defence Press Notices: 29.12.1944.

A serious fire broke out in a rocket magazine in Mogadishu. Captain Latutin of the Somerset Light Infantry suffered severe burns whilst successfully rescuing two men and attempting in vain to rescue a boy caught in the blaze. Latutin died of his injuries the following day, and was awarded a posthumous George Cross.

Further

The officers, who suggested letting off some rockets for New Year's Eve, were from the Corps of Military Police — the Redcaps. Thus the explosion was not "unexplained" but could perhaps best be described as 'friendly fire'. It was the troops, in training under his supervision, which prevented him from trying to rescue the third victim, rather than, as reported, the danger and excessive heat.

©*Royal Academy of Music*

Memorials: Name on Roll of Honour at the Royal Academy of Music, London. Memorial Gates dome, Constitution Hill, London. Museum of the Association of Jewish Ex-Servicemen and Women of the UK (AJEX) in Hendon. Somerset Regimental Museum, Taunton. Interestingly the Regiment was not told of the award until many years later as Latutin had only been stated as belonging to the Somalia Gendarmerie.

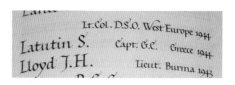

Photo by T Hissey

The VC and GC Memorial Gates and Dome on Constitution Hill in London were built in memory of those nationals who served in either WWI or WWII (but did not necessarily die in them) from the Sub-continent, Africa and the Caribbean as well as those who were attached to Commonwealth Forces in those areas.

Simmon Latutin comes into the second category. There has in fact been some disagreement with the criteria used but perhaps that is always the case with any monument. There are incidences of names left off and postnominals omitted as with Mahoney GC at Plymouth.

One could query why Inayat-Khan, who was not an Indian citizen, is in the list. I leave readers to form their own opinions and welcome their thoughts for additions to the list shown.

Background: *Somalia Gendarmerie and why was Latutin involved?*

In 1941 the British defeated the Italians and formed a British Military Administration (BMA) over British Somaliland, Italian Somaliland, and Ethiopian Somaliland. The BMA disbanded the Corpo Zaptié, the old Somali police corps created by the Italians, and created the Somalia Gendarmerie. By 1943 this force had grown to more than 3,000 men, led by 120 British officers of whom Latutin was one. In 1948 the Somalia Gendarmerie became the Somali Police Force.

After the creation of the Italian Trust Territory in 1950 whereby the United Nations gave the mandate for administration of Somalia to Italy, Italian carabinieri officers and Somali personnel from the Somali Police Force formed the Police Corps of Somalia (Corpo di Polizia della Somalia). In 1958 the authorities made the Corps an entirely Somali force and changed its name to the Police Force of Somalia (Forze di Polizia della Somalia).

Miles and miles of this kind of road faced transports in Somaliland.
From an old colonial newspaper

The East Africa Command and the East Africa Force

The East Africa Command came into being on 15th September 1941 with the purpose of freeing the Commander-in-Chief, Middle East from East African affairs. Essentially an expansion of East Africa Force, the new command comprised Ethiopia, Eritrea (for a short time only), Italian Somaliland, British Somaliland, Kenya, Zanzibar, Tanganyika, Uganda, Nyasaland and Northern Rhodesia. The General Officer Commanding commanded and administered all land forces in this vast area.

Throughout the Second World War, Nairobi was the headquarters of the East African Force and the base for the conquest of Jubaland and Italian Somaliland, the liberation of British Somaliland and the sweep north-westwards to open Addis Ababa for the return of the Emperor. It was also a hospital centre. No. 87 British General Hospital arrived in June 1943 and was still there in December 1945, while No. 150 British General Hospital was there for a period in 1943.

Sources: Margaret Liebert — widow
Martin Sugarman
Somerset Military Museum
Terry Hissey
Janet Snowman of the Royal Academy of Music
The Times
National Archives

Walter Holroyd LEE, GC

Mine rescue, 11th November 1947, Wombwell Main Colliery, Barnsley, Yorkshire

©*Syd Cauveren*

Walter and Elsie Lee at Buckingham Palace.
Courtesy S Vains

Status: Ripper, Wombwell Main Colliery, Barnsley, Yorkshire
Life dates: 29th May 1919, Jump, Barnsley, Yorkshire – 24th May 1984, Wombwell, Barnsley, Yorkshire.
Walter was cremated at Ardsley Crematorium and his ashes scattered in the Garden of Remembrance. **Obit:**
The Times, 9th June, 1984

**Walter and Elsie celebrating 40 years
of marriage.**
Pictures ©S Vains

**Elsie holding granddaughter Alison with
her four daughters Gloria, Pat, Joyce,
Susan and son Brian.**

Biography: Walter was the son of Jack and Kate (Hannigan) Lee. After leaving school, he became a miner at Rockingham Colliery. On the 26th June 1940 he married Elsie Charlesworth and they had four daughters Gloria, Patricia, Susan and Joyce and a son Brian. When the couple married they moved to Wombwell and, due to the poor transport to his old pit, Walter moved over to the Wombwell Main Pit. However, after it closed he moved back to Rockingham Colliery from where he took early retirement not long before the 1984 miners' strike. Those dark days are remembered by his daughter as the family had no coal for fires. Like almost all GC recipients Walter never talked about his award or the action for which he received it.

Wombwell in 1926.
All courtesy M Phillis

Wombwell in 1965.

Wombwell High Street, approx 1930.

Citation: *10th May 1949*
Whitehall, May 4, 1949

The KING has been pleased to award the Edward Medal to Walter Holroyd Lee and to the late George Dorling in recognition of their gallantry in the following circumstances:—

A fall of roof occurred at about 4 p.m. on the 11th November, 1947, at Wombwell Main Colliery, near Sheffield, burying three men. The first rescuer on the scene was a workman, George Dorling, whose calls for assistance attracted a coal-cutter team of three men. Dorling had climbed over the fall in an attempt to reach the trapped workmen and was being followed by the cuttermen when the roof again began to move and a second fall occurred. The cuttermen were just able to withdraw in time but Dorling could not escape and was killed instantly. Shortly afterwards Walter Holroyd Lee arrived on the scene when it was clear from their cries that two of the men trapped by the original fall were still alive. Lee then took the lead in making a way through the fall and after some two hours one of the men was extricated alive. Lee was largely instrumental in saving this man's life and exposed himself to great risks in so doing.

Another medal for pit hero

Other awards: EM (Bronze Mine) – GC exchange named "Walter Holroyd Lee, 194 The presentation of the GC took place on 20th February 1973. Silver Jubilee Me 1977. Walter Lee's George Cross group was sold by Sotheby's on 1st November 19 Walter also received the Carnegie Hero Fund Trust Certificate and £15, the certific being sold with the medals. Walter Lee's Edward Medal is now in Doncaster Museu and Art Gallery, where it is on display in the Coal Mining cases.

*©Doncaster Museum and
Art Gallery*

Background: *Wombwell Main Colliery*
This colliery lay within the South Yorkshire coal-belt close to Barnsley. It closed in 1968.

Doncaster Museum and Art Gallery and Cusworth Park and Museum
While it is believed that Lee's Edward Medal was first donated to Cusworth Park it is now in the hands of Doncaster Museum where it is on display. Doncaster Museum and Cusworth Hall are both part of Doncaster Metropolitan Borough Council. The staff and collections are for Doncaster Museums' Service, not for a specific museum. They both tell the history of Doncaster but Cusworth does it more from the point of view of the people, whereas Doncaster Museum does it more from the civic and archaeological and natural history point of view. Doncaster Museum has a section about the history of mining in the area so that is why the medal ended up there. Cusworth Hall is closed at the moment for refurbishment but it will re-open in 2007.

Sources: Susan Vains — daughter
'Gainst All Disaster by Allan Stainstreet
Doncaster Museum and Art Gallery
Malcolm Wallace — friend
Mark Phillis
Laura Nugent of Cusworth Park and Museum

Raymond Mayhew LEWIN, GC

Air-crash rescue, 3rd November 1940, Malta

Ray Lewin in 1938 beside a Tiger Moth.
Courtesy Aviator Hotel

**We leave him
in God's keeping
The rough road
safely passed**
©Stuart Tamblin

Ray Lewin, the young aviator.

Status: 700404 Sergeant, 148 Squadron (Wellington Flight, Malta), RAFVR

Life dates: 14th January 1915, Kettering – 21st November 1941, Oakington, Cambridgeshire. Raymond is buried in Kettering (London Road) Cemetery, Northamptonshire, Grave Reference: Row 00. Grave 9. John Profumo, then the MP for Kettering, is noted as sending a telegram to the family. **Author's note:** This would not perhaps have been particularly significant were he not subsequently to become a household name.

The Lewin family in 1900. Alfred George, Ray's father is back right with Raymond's grandparents seated in the middle.
©Lewin family

Biography: Alfred Lewin, Raymond's grandfather came from a long line of distinguished Lewins in Kettering. He, following in *his* father's footsteps was an extremely enterprising man owning a great number of businesses ranging from photography (his brother William brought the first magic lantern to the town) to building, grocery, drapers and butcher shops. He was active in setting up the London Road Congregational Church after a break-away from that already in the town in 1892, the Toller Congregational Church. However, his son Alfred George did not have his father's entrepreneural skills but instead married a woman who carried on the name in Kettering to great success.

Alfred George married Clara Frances Mayhew at the parish church in her home town of Stanstead in 1905.

Author's note: This is important as for many years AJEX have considered Raymond to have been Jewish. As his mother, through whom the faith is passed down, was Anglican and all the Lewins for the past three hundred years were not Jewish this information is incorrect and the reason for the error is as yet unclear.

Raymond's birthplace, 167 Rockingham
Road, Kettering.
©R Lewin

COUNCILLOR Mrs. C. F. LEWIN
(Vice-Chairman of the Council)

Ray's mother Clara, 1938.

G & C Lewin van.

Alfred took his bride back to Kettering where they had three sons, Robert, Leslie and Raymond. Clara's obituary is astonishing. She was an Urban Councillor, Chairman of multiple committees, the town's first Deputy Mayor, started the Women's Institute in Kettering as well as setting up the Women's Voluntary Service. Her committment to her adopted town was extraordinary and she was often the first woman to hold the different positions. Meanwhile her husband is described as "running a grocery shop" though it seems that this was a very successful enterprise as he was able to purchase the imposing Stanstead House. Despite her strength of character Clara was known to have 'taken to her bed' when her youngest son was killed.

Raymond joined the ATC at based at Stamford Road School and attended Kimbolton School from 1927-33 as did **Copperwheat GC**. He and his brother Bob flew and kept a biplane at Sywell aerodrome, where he started flying as a member of the Northamptonshire Aero Club on 19th July 1934 and made his first solo flight in DH60-G-ABJT (a De Haviland Moth) on 5th September 1934. Raymond was one of the original members of the club under the instruction of Flt Lt Tommy Rose who went on to become a test pilot.

After leaving school Ray went to work for Boots where he trained as a pharmacist, first at the Kettering Branch then in London. One day, exhibiting the business skills of his forebears, he told his brother how he had analysed the consituents for lemonade — and that they should go into business as the ingredients were quite inexpensive and great profits could be made. The war put an end to all that.

Raymond passed his flying test for the RAFVR on 21st January 1936 and enlisted in Spring 1936 (Class F Reserve). By the time war broke out he had logged 103 hours on such aircraft as the Tiger Moth, Audax, Hart and Hawker Hind. He then commenced training on multi-engined aircraft and after flying 100 hours on Airspeed Oxfords commenced training on Vickers Armstrong Wellington Bombers on 16th January 1940. His operational career began in May 1940 with No 38 Squadron at Marham. His commission was announced in *The London Gazette* on 11th April 1941 as "700400 Sergt. R M Lewin to be Pilot Officer (62254) effective 15.3.41 (seniority 27.1.41)."

After his GC Action Raymond came back from Malta to recuperate from schrapnel wounds. He was soon pronounced 'fit for duty' and was flying aboard Wellington Ic (serial T2552) of 109 Squadron piloted by Flight Lieutenant Brendan P Hennessey, when it crashed trying to land at Oakington, Cambridgeshire. All aboard were killed. When we take note of Raymond Lewin's flying experience the loss is even greater for it took hundreds of hours to achieve his level of expertise. He flew 27 operations from May until September 1940 against targets in Germany and France.

Author's note: The numbers 700400 above and 700404 below are as per the *Gazette*.

Citation: *7th March 1941*
11th March 1941

The KING has been graciously pleased to approve the award of the GEORGE CROSS to: -
700404 Sergeant Raymond Mayhew Lewin, Royal Air Force.

In November, 1940, Sergeant Lewin was the captain of an aircraft on a night bombing mission. Shortly after the take-off the aircraft began to sink and crashed into a hillside where it burst into flames. Sergeant Lewin extricated himself and saw three of his crew of four climbing out of the escape hatch. He ordered them to run clear. He then ran round the blazing wing in which full petrol tanks were burning and crawled under it to rescue his injured second pilot. Despite his own injuries — a cracked kneecap and severe contusions on the face and legs — he dragged and carried the pilot some 40 yards from the aircraft to a hole in the ground, where he lay on him just as the bombs exploded. This superbly gallant deed was performed in the dark under most difficult conditions and in the certain knowledge that the bombs and petrol tanks would explode.

Other awards: 1939–45 Star, Air Crew Europe Star, Defence Medal and War Medal 1939–45. The group was sold on 21st July 1998 by Spink.

The story

Sgt Lewin, pilot of Wellington (serial R1094), took off heavily laden with bombs, from Luqa airfield on Malta just before midnight on 3rd November 1940. The aircraft refused to gain height, crashed and burned at Tal-Handaq. An eye-witness account from *The Times of Malta*.

The bomber, a Wellington, had just taken off during the night on a bombing mission when it crashed into the hillside at Tal-Handaq. On the top of the hill was a heavy anti-aircraft gun position which I was then commanding. Immediately after a small group of gunners from my troop with our two stretchers were detailed to proceed to the scene of the crash which was well lit up by the exploding ammunition and pyrotechnics sending up coloured streaks of light.

Map showing the position of Tal-Handaq and of Luqa. The Malta International Air show now takes place at the airfield at Luqa.

Going down the steep hillside which forms part of Wied il-Kbir was no joke and the bullets whistling past in all directions did not make it any funnier.

We found Sergeant Lewin and the co-pilot whose condition was desperate. Slowly they were brought up the steep rocks on stretchers to the gun position. Sergeant Lewin was placed on my camp bed and given the best first-aid we could ... Sometime later the RAF ambulance men arrived and they found the co-pilot laid on a table with a few candles around him which some reverent gunners had lit. Sergeant Lewin was removed from my bed conscious ... that was the first and last time I saw him.

I hope he survived the war.

Yrs truly

©*RF Jacono*

Malcolm Barrass of the Air of Authority website told me

Malta — The Hurricane Years indicates that the two other pilots killed that night were Plt Off David Ross Allen and Sgt David Pryce Rawlings (although his death is given as 4th November 1940 on CWGC site), both of No 148 Sqn.

Apparently two Wellingtons of 148 Squadron crashed on take-off that night, Lewin's being the first (second aircraft to take off), in which most of the crew got out except the co-pilot. Having rescued the co-pilot, he then found that he was dead. The second aircraft to crash was the fourth to take off and it crashed into a stone quarry and only one crew member was rescued but died later. Both pilots in the second aircraft were killed. Allen and Pryce could have been the two pilots from the second aircraft or one of them could have been Lewin's co-pilot.

Memorials: Association of Jewish Ex-Servicemen and Women Military Museum in Hendon, London erroneously — see note above. No 1101 (Kettering & District) Squadron Air Training Corps presents the Raymond Lewin Cup for the best Group Achievement. This could for instance be in the field of civic service, or sports however, it is not necessarily awarded each year as there has to be a significant achievement of a high enough merit to warrant presentation. At RAF Marham there was, for a short while, a display in memory of Raymond and also at 148 Squadron. In Valletta Museum, Malta there is a further memorial. The portrait illustrated above hangs above the bar of the Aviator Hotel at Sywell aerodrome.

The display that was at RAF Marham.

The Raymond Lewin Cup.
©*Flt Lt Liz Kerr*

Lewin's medals.
Location withheld

Ray's nephew and family historian Reg Lewin and his wife Pam on the Isle of Wight 2006.
©R Lewin

Background: *Kettering ATC at Stamford Road School*

February 1941 saw the formation of the Kettering and District Air Training Corps. The cadets were teenagers, learning to fly, navigate and observe, etc. The meetings took place at Stamford Road School and the cadets paraded and took instruction in the school. There was a close association with RAF Wittering but soon other aerodromes were also to be connected with the Corps including Sywell and Desborough. Now in 2006 the Corps includes girls and the headquarters has been permanently established since 1955.

Sources: Stuart Tamblin

Brian Oram

John Lewin — great-nephew

Reg Lewin — nephew

Northamptonshire Advertiser

Flt Lt Liz Kerr of 1101 (Kettering & District) Squadron ATS

Geoff Coles

Roy Wood — Aviator Hotel

RAF Marham

The Pathfinder Cranswick by Michael Cummings

Britain's wonderful airforce edited by Air Commodore PFM Fellowes DSO

Evening Telegraph

Malcolm Barrass

Wellington bomber.

16

Robert Stead (Bob) LITTLE, GC

Industrial rescue, 11th January 1939, British Dyestuffs Corporation Ltd, Blackley, Manchester

AUGUST 1939

Mr. Robert Little leaving St. James's Palace
After receiving the Edward Medal.
Courtesy ICI and Catalyst

Status: Process worker, British Dyestuffs Corporation Ltd — part of Imperial Chemical Industries, Blackley, Manchester

Life dates: 14th November 1897, Bradford – 31st May 1976, Wallasey, Cheshire. Robert was cremated at Landican Crematorium on 7th June 1976 and his ashes scattered in Bed 21.

Biography: Robert was the son of Robert and Mary Jane (Stead) Little, he had four siblings. His father was a provision dealer. Bob attended Birley Street School. He served with the Lancashire Fusiliers in WW1 as Private No 19786, enlisting on 29th May 1915 and being discharged on 12th December 1918. He was first employed at Levenstein Blackley Works in January 1919 and worked there until 16th November 1962 (some books say 1963). Most of this time was spent in the Thionol Department working on Sulphur Blocks and Colours and Chlorazol Colours. On his retirement he was presented with a Long Service Certificate, a radio, an electric razor and bathroom scales.

Robert's wife's name is sometimes given as Edith and other times as Jessie.

Citation: *5th May 1939*

Whitehall, April 19, 1939.

His Majesty The KING has been graciously pleased to award the Edward Medal to Robert Stead Little, in recognition of his gallantry in the following circumstances: —

On the 11th January, 1939, a fitter engaged on repairs in a chemical reaction pan at the works of the British Dyestuffs Corporation at Blackley, Manchester, fell into the pan. Little, who was in charge of the shift, was called and while rescue apparatus was being brought, he descended into the pan at great risk to himself and carried his unconscious fellow-worker up the ladder. Unfortunately, however, another man who had started to go down the manhole collapsed on the top of Little and the rescued man, knocking them both to the bottom where all three remained unconscious. The rescue party then arrived and brought them to the surface. Two of them were dead, but Little recovered.

On pursuing the Michigan link no museum so far has been able to confirm acquisition of the medal.
Courtesy ICI

Other awards: EM (Bronze Industrial) – GC exchange. The Edward Medal was presented in July 1939 and the GC on 20th February 1973. Carnegie Hero Fund Trust Certificate with a monetary reward. ICI Medal for Bravery (12th May 1939, as recorded in the *ICI Magazine* of June 1939), 1914–15 Star, British War Medal and Victory Medal. The GC was sold at Spink in 1984 to Max Brail. In early 1992 the other bravery medals came up for sale at Christie's. Extensive searches have been done in a number of Michigan museums by a friend of Brail's to track down Little's medal but to no avail.

Letter from Max Brail re the GC.
©ME Brail

At first Max Brail was not sure of the GC's authenticity and was in fact told by a researcher in London that it was not genuine. However, further research by Spink published in their *Numismatic Circular* confirmed that it was.

The story

Little was working on the Thionol Plant in Blackley. The two men had been overcome by poisonous gas in a wrought-iron reaction vessel/pan which formed part of the sulphur black plant. It was out of commission at the time. Wilfred J Martin, the fitter, had collapsed at the bottom of the vessel.

Foreman Harry Davies then takes up the story as he

Robert S. Little, a process worker, who was working on the stage outside the building, was informed that Martin had collapsed and at once sent for further assistance. Little thereupon covered his mouth and nose with two handkerchiefs saturated with water and descended, through the manhole, down the ladder to the bottom of the reaction pan to Martin's assistance. He found Martin's head trapped between the blades of the agitator and the heating coils. He disengaged Martin and was in the act of carrying him to safety up the ladder when William Wynne, an engineering labourer, coming also to the rescue (but unfortunately without any precautions against gassing), was descending the same ladder. Wynne appears to have become affected with gas almost immediately he entered the pan, and fell headlong down the ladder, knocking both rescuer and rescued off the ladder again into the bottom of the reaction vessel.

entered the pan and quickly examined the three men. He noticed Little was moving and removed him from the pan first, thus saving his life. He entered the pan on two further occasions, bringing out the remaining two men, Martin and Wynne, who unfortunately were dead. These three, Foreman Harry Davies, Process Worker Robert S. Little and Engineering Labourer William Wynne exhibited great personal bravery and sublime unselfishness, and the Blackley Works Council therefore recommended to the Board of I.C.I. (who have agreed) that they should be given the Company's bravery award. The Council, I think, will be pleased to learn also that His Majesty the King has awarded to Mr. Little the Edward Medal for gallantry. (Great applause.)

©ICI Magazine June 1939

The hearing

At the Coroner's Court in Blackley the story was told, witnesses were called and the cause of the accident identified as a leak of gas through a faulty valve in the pipe. A suction machine drew the fumes out of the four pans passing them down the pipe to be treated. A series of valves controlled this and when a pan was not in use the others went on working. A chemist, A W Burger, told how the vessel had been cleaned out and tested for the presence of gas with a "*mouse in a cage which had been in the pan (vessel) suspended three feet from the bottom. The mouse was breathing normally and active*". The test of the valves was done on both previous days, the Monday and Tuesday and again on Wednesday morning the day of the accident.

The Coroner asked, "If fumes had been present what would have happened to the mouse?"

Burger replied "It would have died."

Robert Little stated when called, "*On Wednesday morning the last time I inspected the machine was 10.30 and everything was in order then. The valves had not needed any alteration, and they were not altered. I did not notice any gas coming from the top of the manhole s... When I saw Martin at the bottom I asked Jack Whalley, another fitter, for a handkerchief, and, with my own, wrapped it round my face. I entered the pan and released Martin's head which was underneath part of the machine. I came up again for a breather and then went back. Someone was coming towards the pan. I lifted Martin up on to my shoulder as well as I could. When I got him to the bottom of the ladder someone was coming down. The man coming down collapsed three or four rungs from the bottom and put us all back where we started. I do not remember anything more.*"

Conclusion

Two men had died of sulphuretted hydrogen — a deadly gas. The jury were advised to return a verdict of 'accidental death' in the case of Martin and 'death from misadventure' for Wynne. The jury complied and added, "*We also recommend that during the period of repairs the weak point in the system, which is the drive in the belt, should be watched*".

Background: *dyestuffs* — when the color of a substance is deposited on another substance in an insoluble form from a solution containing the colorant it is said to be a dye.

Thionol — a red or violet dyestuff having a greenish metallic luster. It is produced artificially by the chemical dehydration of thionine as a brown amorphous powder.

Chlorazol — a black dye for staining fungi and some human tissues to make them visible under a microscope.

Sulphur dyes — sulphur dyes have been generally regarded as those dyes which are applied to the fibre by the aid of the alkaline sulphides, the most common, and, in fact, the sulphide of universal use is the well-known sodium sulphide of commerce. There are two main ways to manufacture sulphur dyes.

1. Baking, roasting or so-called dry fusion process producing Sulphur Browns, Sulphur Tans and Crutches and Sulphur Yellows of the redder shades.

2. Wet fusion process, producing Sulphur Blacks, Sulphur Navy, Sky and Brilliant Blues, Sulphur Bordeaux and Sulphur Green.

A man working next to the vats in the Blackley plant.

The offices and sheds of the Blackley plant.
Photos courtesy of Avecia Limited

Man in the Blackley works.

Inside the Dianol shed.

The Blackley works sheds.

ICI

ICI came into being in 1926 after a merger which included British Dyestuffs Corporation Ltd (BDC). It was the brainchild of Sir Alfred Mond and Sir Harry McGowan. There were two main divisions, chemicals and explosives. Until the 1930s BDC was seen as the poor relation of the group and, though it had a strong research team, the company in Blackley was poor compared to other plants in the country. However, all was to change in the 30s when organic synthesis took over from the nitrogen industry. Its success was aided by the extension of the Dyestuffs Act and by the Cartel Agreement of 1932 which allowed them to compete equably with Germany and Switzerland. Blackley not only made dyes but also had laboratories for testing such products as rubber.

Sources: *The Times*
Josephine Banks — *ICI*
Eric S. Perkins, Michigan Historical Museum
Middleton & Blackley Guardian
ICI Magazine and *Hexagon Courier*
www.coloranthistory.org

Dr Lisa White
Paul Meara
Bridget Hall of Avecia Ltd
Imperial Chemical Industries, A History by WJ Reader
Local Heroes by James W Bancroft
Tom Johnson

William (Bill) LlOYD, GC

Industrial rescue, 3rd October 1927, Quibell Brothers Ltd., Newark-on-Trent, Nottinghamshire

©*Leanne Shaw*

Status: Sub-foreman, Quibell Brothers Ltd., Newark-on-Trent, Nottinghamshire

Life dates: 6th March 1905 West Derby (this has still to be verified) – 16th June 1978, Newark, Nottinghamshire. Bill was 73 when he died. The funeral took place at St Mary Magdalene, Newark Parish Church on 20th June 1978 and he and his wife share Grave 412, West Row B in Newark Cemetery. **Obit:** *Daily Telegraph* 20th June 1978

Biography: Too young for WWI Bill first went to work in the drawing office at Ransome & Marles Ltd (which became Ransome Hoffman Pollard — RHP) which produced ball bearings. However, most of his life was spent as the Licensee of two pubs, the Watermill (from 1946, owned by James Hole & Co) and later Spring House (1957–73 also a James Hole & Co pub), in Newark. He also owned Bill Lloyd's Fishing Shop in Castlegate, Newark.

Though a personable man it was well known that Bill's wife Ireena Doris (Green), known always as Dolly, "did all the work" in the pub. Bill was a keen golfer being a member of the Newark golf club. He was also known to be quite an obstreperous man though those who were his friends got on well. His friend **Barry Wright** recalls how Bill was quick to call the police one day when his automatic car had disappeared from ouside his home only to find that he had left the handbrake off and it had rolled down the street!

He was also keen on rifle shooting and though not an angler was a member of the Piscatorial Federation through his fishing shop.

As Bill died intestate and as his wife had died, his brother George became his heir. Bill had at least two brothers and two sisters.

Citation: *9th December 1927*

His Majesty The KING has been graciously pleased to award the Edward Medal to William Lloyd and Frank Boot, employed by Messrs. Quibell Brothers Limited, Nottingham, in the following circumstances:—

On the night of the 3rd October, 1927, a man named Taylor was engaged in attending, at the works of Messrs. Quibell Brothers Limited, a grease extracting plant used for extracting grease from bones by means of petroleum benzine. Noticing that benzine vapour was escaping from the extractor through the lid which had been incorrectly left open he endeavoured, with the help of a fellow workman, to close the lid. The fellow workman was affected by the fumes and on the suggestion of Taylor left the room. On recovering and finding later that Taylor had not followed him he gave the alarm. William Lloyd, a sub-foreman of the works, who was not on duty but was passing the works on his way home, hearing that Taylor was in the building, put a scarf round his mouth and ran to the upper floor of the building where he found Taylor lying unconscious near the lid of the extractor. He succeeded in dragging Taylor down three steps to a lower floor but was himself overcome, and collapsed, and was later taken out of the building by other men. Frank Boot, the foreman of the works, who was not on duty but had been summoned from his home, meanwhile arrived at the works, and having put a handkerchief round his mouth went into the building where he found Taylor in the position in which Lloyd had left him.

Boot then dragged Taylor to a point where other men could reach him, but he himself became affected with the fumes. Lloyd and Boot in rescuing Taylor, displayed a high degree of courage. It was stated in evidence at the inquest on Taylor, who did not survive, that at the time of the rescue the building was full of benzine fumes and that a cloud of fume was also visible outside the building. Apart from the risk of suffocation there was the exceptionally serious risk of an explosion, and both men were well aware of these risks. The Coroner and the Jury spoke in the highest terms of the bravery shown by Lloyd and Boot and asked that it should be recognised.

Other awards: EM (Bronze Industry) – GC exchange. William Lloyd also received a Carnegie Hero Fund Certifcate for his EM action. 1977 Queen's Silver Jubilee Medal. The GC was presented by HM The Queen on 20th February 1973. Boot did not live to exchange his EM for the GC.

Background: *Quibell Brothers*

Mr. James Snow, a Chemist, originally founded the Company in 1814. John Harvey joined with James Snow and the business traded as Snow & Harvey until the 1850's. William Oliver Quibell was articled to John Harvey and eight years later in about 1855 became a partner in the business, which from about 1860 traded as Harvey & Quibell. After John Harvey's death, William's brother Thomas Oliver Quibell joined the firm and the business traded as Quibell Bros.

British Glues and Chemicals acquired this Newark family glue-making business in 1920. The name Quibell, however, continued to be used for trading purposes until as late as the 1960s. Quibell's glue factory was located beside the Trent close to the old Bottom Lock, some distance off Winthorpe Road. Part of the premises survive to this day. Glue was made by extracting grease from bones using petroleum benzine. The name Quibell is still found today on chemical products such as pesticides and fertilisers.

A model Quibell Brothers railway wagon.

A blue Quibell's bottle for infallible disinfectant. Poisons were nearly always sold in blue bottles.

piscatorial — to do with fishing or angling, a club for anglers or those connected therewith

Spring House pub, Newark

This public house opened in 1832 and is still a selling hand-pumped beer. It is situated on Farndon Road and if you should visit it do mention you read about its famous publican in this book.

Courtesy John Marrison

Sources: George Quibell   John Marrison
Barry Wright — friend   Leanne Shaw
Mark Wells of the Spring House Pub   *www.newarkadvertiser.co.uk/warner/warner44.htm*

George LOCK, GC

Industrial accident rescue, 8th October 1925, Oxford Street, London

DEATH		Entry No. 152

Registration district Colchester

Sub-district Colchester   Administrative area County of Essex

1. Date and place of death Tenth June 1974.
Lime Court. Lime Avenue
Dovercourt. Harwich

2. Name and surname George Lock   3. Sex male

4. Maiden surname of woman who has married ———

6. Date and place of birth 15th march 1892
London.

Extract from George's death certificate.

Status: Leading hand, steelwork erector employed by Dorman Long & Co. Ltd

Life dates: 15th March 1892, Chelsea, London – 10th June 1974, Colchester, Essex. George was buried on 18th June in Dovercourt Cemetery, Grave 788. There is no headstone. George's name is often spelt incorrectly as Locke.

Biography: There is only one George Lock aged 9 listed in London on 31st March 1901 when the Census was taken. He was living in Kensal Green with his father Horatio, mother Martha, two sisters (one of whom was married), a brother and a nephew. His father was a general labourer at the time. There was no George Locke born in London in 1892 so the e used in the Citation is erroneous as is corroborated on his death certificate.

Citation: *2nd March 1926*

Whitehall, February 25, 1926

His Majesty The KING has been graciously pleased to award the Edward Medal to George Locke (*sic*), leading hand of steelwork erectors, employed by Messrs. Dorman Long and Company Limited, in the following circumstances:—

On October 8th, 1925, Locke was engaged in the erection of steel work for the rebuiliding of the premises of Messrs. Bourne & Hollingsworth in Oxford Street. He and another workman named Frederick Dowser were standing on parallel girders on the fourth floor level when Dowser tripped and fell, striking his head in his fall and lying stunned on the girder. The girders on which the men were working were only 7 inches in width and were no less than 7 feet apart. Locke, on seeing his comrade fall, with great presence of mind immediately leapt across the intervening space and throwing himself upon the legs of the fallen man pinned him to the girder until help arrived and they were dragged back to safety. But for Locke's prompt action there is little doubt that Dowser would have fallen to the ground and been killed. Locke's action was a very brave one and he showed total disregard of his own safety. To spring from one girder to the other at a great height was no small feat and he must have recognised, in holding down his comrade that any struggle on the latter's part must endanger the lives of both.

Other awards: EM (Bronze Industry) – GC exchange. Sadly George Lock died about a month before he was due to be invested with his exchange GC. However, it was presented to his next of kin. He also received the Carnegie Hero Fund Medal for Bravery and a gold watch from his employers.

The story

In the *Evening News* of 5th January 1974 Lock described the events.

"I was the foreman at the time and he (Dowser) was the erector. We were 4 floors up walking on parallel steel girders about 7 feet apart when he slipped and fell. He was lying across the girder and I jumped over from my girder and held on to him until the other lads helped us."

Background: *Bourne & Hollingsworth*
One of the iconic department stores of Oxford Street, London which is sadly no more. The Plaza shopping centre now occupies the site. From one store selling everything to multiple stores selling most things.

Bourne & Hollingsworth Department Store, Oxford Street.

Sydney Harbour Bridge taken on Sunday 13th February 2005 aboard round-the-world yacht race winners BG Spirit as they crossed the finish line in first place, by crew member Dr Lisa White.

Dorman Long & Co
Best known for its bridge building, this large constructural engineering company built the Tyne Bridge which opened in 1928, the Sydney Harbour Bridge in 1932, and was part of the consortium which built the Cleveland Bridge in the late 1950s. However, the Company also undertook large-scale building work such as the Bourne & Hollingsworth Department Store.

Sources: *Evening News*
Dr Lisa White
Paul Markham at Glengate Holdings

John Niven Angus LOW, GC

Self-sacrifice in submarine, 29th April 1940, North Sea

©*Royal Navy Submarine Museum*

Status: Lieutenant, H.M. Submarine *Unity*, Royal Navy

Life dates: 25th (Ipswich School says 20th) August 1910, Tendring, Essex – 29th April 1940, North Sea **Obit:** *The Times*, 18th May, 1940

Biography: John was the eldest son of Captain William Augustus John and Annie Cook (Snowball) Low, of Dovercourt. John's father was a Trinity pilot and the family lived in Harwich. He attended Ipswich School from 1922–25 where he was a good all-rounder on the sports fields and on the water though his interests were many and varied. He left to train on HMS *Worcester* for the Merchant Navy when he was 14 on 7th May 1925 leaving on 14th April 1927 as a 1st Class Cadet Captain.

By the 1920s HMS *Worcester* was berthed off the village of Greenhithe with the shore base at Ingress Abbey. It had been founded in 1862 as the Thames Nautical Training College for the training of pre-sea young men who were seen to have the potential to become officers. Most joined the Merchant Navy though a percentage always went into the Royal Navy until the outbreak of war when the percentages were reversed. The College closed in 1968.

Stephen Rabson of the National Maritime Museum found Low's records.

JNA Low joined the New Zealand Shipping Company, rather than P&O and it appears from the NZSCo records that he did this from another shipping company, Kaye Sons & Co Ltd rather than direct from *Worcester*. Kaye's had no link with NZSCo or P&O.

01.12.30 Low joined NZSCo as 4th Officer in Cambridge, later served on *Otaio*, *Remuera*, *Hororata*, *Somerset* and *Kent* as well as some periods on dock office duty, some on sick leave (he hurt his back falling overboard in November 1932 and the injury continued to trouble him, and he also contracted chickenpox) and some with the RNR, although the last is not mentioned before June 1934 (drill) and August 1935 (leave).

The record shows that he passed his 2nd Mate's certificate on 22nd April 1930 and his 1st Mate's on 6th July 1932. He was promoted Third Officer on 1st April 1933 (acting from 10th February) and resigned on 15th July 1936.

There is *no* mention in the P&O records of him having served with the company as is often reported.

30.9.32 Probationary Sub-Lieutenant (RNR)

25.8.34 promoted Lieutenant (RNR)

1.11.35 joined Submarine Service — Lieutenant (RNR) Submariner Course at HMS *Dolphin*

14.6.36 joined HM Sub *Sturgeon* (6th Flotilla, Portland)

19.4.37 joined HM Sub *L54*; transferring from RNR to RN as a Lieutenant

1.10.37 joined HM Sub *Seahorse* (2nd Flotilla, Portland)

22.5.38 joined HM Sub *Narwhal* (2nd Flotilla, Devonport)

14.4.39 joined HM Sub *Unity* (operating from Portsmouth) as second-in-command, working from the Depot Ship HMS *Titania*. *Unity* moved to HMS *Elfin* in Blyth in December 1939. Low was the First Lieutenant.

He married Margery Russell-Walling of Mayfield, Dundee who was a 3rd Officer, W.R.N.S.

Citation: *16th August 1940* **Author's note:** This is also Henry Miller's story, later in this book.

The KING has been graciously pleased to approve of the following posthumous Awards for gallantry in one of H.M. Submarines: —

The Medal of the Military division of the Most Excellent Order of the British Empire, for Gallantry.

The late Lieutenant John Niven Angus Low, Royal Navy, H.M. Submarines.

The late Able Seaman Henry James Miller, P/J-55387, H.M. Submarines.

Other awards: EGM (Military) – GC exchange. 1939–45 Star, Atlantic Star and War Medal 1939–45. The exchange took place on 23rd April 1948.

The story

On 29th April 1940 the submarine *Unity* on patrol duty in the North Sea, was in collision in the dark with the Norwegian freighter *Atle Jarl,* and sank a few minutes later. Lieutenant Low and Able Seaman Miller were the two men on duty in the submarine control room. When the order to abandon ship was given by the submarine's Commander they were instrumental in helping every member of the submarine to escape — except themselves.

Further

Submarine *Unity* was laid down on the 19 February 1937, launched 16th February 1938 and commissioned the following August. Just nine days before her final voyage, Lt Francis Brooks had taken over command. HMS *Unity* had put to sea from Blyth at 1730 hrs on the 29th April 1940. Sailing on the surface, by 1830 visibility was down to 100 yards due to a heavy mist closing in. At 1907 a prolonged blast of a ship's siren at 50 yards was heard on *Unity's* bridge. Neither vessel was aware of the other until the submarine spotted the Norwegian freighter *Atle Jarl*, sailing from Methil in Fife for Tyne. There was just time to shut the bulkhead doors and order the engines astern before the freighter, sailing at a speed of 4 knots on a collision course, smashed into the submarine in the area of the port forward hydroplane.

The order to abandon the submarine was given at 1910 and most of the crew made their way topside and were crowded on the bridge.

According to Engineroom artificer (ERA) **Rob Roy McCurrach**.

"There was no panic, indeed, such a thing would be unforgivable. Personally I thought the whole thing another exercise. As far as I can recall, I was the last but one up the ladder. (Henry) Miller followed me.

As I stepped out onto the packed conning tower I heard the Captain say: *"I must have the main motors stopped"*.

As I went to go back down to do this, I almost trod on Miller's head.

"I'll go, Bob. I'm better placed", said Miller. He returned below. I then swam away from the boat. Turning, I waited to see if there would be some suction as she went down. There was none. When the motors stopped, she went down. Her stern rose high, water streaming from props, hydroplanes and rudder."

HMS *Unity* had taken an angle of 25 degrees and sank within four to five minutes. Although all the members of HMS *Unity*, bar Lt Low and AB Miller, escaped from the stricken vessel, Leading Seaman James Hare and Stoker 1st Class Cecil Shelton were not picked up by the crew of the *Atle Jarl* during the subsequent search and drowned. A subsequent investigation revealed a breakdown in internal communications between the Submarine and the fact that the Methil-Tyne convoy was due off Blyth at approx 1930.

Memorials: Portsmouth Naval Memorial, Southsea, Hampshire, Panel 37, Column 1. Low's name is listed with those who lost their lives in the Second World War on a memorial plaque in the School Chapel at Ipswich School. War Memorial in the Crypt at All Hallows-by-the-Tower.

The War Memorial in the Crypt at All Hallows-by-the-Tower.
From the College Magazine, *The Dog Watch*.
Courtesy Graham Smith of the Association of Old Worcesters

©Ipswich School, courtesy G Peck

Portsmouth Naval Memorial.
©M Hebblethwaite

Sources: Debbie Corner of Royal Navy Submarine Museum
Beneath the Waves by Rob Roy McCurrach
Graham Smith of the Association of Old Worcesters
Graham Peck of Ipswich School
Stephen Rabson, National Maritime Museum ff.23 and 56 of
NZS/33/4 at the NMM

Alfred Raymond (Alf) LOWE, GC

Sea rescue, 17th October 1948, Portland Harbour, Weymouth, Dorset

Alf and his Dad.
All pictures courtesy of AR Lowe unless otherwise noted.

Alf and his sister June after he received the Albert Medal.

Alf Lowe GC, 1974.
©Flatow estate

Status: P/JX 819579 Boy 1st Class, HMS *Illustrious*, Royal Navy
Life dates: 14th June 1931, London
Biography: Alf Lowe tells his own story

Alf was the eldest son of Alfred Joseph Henry and Emma (Elliott) Lowe who lived in Silvertown, Custom House, London. Alfred was a labourer with Tate and Lyle Sugar Refinery while Emma had worked as a housemaid before her marriage. Alfred Junior and his eldest sister June and younger sister, by one year, Joyce were put into a Barnado's Home in Poplar in September 1936 as their mother was going into hospital with pregnancy complications while carrying her son Geoffrey. Despite the responsibilities of her family Emma served her country with pride in the WVS during WWII. (Velda the youngest daughter was born later during the War). The short period in Dr Barnardo's was to become one of the most significant events in Alf's life as we shall see. Within ten days of their stay in the Home Alfred and Joyce were fostered by a Mr and Mrs Beguely who, by chance, had carefully selected one boy and one girl. As they later drove away from Ipswich station in a taxi to their new home Joyce started to cry. Alf comfortingly said, "Don't cry Joyce it will be all right".

Amazed Mrs B asked, "Do you know this little girl?"

"Yes, she is my sister".

The stay was to last 6 months until they were returned to their parents in Dagenham where Alf attended his only few months of schooling until 1943 when he was nearly 12. What followed over the next four years was a series of evacuations and reunions. Firstly to Lowestoft to which the elder two children travelled on a paddle steamer, the *Royal Daffodil*. On arrival the reception they received and the experiences they endured were repeated again and again all over England to the shame of those in charge. They were but two children representative of thousands

Put up at first in a schoolroom the children were bedded down on straw with one blanket and, were it not for the generosity of local teachers who bought them fish and chips, the food was bread and cheese and little else — but this was a feast compared to what was to come in later years. Alf hungry, but not unhappy, did not go to school, and, on the whole, remembers the kindnesses of most of the families who took him in. He learnt from the son of a poacher how to live off the land, to catch pheasants, to watch where squirrels hid their nuts, to tickle potatoes (stealing just a few from each), to take the odd egg from hen houses and which berries in the headgerows to eat.

These lessons were to stand him in good stead on his next two evacuations to Somerset where the food was sometimes extremely poor and the hygiene so bad that the children contracted scabies. Twice he had to return to his parents because of the disease. Once his brother Geoff, who had by now joined him had to go into a sanatorium to recuperate.

While in Somerset, now aged nearly 9, a German Dornier had crashed and Alf managed to get some ammunition off the plane, of course the police tracked him down and moved him on to yet another billet —

this time a farm where he at last received a large breakfast every day after early morning milking. As he was dropped off he heard the policeman say to the farmer "*tire the b... out*".

DAGENHAM SEAMAN WAS HERO AT "ILLUSTRIOUS" TRAGEDY
Gallant Attempt to Save Midshipman
Home, this week-end on leave was 17-year-old Boy Seaman Alfred Raymond Lowe, of 127 Cornworthy Road, Dagenham, one of the survivors from the pinnace which sank in Portland Harbour while returning with liberty men from the aircraft carrier "Illustrious." In hushed tones, he described to our reporter his heroic efforts to save from the gale-swept sea the midshipman in charge, who later died on board. "It was a horrible experience," he said.
The local hero.

HMS *Ganges* — naval training school.

Eventually, at what was to be their last billet, one of the boys of the family started to bully young Geoff. Alf had had enough and beat the boy up. The two young evacuees had this time been nearly starved and had again to resort to supplementing their diet. Remember Alf is still not in school and only just 10 years old and if it sounds like a Roald Dahl story it too has a happy ending. A second dose of scabies and Alf's behaviour finally resulted in the two boys returning to London. Here Alf ran wild with older boys and before long came to the notice of the police again who put him on probation. Now comes the lucky break. The Probation Officer, who discovered he had been a Barnado boy, asked him what he wanted to do with his life and the reply came back swiftly.

"*When I grow up I want to join the Navy*".

HMS *Watts*.

At Dereham.

Arrangements were shortly made for him to join the *Watts* Naval School at East Dereham in Norfolk where the intake was reserved for boys from Dr Barnado Homes and other similar institutions — read more about it in **McCarthy GC's** story. The date he joined, 12th September 1943, is etched on Alf's memory. There was strict discipline but superb teaching which enabled this 11 year old boy who started in the lowest class in the school to win a scholarship at the age of 14 to the Royal Navy and he joined HMS *Ganges* in Ipswich on 7th January 1946.

After eleven months of training and schooling at *Ganges* at Shotley Point Alf was drafted to his first ship, a light cruiser HMS *Diadem* — but to his great disappointment the ship did not go to sea for the entire 6 months he was on her. At last in March 1948 on board HMS *Illustrious* — a big fleet aircraft carrier — he set sail in the English Channel — his dreams were coming true. All summer was spent working with the aircrews as they learnt to land and take off — a number of planes crashed on a daily basis — mostly on deck. From Alf's perspective this was very exciting as being at the time the bridge messenger he witnessed many of these, sometimes spectacular, events.

The day the Admiral came on board *Illustrious*.

Then comes the story of Alf's heroism which is detailed below.

By March 1949 Alf had been posted to HMS *Implacable* and it was while they were anchored in Aberdeen that he learnt of the award of the Albert Medal.

In May 1950 Alf joined the troop ship *Empire Orwell* to take troops and 150 sailors to change over the crew of HMS *Concord* in Hong Kong. Before leaving home he had become engaged to Hilda May Denham. Then he left for a two and a half year stint in the Far East. Returning in 1953 the couple married but by now the Navy was shrinking rapidly and many young officers were being paid off and Alf's prospects looked slim so he decided to leave the Navy and was finally discharged by purchase 1 year before his 12-year contract was up with a final rank of Leading Seaman. During the last few months prior to leaving he had been at HMS *Collingwood* as acting P/O but this was never finalised. He became a commercial salesman in Portsmouth.

Alf's yacht *Gemini* — once a sailor, always a sailor.

By 1963 the Lowes had two children and unhappy with the persistent class system, the lack of opportunity and perhaps also the lure of somewhere new they emigrated to New Zealand and settled on North Shore, Auckland. Here followed a very successful commercial travelling career.

In 1982 May and Alf were divorced after a period of unhappiness. He also bought a house, built a boat, built a house, sailed a boat round the Pacific Islands and in November 1998 married Philippa (Grisé, maiden name Newbery) and at last found peace and contentment.

There is however one story from long ago that only gets better as the years go by.

One Sunday while in Hong Kong Alf, along with some of his companions, was invited to afternoon tea with the Earl of Dalkeith at his private residence. Amongst the guests were a number of young ladies. One explained to Alf that there was a shortage of presentable young men in HK and perhaps he would take her to the dubutantes' dance the next Saturday.

"You do have a civilian suit don't you?"

"Yes of course," he replied, not even owning a civilian handkerchief. As they were leaving in the truck to return to the ship she slipped a piece of paper into his hand with the address.

"Fat chance you have of mixing with the high society of HK," said the sailor sitting next to him.

Come the Saturday, while strolling around the afterdeck along came the First Lieutenant in a civvy suit with a holdall in his hand.

"Lowe" he said "I believe you are duty coxswain tomorrow."

"Yes sir."

"Fine pick me up at the King's Stairs at 7.30 tomorrow mornng." And with that he walked off and got into the motor boat and went ashore.

As the boat disappeared Alf thought, "Just my size, I wonder if he's got another suit — I can be back by midnight."

He went down to hthe Lieutenant's cabin and there was a lovely blue pinstripe suit, the whole kit was before him, a shirt, socks, shoes and tie. He packed them into an attache case and shortly afterwards went ashore to the China Fleet Club where he changed, had a few Tom Collins for fortification, took a rickshaw to the Royal Jade Gardens and found his girl waiting in a beautiful long blue dress and looking much older than her 18 years.

Greatly relieved she told him "I am so glad you came as I was beginning to think I would be another wallflower." They went into the dance and as they started to dance there was a tap on his shoulder and the First Lieutenant said "that's a nice suit you're wearing Lowe!"

Alf with his daughters Teresa and Rebecca and grandson Matthew.

Alf and Philippa in the author's garden 2005.
©*M Hebblethwaite*

Citation: *8th February 1949*

The KING has been graciously pleased to approve the following award: —

Albert Medal

Boy First Class Alfred Raymond Lowe, P/JX 819579, for gallantry in attempting to save life at sea.

At 2245 hours on 17th October 1948 a liberty boat returning from Weymouth Pier to H.M.S. *Illustrious* in Portland Harbour overturned and sank 50 to 100 yards from the ship's stern, with 51 men on board. Boy Lowe was trapped under the canopy, struggled free and surfaced. He saw a lifebelt a short distance from him which had been thrown from H.M.S. *Illustrious* and swam to it. He then removed his overcoat and shoes and swam towards the ship. When he was under the stern a line was thrown to him. At this moment he heard a faint cry of "Help" and on looking round saw that a Midshipman who was about ten yards away, was in great difficulty.

He grabbed the line and swam to the Midshipman who was unconscious by the time he reached him.

He endeavoured to turn him over to keep his head above water but found this impossible and still holding him was pulled to the ship's side. A fog buoy was then lowered and he managed to drag the Midshipman on to this and to hold on to him until a Petty Officer came down the rope to assist him. Together they secured the Midshipman who was then hoisted on board.

The accident took place in eight fathoms of water, in a rough sea with a strong wind blowing. Although the midshipman subsequently died, Boy Lowe acted with complete disregard for his own life in leaving his place of safety in an attempt to save him. His action in endangering his own life in this accident in which 29 men lost their lives was in accordance with the highest traditions of the Royal Navy.

Other awards: AM (Bronze Sea) – GC exchange. Korea Medal with oak leaf (MiD *LG* 03/10/52), United Nations Medal with clasp 'Korea', QSJM, New Zealand 1990 Commemorative Medal and QGJM.

©HMS Raleigh

©A Lowe GC

Lowe's Albert Medal was presented on 1st March 1949 and is currently on display at HMS *Raleigh*, Plymouth. In Lowe's file at the IWM there appears the fact that he received the British Korea Medal with the Commonwealth *palm leaf*, from the actual medal to the left with its oak leaf this is obviously incorrect.

To have this decoration (or any other for that matter) ensconced in a glass case to be viewed with awe would be an embarrassment to say the least. If it should serve as an inspiration and encouragement to those that may regard themselves disadvantaged which is a cry often heard from todays younger generation. If it could say that everyone has the potential to be whatever they desire, provided they have the right mental attitude then I think it would serve a more useful purpose than at the back of some obscure drawer.

Alf's letter to HMS *Raleigh*.

The story

The background to the Albert Medal needs some telling from Alf himself.

P/O Saunders, engine room artificer, was trying to pass officer exams. Alf had been teaching him seamanship and in appreciation of this he took Alf ashore while they were anchored in Portland Harbour. They went for a pint and some dinner but because Alf was still only 17 his leave expired at 11pm so late in the afternoon he went down to the ship's pinnace (liberty boat — an open boat that collects and delivers sailors to shore on such occasions). Meanwhile a storm had blown up and already by the time the boat was beside the jetty some quantity of water was baled out of the boat.

The boys were to board first and to go in under the canvas canopy — Alf was the first in so at the back over the engine. Everyone packed in tight, it was now raining and as the boat came out from the lee of the breakwater they hit the weather. The conversation took on a new note of anxiety, "*the water is coming in over the bow, it is filling up!*"

Those out in the open up in the bow were now soaked to the skin and the waves were breaking over them. "Come aft!" was the order and this was interpreted as an order to come to the aft cockpit with the disastrous result that they clambered over the canopy which collapsed on all those beneath it, meanwhile the water was rising in the boat below them. Trapped between the bodies above and the water below and further having one of the collapsed bars from the canopy pinning him to the engine box Alf started to think *"I've had my chips now"* as he heard the cry *"the boat is sinking"*.

He took a deep breath and all went quiet and Alf knew he was sinking but a consequence of this was that the air under the canopy released the bar and he could move. He ducked down and swam under all the legs until he surfaced only to be grabbed by drowning men all around him. His training had taught him to sink if this happened and the third time he swam away into a clear space in the heaving sea. He will never forget the terrible noise of the wind and the waves and the cries of the drowning men, the foam and the dark lit intermittently by flood lights. It was only then that he took off his overcoat and shoes.

Mentioned in Despatches, 1952.

Alf's lifeboatman certificate.

Statement accompanying the story of the disaster.
© *The Echo*

Alf started to swim to his ship, diving under the enormous waves. Fortunately he was seen before he could be smashed against the side, thrown a heaving line and pulled astern. Then out of the chaos of the night he heard a cry of help, looked to his right and saw a hat. He shouted to the ship to let him go. Neither they nor he let go. He let the rope slide through his hands as the marine let out more and swam to the Midshipman. The hat had gone but as he still wore his oilskin lifting his head was too difficult, somehow the two hung on to the rope as they were slowly pulled to the ship's side. A fog buoy had been lowered and a P/O came down to assist and pulled the MSM up to the deck but Alf was still in the water. Without warning the buoy banged his head and he was swept away, stunned but not unconscious, somehow still able to keep his head above water, he was now back 30 meters astern again. And all the while the storm raged. He will never know where he found the strength to swim back along the ship until he found the accommodation ladder where, exhausted, he was finally in safe hands. Too weak to stand he was taken to the quarter-deck then to the sanatorium where he found P/O Saunders.

The Midshipman died of shock half an hour after coming on board. Alf was the last to escape the liberty boat and one of only 22 of the 51 on board to survive.

Outside Buckingham Palace 1947, the Lowe family.
The small girl in the front is his sister Velda who now lives in Virginia USA, behind her is his mother Emma Lowe, standing behind her is his sister Joyce. Then Alf, brother Geoff, and behind him sister June and proud father Alfred J.H. Lowe.

Courtesy G Lowe

A witness to the story — Clive Buckle — son of Henry Buckle GC

"I can tell you it was a really dirty night when he (Lowe) earned his medal.

I was one of those who went out searching for survivors after the launch sank. I thought there had been more people in the boat than reported in our local paper — nearer 100 than the 51 (of whom 29 died) reported.

Our house in 1948 was above (on a very steep slope) the Weymouth lifeboat berth. When the lifeboat was called out two double maroons were let off. As just a teenager I went to investigate. It was evening so there were more (volunteer) crew showing up than were needed. A few of the crew, who were mainly professional fishermen, hearing the details decided to take their own boats to see what could be done. I was known as a kid who was always in boats so was asked along.

Frankly it was a forlorn hope. Fishing boats did about 6 knots in fine weather. The weather was awful and we had to use the East entrance to Portland harbour rather than the North one so from where the boats berthed to where the Navy launch sank was about 7 miles. It must have been at least two hours before we were effectively on task. We found nobody.

For the 10th anniversary of the D Day landings on the South of France I was a Midshipman of a boat which I believe was similar to the one which sank at Portland. The weather turned nasty and my boat was the only one left running of the combined NATO fleet assembled for the commemoration. The boat had a fair weather capacity of 105 including the 5 crew. I limited the number of passengers to 60 and made them wear lifejackets. I also turned away any I thought had too much drink to wait for the next trip (or later when they had sobered up a bit). There was no way I wanted the responsibility of another Portland.

(Overladen boat, no life jackets and drunks were alleged in the newspaper to have contributed to the loss of life at Portland.)"

©*Clive Buckle*

Memorials: Accommodation building at HMS *Collingwood* opened in 2005 by the 2nd Sea Lord.

The Lowe building, HMS *Collingwood*.

The plaque next to the tree planted by Alf in front of the Lowe building.
Both pictures M Hebblethwaite

Sources: AR Lowe GC
Clive Buckle
Geoff Lowe — brother

Danger over Dagenham 1939–1945 by the Borough of Dagenham
An Unknown Few by Phillip P O'Shea

At Alf and Philippa's wedding the Lowe family turned out in style and travelled from across the world.
Left to Right — Velda Lowe, Chas Lowe, Joyce Lewis (Lowe), Heather Lowe (wife of Chas), June Comben (Lowe), Ann Lowe (wife of Geoff), cousins Iris and George Phillips, Geoff Lowe and sitting, Alf & Philippa.
©*G Lowe*

If I were invited to say a few words to the new trainees of H.M.S. Raleigh about my time in the Royal Navy I would tell them:

"It was not until I left the navy that I realised what a great life it was, my only regret would be that I did not understand earlier of the possibilities before me, I know now that discipline was the most important factor I was to learn. Discipline is probably the hardest thing to learn, self discipline is even harder. Self discipline will give you self confidence, courage, determination. With these mental attitudes you have the potential to do anything, The Royal Navy did this for me of which I will be eternally grateful. It will do it for you, if you desire it."

Alf has the last word.
©*AR Lowe*

Alfred Herbert (Joe) LUNGLEY, GC

Earthquake rescue, 31st May – 1st June 1935, Quetta, India

©*Syd Cauveren*

Status: 1426460
Lance-Sergeant,
24th Mountain
Brigade, Royal
Artillery

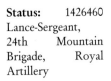

Joe's clothing list in his pay book.

All pictures courtesy Lungley children

Educational Attainments, Trade Qualifications, Medals, &c.

Joe's CV.

Life dates: 20th October 1905, Wix in the district of Manningtree, Essex – 31st December 1989, Norwich, Norfolk. Alfred was cremated at Earlham Crematorium. **Obit:** *The Daily Telegraph,* 11th January 1990

Biography: Alfred (known as Joe) was the son of Frederick and Eliza Maria (Haggar) Lungley. Frederick was a farm labourer and the family lived in Wix in Essex. Joe attended the local school and on leaving school at 12 and worked on the farm and then joined the 24th Mounted Brigade, Royal Artillery in 1921. At the time of the earthquake he was a Lance-Sergeant. He later rose to the rank of Battery Sergeant Major and served in the 1939–45 War.

The first page of Joe's pay book.

Date and information on discharge.

He married Lilian May (Moore) at the Holy Trinity Church in Norwich on 23rd September 1939 and they had two sons, Barry and David and a daughter, Christine. As his Battery was based in Norwich Joe was to spend the rest of his life in the city.

After the war Joe worked as a fitter for British Rail Eastern Region, in the coach works, until his retirement in 1964. During his time in the Army he was a keen rugby player and also an enthusiastic tug-of-war participant.

Joe and Lilian Lungley with their extended family.

Alfred in his railway overalls.

Joe's main love though was his family and being a keen gardener and allotment holder, until very late in life, he was able to bring home fresh produce for them. He loved to cycle around and though he had a driving licence never owned a car. He supported Norwich City, his local football club.

Alfred and Lilian in 1972,

and their memorial stone in Earlham Crematorium.
Courtesy B Lungley

Citation: *19th November 1935*
No. 1426460 Bombardier (Lance-Sergeant) Alfred Lungley, 24th Mountain Brigade, Royal Artillery. In Bruce Road, Quetta, on 2nd June, 1935, at about 12-00 hours a survivor was located in a house on the east side of the road. In order to extricate the survivor it was necessary to go to the bottom of a deep hole surrounded and overhung by tottering masonry. This was liable to collapse at any minor shocks, some of which occurred during the work. Lance-Sergeant Lungley showed the greatest zeal and disregard for his own safety, although he was already suffering from a severe injury to his foot. The survivor was extricated alive.

©*B Lungley*

Other awards: EGM (Military) – GC exchange. 1939–45 Star, France & Germany Star, Defence Medal, War Medal 1939–45, 1953 Coronation Medal, QSJM and Army Long Service and Good Conduct Medal (GVIR) Regular Army.

Awarded the *Empire Gallantry Medal* in the same incident:

— see the **bold** entries for exchanges to the GC.

LAC Norman Breadon, Pte **Arthur Brooks**, L/Naik **Mata Din**, Pte **Ernest Elston**, L/Naik Chitrabahadur Gurung, L/Cpl **George Henshaw**, Naik Nandlal Thapha and Havildar **Ahmed Yar**.

Awarded the *Albert Medal* in the same incident: Miss **Florence Allen**, Lt **John Cowley**, L/Naik Hukam Dad, Pte Harry Fitzsimmons, L/Naik Firoze Khan, L/Naik Kabul Singh, Pte **Robert Spoors** and Rfn Harkbir Thapa.

The story

The men of the 24th Mounted Brigade put down their rifles and joined the local people to rescue survivors, put out fires, prevent looting and speed up the clearance of the area and disposal of the dead to avoid further death, injury and disease.

'Joe'—hero of the great Quetta 'quake

Headline from the *Eastern Evening News*.

On the fourth day Joe with a badly injured hand heard a noise from under the rubble and started to dig. All the time earth tremors brought down more debris. Joe found a man, dragged him onto his back and hauled himself to daylight. After others came to help and took the rescued man to hospital it never occurred to anyone ever to tell Joe if the man survived.

Background: *Quetta before and after*

Under each entry for Quetta I have included some different information. Here I thought it would be interesting to discuss the aftermath; the disease prevention, the salvage work and the refugees.

This peaceful picture was taken in Quetta before the earthquake.

Refugees beside their tents on the racecourse.

Masks worn to cope with the smell and to prevent disease.

Before the Earthquake the city of Quetta was home to over 50,000 people. In addition there was the substantial military presence and the European adminstrators along with many of their families. The immediate effect of the earthquake was to cloud the city in dust, having reduced the buildings to rubble. As the power station was destroyed there was also complete darkness. General Karslake directed operations from a relief HQ at the Quetta Club.

Rescue of those trapped was the first priority. Communications with the rest of the world, provision of water, food and medical supplies needed to be addressed. Looting and the prevention of access to the city from outside had to be controlled. As the police and civil authorities had been virtually wiped out these tasks fell to the military.

The city was divided into 8 sections for rescue teams and survivors were evacuated to the racecourse where tents were erected and emergency medical stations opened. By the next day the erection of a barbed wire fence around the city was begun which took 2 weeks to complete. This then sealed off the entire area. Looting was thus inhibited though guards were additionally placed at Banks.

Food was a serious issue and the supplies, which had been held in the Supply Depot for possible use in case of mobilisation of the troops under different circumstances, were rationed and distributed. A dairy was opened made up of abandoned cows.

Salvage operations were carried out by both Government and private labour and all the while there was the risk of disease from the decomposing bodies — up to 30,000 of them. In order to prevent disease the entire population was innoculated against Cholera though an added precaution was that no water from wells was to be used. All fresh fruit given to the refugees was washed with a solution of Potassium Permanganate.

Further innoculation against Smallpox was carried out in June and July as well as anti-Malaria work in the form of draining of stagnant water, the oiling of water courses and dispensing of quinine to all those suffering from Malaria. An anti-fly campaign was carried out which was 'strikingly successful'.

Further information on Quetta will be found in the entries for all the other recipients from this event.

Sources: Barry Lungley — son
David Lungley — son and Christine Male — daughter
Report on The Quetta Earthquake of 31st May 1935 by Capt LAG Pinhey IA
Thirty Seconds at Quetta by Robert Jackson

Joseph (Joe) LYNCH, GC, BEM

Saving life, 26th February 1948, Port Stanley, Falkland Islands

Joe as a young cadet.
Courtesy I Lynch

©A Flatow estate

Ian Lynch with his grandfather Joe in 2006 at the 50th anniversary of the GC.

Status: D/JX 133231 Chief Petty Officer, HMS *Nigeria*, Royal Navy

Life dates: 6th November 1912, Wallasey, Cheshire – 7th October 2006, Wallasey, Cheshire. Sadly Joe died while I was in the process of writing this book. His grandson Ian arranged a fine funeral for him with a procession which started at the RNA Wallasey HQ and processed to St Paul's Church, Seacombe with standard bearers from the RNA and the British Legion, a bugler sounding the *Last Post*, officers from HMS *Eaglet* (local naval base for reservists), the Mayor and the Dean of Wirral. A worthy tribute to a worthy man. The cremation took place at Landican Crematorium. **Obit:** *The Daily Telegraph*, 11th October 2006

Biography: The son of Bernard and Esther Lynch Joe went to Somerville School, Wallasey leaving at 15 to work in what is now known as the retail sector. However, on 29th May 1929 he joined the Royal Navy as a cadet at HMS *Ganges*. He served in the Atlantic and North Sea during WWII.

Joe married Elizabeth Bennett in July 1939 and they had one son, Joe, who predeceased him. After 24 years in the Navy, with the rank of Chief Petty Officer, Joe retired. He then took a job at Cadbury's for a short while until becoming a Customs & Excise Officer based at Albert Docks, Liverpool. Also worked at Heathrow for about five years dealing with the duty on cargoes coming into Britain. He worked there until his retirement in 1976.

A keen sportsman Joe retained his interest and became involved in less physical acitivites such as the Royal Naval Association in Wallasey where he served his term as Vice-President and as welfare officer. He was honoured with the Freedom of The Wirral. His last years were spent peacefully in a residential home where his grandson Ian was a frequent visitor.

Joe was well-known in his local community and fitting tributes were paid to him. He liked a heated debate, world politics, keeping watch on the Stock Market and watching the snooker and climbing trees to prune the branches until in his eighties. Ian was surprised to find that he prayed every night. Through his welfare work he assisted in the research and recognition of forgotten Royal Navy heroes and endeavoured to give them proper service.

From **Doug Arman**

Here's another small snippet for you which appears in the record for William Dowling VC. A memorial plaque was dedicated in his honour at the Church of St. John the Evangelist, Liverpool, on 13th October 1991, unveiled by Lieutenant Commander Ian Fraser VC DSC. The service was conducted by Revd. Father M. Reilly and those in attendance included Mr. Peter Gilfoyle MP and Mr. Joseph Lynch GC BEM.

Citation: *15th June 1948*

The KING has been, graciously pleased to approve the following award:

Albert Medal in Bronze

Chief Petty Officer Joseph Lynch B.E.M., D/JX 133231, for gallantry in saving life at sea.

While H.M.S. *Nigeria* was lying at anchor at Port Stanley, Falkland Islands on the night of 26th February, 1948, a Rating missed his footing on the Jacob's ladder while disembarking from the motor cutter at the port boom and fell into the sea. It was after dark and the sea was rough, and at a temperature of 42° Fahrenheit with the wind blowing a fresh gale.

The Rating, Leading Seaman Hughes, managed to retain his hold on the Jacob's ladder but, as he was dressed in heavy oilskins, was unable to pull himself up, nor could he make for the cutter owing to the cold state of the sea and the fear of sinking in his heavy clothes.

C.P.O. Lynch heard the pipe for the life-boat while sitting in his mess. Dressed only in a singlet and trousers he immediately went on deck and, on seeing the situation, made his way out along the boom, down the ladder and into the water alongside Hughes. He persuaded Hughes to let go of the ladder and supported him to the motor cutter. To keep out of the way Lynch then swam back to the ladder to wait until Hughes had been hauled into the boat. When Hughes was safe Lynch swam back to the motor cutter and was himself hauled to safety.

BEM citation: *9th October 1942*

13th October 1942

The KING has been graciously pleased to approve the award of the British Empire Medal (Military Division) to: Petty Officer Joseph Lynch, D/JX. 133231.

For bravery in rescue work while serving in H.M.S. *Wallace.*

Other awards: AM (Bronze Sea) – GC exchange. BEM (Mil) for Gallantry (13/10/42, presented 16th March 1943), 1939–45 Star, Atlantic Star with clasp 'France and Germany' (clasp added post 1993), Defence Medal, War Medal 1939–45, Royal Naval Long Service and Good Conduct Medal (GVIR), 1953 Coronation Medal, QSJM, QGJM. Joseph Lynch's Albert Medal is located in the Imperial War Museum, London. The investitures took place on 14th November 1951 and on 20th February 1973.

Joe's medals.
©I Lynch

Joe's Albert was stolen, but recovered.
Courtesy Imperial War Museum

The story

Joe always told how he understood the phrase "frozen to the marrow". When he realised that he could not get into the cutter the first time he knew he had to keep moving or he would die of cold which is why he swam back to the ladder. As soon as Hughes was hauled up into the cutter he swam back and once in helped to rub Hughes which in itself kept him moving too. Once back on board ship he was admitted to sick bay for 24 hours to warm up while Hughes was there for double the time. He told his grandson Ian "I was in the right place at the right time".

The BEM story

Joe was serving on the destroyer HMS *Wallace* off the East Coast of Britain endeavouring to prevent the merchant ships from coming under German attack. The ship was equipped with Bofors guns and it was during one of the Luftwaffe attacks that a merchantman crashed into HMS *Wallace* damaging the boiler. Joe had, with foresight, run to the opposite side of the ship and as soon as the steam which gushed from the broken boiler lessened he went below decks. One man had been killed and two others stunned and burnt. These he helped to safe hands but he then heard the First Lt calling. With another crew member he again went below this time to wedge timber baulks against the damaged hull of the ship. There was no guarantee that the measures the two men were taking would prevent a catastrophic crack and subsequent flooding and capsizing.

Background: *Jacob's ladder* — a rope ladder with wooden rungs which hangs over the side of a ship

42° F — 5°C

motor cutter — a single masted ship's sailing boat which was powered by a motor

Why was HMS Nigeria in the Falklands?
In 1948, further fears were expressed inside the Foreign Office and in other Government departments that conflict might erupt in the Antarctic. Indeed in 1948 an agreement was signed in London by Britain, Argentina and Chile preventing the use of warships south of 60°S in response to fears of naval clashes.

However, the British came up with arguments that Argentina was a threat to British interests in Antartica and in particular South Georgia and the Falklands so was seen as "*sending warships (such as HMS Nigeria in 1948) to defend the imperial fantasies in the South Atlantic*".
Klaus-John Dodds

Paul Hunter
For those with other interests the obituary for Paul Hunter, the young snooker player who won the Benson & Hedges Masters three times, is on the same page of the *Daily Telegraph*. He died at the age of 27, of cancer, a different hero but a hero too, to many and whose death Joe too would have mourned.
Sources: Ian Lynch — grandson
Geopolitics in the Foreign Office: British representations of Argentina 1945–1961 by Klaus-John Dodds
The Daily Telegraph

Ghulam MOHI-ud-DIN, GC will be found in the S book along with all other Punjabi GCs

Horace William (Slim, Bill) MADDEN, GC

Resistance under torture, 24th April – December 1951, PoW, Korea

©*Australian War Memorial,*
courtesy R Yielding

©*Mark Adams*

Status: 2/400186 (NX173860) Private, 3rd Battalion, Royal Australian Regiment (RAR)
Life dates: 14th February 1924, Cronulla, Sydney, NSW, Australia – see below. Plot 36, Row 9, Grave 2978, which is within the UN Military Cemetery, Tanggok, Pusan, Korea. **Obit:** *The Times*, 30th December 1955

> Pte MADDEN was held prisoner by the enemy until 6th November 1951, when he died of malnutrition and the result of illtreatment. During this period he openly resisted all enemy efforts to force him to collaborate, to such a degree that his name and example were widely known through the various groups of prisoners. Testimonials have been provided by Officers and men from many units of the Commonwealth and Allied forces which show that the heroism he displayed was quite outstanding.

Extract from the Recommendation for the George Cross with the date of death (later refuted) as 6th November 1951.

Guthrie thinks that Madden died on the 25th November, 1951, and is confident that there would not be an error of more than one day in fixing this date."

3. The casualty questionnaire completed by Col HARRISON, USAF on 8 Aug 53 states that Capt A.H. FARRAR-HOCKLEY, GLOSTERS told him that Pte MADDEN died on 30 Nov 51 at the hospital to Camp No. 3, 10 miles EAST of CHANGSON.

4. BRPWIU report will not be available for at least 6 weeks but it may include further details from Capt FARRAR-HOCKLEY.

5. It appears definite that the date given by Pte PARKER (5 Nov 51) is in error and the actual date of death was between the 25 Nov 51 and 30 Nov 51.

11 Sep 53

Dear Mrs Regan,

I am writing to you as the next of kin of Private Madden, 3 RAR. I was with your brother when he died in the hospital of POW Camp No 3 on the 3rd December 1951.

When did he die?
The extract on the left is from the Interrogation Reports dated 20th November 1953. There was much confusion in the reports from various witnesses. Perhaps the above letter to Slim's sister from Capt Farrar-Hockley is definitive?

© *National Archives*

Thanksgiving is on the 4th Thursday of November and according to Farrar-Hockley's book *The Edge of the Sword* Madden died "a few days later". In the book he does not mention that he was with him.

Biography: Horace was the son of Charles Bernard and Pearle Ellen (Clemson) Madden. He had a younger brother Alan who was born in 1928 but who died in 1931 and a sister Florence Bernice who married Thomas William Regan. Florence in turn had 3 children Robert, Julie Ann and Sharyn. Slim, the nickname he acquired due to his slight build, was described as a fruiterer's assistant when he was mobilised on 26th May 1942. He was posted to the 114th Australian General Hospital at Goulbourn in July. Then, after a period of illness, he was transferred to the Army on 10th August 1943, then the 8th Field Ambulance in November embarking for Milne Bay and operations in New Guinea on 17th November. Here he contracted malaria and not long after recovering was posted to the Cook Group II in June 1944 then to the Motor Ambulance convoy on Bougainville.

A Japanese petrol wagon captured by Australian troops during the unsuccessful enemy attack on Milne Bay.

Milne Bay, New Guinea. The Australians were the first to effect a defeat on the Japanese on land.

From an old colonial newspaper

Thereafter Bill served with a number of medical units in New Guinea, Moratai, Borneo and Japan being discharged from the 2/AIF (Australian Army) on 2nd June 1947. He then took a job as a nursing orderly at the mental hospital at Morriset though he later worked there as a moulder.

When the Korean War broke out Bill re-enlisted on 19th August 1950 into the Australian Korea Special Force and after a short spell in Japan joined 3 RAR in Korea, initially as a Driver. On 11th September he emplaned for Japan being promoted to Lance Corporal on 11th October but within a month, at his own request, he reverted to Private and joined the 3 RAR A Company at Signaller Bn HQ.

On 5th November 1950 he emplaned from Japan for Korea as part of the United Nations advance over the 38th parallel into North Korea and then the withdrawal past Seoul into South Korea. On 24th April 1951 he was reported missing in action at Kapyong after twice being concussed by grenades (see also **D Kinne GC**).

Capt Farrar-Hockley of the Gloucestershire Regiment, who had told Florence Regan, Madden's sister that he was with Slim wrote:

"let me assure you that he did not die in pain; and was only semi-conscious throughout the last two days of his life, at the end of which, unable to withstand a final bout of enteritis, he passed away".

So we have various dates of death ranging from 25th November 1951 to 6th December 1951 (even erroneously as early as 6th November). Will anyone ever know for sure? Was he alone or was he not? Again we may never know.

Citation: *27th December 1955*

30th December 1955

The QUEEN has been graciously pleased, on the advice of her Australian Ministers, to approve the posthumous award of the GEORGE CROSS, in recognition of gallant and distinguished service whilst a prisoner of war in Korea, to:-

2/400186 Private Horace William Madden (deceased) 3rd Battalion, Royal Australian Regiment.

Private Madden was captured by Chinese Communist Forces on 24th April, 1951 near Kapyong. He was a signaller attached to Battalion Headquarters at the time and received concussion prior to capture.

Private Madden was held prisoner by the enemy until about 6th November, 1951, when he died of malnutrition and the result of ill treatment. During this period he openly resisted all enemy efforts to force him to collaborate, to such a degree that his name and example were widely known through the various groups of prisoners. Testimonials have been provided by Officers and men from many units of the Commonwealth and Allied forces which showed that the heroism he displayed was quite outstanding.

Despite repeated beatings and many forms of ill-treatment inflicted because of his defiance to his captors, Private Madden remained cheerful and optimistic. Although deprived of food because of his behaviour, resulting in severe malnutrition, he was known to share his meagre supplies, purchased from Koreans, with other prisoners who were sick.

It would have been apparent to Private Madden that to pursue this course must eventually result in his death. This did not deter him, and for over six months, although becoming progressively weaker, he remained undaunted in his resistance. He would in no way co-operate with the enemy.

This gallant soldier's outstanding heroism was an inspiration to all his fellow prisoners.

Slim Madden in snow-laden trench.
© *Australian Korean War Album Search Engine*

Other awards: 1939–45 Star, Pacific Star, 1939–45 War Medal, Australian Service Medal 1939–45, Korea Medal and United Nations Medal with clasp 'Korea' and United States Presidential Unit Citation. The George Cross was presented to Slim's sister Florence Regan on 9th May 1956 by the Governor of NSW, Sir John Northcott the announcement being made by the Governor-General Sir William Slim.

The story

Pte Madden, along with several others, was captured by Chinese Communists and taken prisoner on 24th April 1951 during the Battle of Kapyong. On 27th April 1951, he was left behind due to ill health, when the other prisoners were forced to march from the Bean Camp to Camp 5. He was later rounded up with prisoners from other camps who were left behind and taken to the Caves camp at Kangdong. These men were then forced to march 300km to the Yalu River, at the end of the column those too ill to march were carried on a cart.

During the battle of Kapyong, he was at Battalion Headquarters when it was shelled and he was concussed. When the signals platoon was ordered to withdraw, Madden dropped behind probably stressed from his concussion. Surrounded by Chinese and forced to surrender, he was the only Australian PoW to die in captivity, but 50 other Commonwealth PoWs died and the Americans lost a staggering 2,701 PoWs from 7,140 taken prisoner. One of 29 Australian PoWs, he was also one of the 339 Australians killed in Korea, where deaths on both sides of the conflict numbered more than two million.

Madden was slightly built but nonetheless recovered fairly quickly and demonstrated his fitness by helping other prisoners as they marched at the rear. Madden died of malnutrition and the result of ill-treatment seven months after being captured.

Inhuman treatment was the regular lot of the UN prisoners, and it took men strong in both body and mind to survive.

Memorials: On 11th November 1997, the Korean Veterans' Association of Australia unveiled a plaque in honour of Private Horace William Madden GC. The plaque in the Remembrance Garden at the Heidelberg Repatriation Hospital is to honour the most highly decorated Australian soldier of the three-year war on the Korean Peninsular. There is also a memorial to him at the Singleton Returned Servicemen's Club.

Bill Madden is mentioned several times in Farrar-Hockley's book *The Edge of the Sword.* The Soldiers' Club of the 3rd Royal Australian Regiment is called *The Madden Club* — also known as 'The Shat' due to it being a building outside of the unit area — a chateau. Of him his fellow captive Keith Gwyther said "He became a sort of legend".

The club's objective is to provide a place for soldiers to rest and recreate during off-duty periods. Facilities include a bar, video room, Nintendo, billiard table, beer garden and BBQ area. The Club committee runs a variety of functions for soldiers throughout the year such as band nights and theme parties, as well as regular pool and dart competitions. The Club operates as a Non Public Monies Account with a committee of 3 RAR soldiers. It raises money through bar sales and fundraising and returns profits to the soldiers of 3 RAR.

Sources: Mark Adams — cousin
Australian War Museum
The Imjin Line, Newsletter of the Herts & District
Branch British Korean Veterans Association
www.anzacday.org.au/history/korea/kapyong.html
www.korean-war.com/australia.html — *Australians in the Korean War*

The Times
Australian Dictionary of National Biography
www.army.gov.au/3rar/Regt_Inst.htm
Lt Col Neil Smith
The Edge of the Sword by Capt A Farrar-Hockley
Tony Gill

Herbert John (Bertie) MAHONEY, GC

Shipboard action, HMS Taurus, 1927

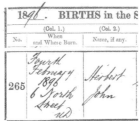

Date of Birth	Place of Birth
4.6.1892	Plymouth Devon

Extract from Herbert's death certificate.

Extract from Mahoney's service record showing his OBE (EGM) and the end of this record. In 1933 his record was transferred to ? Prison Commission.

Extract from birth certificate.

Status: ONK 8540 Petty Officer Stoker, HMS *Taurus*, Royal Navy

Life dates: 4th February, 1896, Plymouth – 1st June 1940. Herbert died on board HMS *Basilisk* which was sunk returning from Dunkirk. The date of birth on his death certificate is incorrect.

Biography: Herbert was the son of John and Ellen (Chambers) Mahoney. John is listed as a street sweeper in 1901 (but as a Scavenger in 1896) and the couple had four children at that time, Alice, Beatrice, Bertie and Ellen. Herbert's service record states that he was a coal labourer at the time of his engagement on 30th August 1910. He first served on the *Vivid II* (and again a number of times during the next eighteen years) as a Stoker. He also served on *Hood, Concord* and many other ships becoming a Stoker Petty Officer in 1917. Herbert's wife's name was Emily.

Citation: *23rd December 1927*

The KING has been graciously pleased to approve of the Award of the Medal of the Military Division of the Most Excellent Order of the British Empire to the undermentioned :— *For Gallantry*.

Stoker Petty Officer Herbert John Mahoney, O.N. K. 8540 of H.M.S. *Taurus*.

H.M.S. *Taurus* was steaming at high speed when the supports to the starboard Fore Turbo Fan fractured from the bulkhead, causing the fan to drop; this in turn severed the main auxiliary exhaust steam pipe and several smaller exhaust pipes.

Stoker Petty Officer Mahoney ordered the boiler room to be cleared at once, but remained behind himself, at great personal danger, to close stop valves and take other necessary action.

The boiler room was enveloped in steam, and large pieces of metal were being hurled about by the Turbo Fan which was still running. By his promptitude and resolute behaviour Stoker Petty Officer Mahoney at grave risk to himself averted what might have been a serious disaster.

Other awards: EGM (Military) – GC exchange. Long Service and Good Conduct Medal. The GC was presented to his widow and first sold by Christie's on 23rd November 1965 to Spink and since then has been auctioned a number of times the last being in 2003.

Memorials: Plymouth Naval Memorial, Devon; Panel 40, Column 3. Mahoney's name doesn't bear the postnominals to which he was entitled.

Plymouth Naval Memorial.
©*Iain McKenzie*

Background: *HMS Basilisk*

The destroyer HMS *Basilisk* under Cmdr M Richmond, along with three others, was sunk by German Stuka dive bombers off the beaches of Dunkirk while she was taking part in the evacuation of the British Expeditionary Force. Preparations for evacuation had begun on 22nd May 1940 with mass boarding of ships both large and small on the 27th. She survived many air attacks during the evacuation but was eventually sunk in shallow waters off the beaches. HMS *Whitehall* destroyed her wreck by gunfire. 140 officers and men were lost. The wreck is still there a mere 7 metres below the surface.

HMS *Taurus*.
Author's collection

HMS Taurus

She was a torpedo-boat destroyer with a displacement of 1,000 tons and armaments of 8x4inch torpedo tubes. She was completed in 1917. While the ship in this photo bears the number H30 this was not a permanent number and there are other photos where the number is F39. The one black band round the after funnel denotes a unit of the 1st Flotilla, Mediterranean Fleet.

A later HMS *Taurus* was a submarine during WWII.

Background: *Naval Memorials*

At Plymouth, Portsmouth and Chatham there are Naval Memorials to those who died in both World Wars.

After WWI the Admiralty wished to find an appropriate way of commemorating all those whose lives were lost at sea or who had died while serving on board an RN ship (though not merchant ships). Three identical memorials were built.

After WWII the memorials were each extended though not identically, to include those that perished in that war. Further pictures of Plymouth and Portsmouth can be found in Volume 4.

Portsmouth Naval Memorial.
©*M Hebblethwaite*

Sources: Iain McKenzie
www.plymouth.register.office
Royal Naval Association

MALTA

Many books have been written on the part played by Malta during WWII so the information here is by definition selective and only a very short selection at that. I also suggest that you read the entries of the individual GCs whose actions contributed to the story of Malta, they are Mason, May, Lewin, **Gregson**, **Copperwheat**, **Eastman**, **Dowland** and **Jephson-Jones** (remembering that bold indicates a different Volume from this one).

Malta received the first of only two Collective Awards of the George Cross. These have been awarded on the express recommendation of King George VI in 1942 to the Island of Malta and by Queen Elizabeth II in 1999 to the Royal Ulster Constabulary.

Malta played two strategic roles.

1. In defence of the route to North Africa and as a safe harbour for ship-repairing

2. In attack against the enemy forces, both the Italians and the Germans.

However, the Island could not carry out either of these alone and Churchill was not immediately prepared to provide men and machines. It was not even obvious that four Gloster Gladiator bi-planes would be insufficient and it was only after much negotiating that even they were allowed to stay on the Island. Three famously became known as *Faith*, *Hope* and *Charity*, being named by Flying Officer John Waters after the 7th, and most successful, raid on the 11th June 1940. Defences were eventually upgraded with the arrival of Hurricane and Spitfire fighters.

Faith, the sole survivor of the three aircraft *Faith*, *Hope* and *Charity*, which became world famous during the defence of Malta 1940-1941.

© *Valetta Museum, picture by I McKenzie*

Before long however, the Luftwaffe joined the Italians and through 1941 and 1942, 3,000 enemy raids took place. Buildings were flattened, particularly the industrial areas around harbours, and it has been stated that proportionately Malta was the most heavily bombed place on earth. This had a devastating effect on the population which was beginning to suffer severe shortages of food and medicine. It became essential for convoys to get through to deliver these essential supplies though it was not until the end of 1942 that substantial aid finally began to reach the stricken islanders.

In April 1942 King George VI, in a dramatic and unprecedented gesture (this was the only award of the George Cross which was not published in *The London Gazette* but was made by King George VI personally) conferred the George Cross on the brave people of Malta. The award was made in a letter dated 15th April 1942 from His Majesty to the Governor of Malta, Lieutenant General Sir William Dobbie GCMG KCB DSO, which read as follows:

"To honour her brave people I award the George Cross to the Island Fortress of Malta to bear witness to a heroism and devotion that will long be famous in history."

The Maltese Flag was altered to include a depiction of the George Cross and the Island appended the post-nominals GC, but this was not extended to every citizen.

The *Sunday Times of Malta* of 19th April 1942 announced the award of the George Cross thus:

King Sets Seal on Living History alongside a picture of the GC and King George VI.

On hearing the news the Governor Sir William Dobbie replied;

"The people of MALTA are deeply touched by Your Majesty's kind thought for them in conferring on the Fortress this signal honour. It has greatly encouraged everyone and all are determined that by God's help MALTA will not weaken but will endure until victory is won. All in MALTA desire to express once again their loyal devotion to Your Majesty and their resolve to prove worthy of the high honour conferred."

General DOBBIE, Governor

While these sentiments are now again evident in Malta there was a period during the Mintoff Premiership when this was not universally so.

The George Cross was actually presented by Field Marshal Lord Gort VC GCB CBE DSO MVO MC (see below **), who had only recently replaced Dobbie as Governor, to Sir George Borg MBE, Chief Justice, who accepted it on behalf of the People of Malta on the 13th of September 1942 in the ruins of the Palace Square, Valetta. The George Cross was subsequently taken to every part of the islands so the Maltese could see their country's award.

Sterling silver £5 coin that was produced for Malta in 1992 commemorating the 50th Anniversary of the Island receiving the George Cross. It is superb, with a mirror finish and frosted relief details, including the GC and the scroll written by KG VI.
All photos here courtesy D Hollowday

The Maltese flag.

On his visit to Malta in December 1943, President Roosevelt read the following citation,

"In the name of the people of the United States of America I salute the Island of Malta, its people and defenders, who, in the cause of freedom and justice and decency throughout the world, have rendered valorous service far above and beyond the call of duty.

Under repeated fire from the skies, Malta stood alone but unafraid in the center of the sea, one tiny bright flame in the darkness — a beacon of hope for the clearer days which have come. Malta's bright story of human fortitude and courage will be read by posterity with wonder and with gratitude through all the ages.

What was done in this Island maintains the highest traditions of gallant men and women who from the beginning of time have lived and died to preserve civilization for all mankind."

December 7th 1943,
Franklin D. Roosevelt

On the occasion of the 60th anniversary of the award in April 2002, 15 members of the Victoria Cross and George Cross Association were invited by the Government to visit Malta for a week of celebrations.

The Siege Bell Monument was built on the initiative of the George Cross Island Association. It was dedicated jointly by H.E. Dr. Censu Tabone, President of Malta and H. M. Queen Elizabeth II, Head of the Commonwealth, on 29th May 1992.

The Monument commemorates the award of the George Cross to Malta and honours over 7,000 service personnel and civilians who gave their lives during the Siege of Malta 1940-1943. The plaque was unveiled by H.E. Professor Guido de Marco, President of Malta, on 15th April 2002, the 60th anniversary of the award.

An interesting envelope sent from Malta to Germany in 1961.

A stamp to celebrate the life of Winston Churchill.

The George Cross and the original letter from King George VI are on display in the National War Museum, Valetta.

Photographs taken by Iain McKenzie

✳✳

How the GC got to Malta

From **Bill Flynn** of Moorooduc, Victoria, Australia
On the 50th anniversary of the GC award to Malta, in 1992, I was invited by my father to attend a celebration at Broadmeadows Town Hall in Victoria, Australia. He was invited to receive a medal struck by the Republic of Malta commemorating this anniversary and awarded to those who had contributed to the war effort in those dark days of WWII.

As part of the proceedings a retired Aussie pilot told the story of how he personally delivered the actual GC medal to Malta aboard a seaplane flying over hostile skies.

I then read the following letter in the *Times of Malta* about some historical controversies and inconsistencies as to who did what and who actually received the medal when.

I seem to vaguely recollect the pilot's story and that he was actually summoned to Buckingham Palace to collect the medal so he could deliver it.

Joseph Mary Wismayer, Sliema, wrote
I refer to the brief letter by Elizabeth Abela Smith (28th October) on the George Cross. Mrs Abela Smith, the granddaughter of Lord Gort VC, declares that it was Lord Gort who had brought with him to Malta the George Cross awarded by King George VI to the Maltese islands.

Lord Gort VC arrived in Malta from Gibraltar on 6th May 1942, at the height of the siege, by flying-boat from No. 10 Squadron, Royal Australian Air Force captained by Flight Lt. Stokes. Field Marshal Lord Gort VC was the Governor of Gibraltar.

He came to replace the Governor and Commander-in-Chief Sir William G.S. Dobbie who flew back to the UK by the same plane on the morrow.

Both flights were conducted at night time. Lt. General Dobbie, KCB, GCMG, DSO, had previously arrived in Malta as Acting Governor and C-in-C on 28th April 1940, and it was during his governorship that Malta was awarded the George Cross.

In his memoirs published under the heading *A Very Present Help*, published in London in 1944 by Marshall, Morgan and Scott, Lt. General Dobbie had complained bitterly that when he had handed the governorship of the Maltese islands to Lord Gort at Kalafrana air-base, Lord Gort refused to show him the George Cross! Lt. General Dobbie did not know that in fact Lord Gort did not have it in his possession.

Although the original Royal Command was that the coveted award was to be brought to Malta by Lord Gort which would have been more proper and dignified, this was made impossible due to wartime logistical and timing exigencies, demanding that the then Flying Officer, Victor Betty, was in a better locality to collect the George Cross than Lord Gort.

In fact, FlgOff Betty was ordered to collect the George Cross from the Air Ministry and report to RAF Hendon and from there to fly to RAF Portreith, in Cornwall. From there he flew to Gibraltar from where he left a few hours after Lord Gort to RAF Luqa where he arrived on board a Hudson MK III piloted by FlgOff Honeman in the evening of 7th May, 1942.

As (now) Squadron Leader Betty, K.S.J., RAF (Rtd) concluded, "what the arrival of the George Cross in Malta lacked in dignity, it was compensated in its safety".
©Joseph Mary Wismayer

The story is further corroborated by letter and the author's personal conversation with the following correspondent/witness.

From **Marquis Godwin Drago d'Aragona**, GCSJ DCSL BE&A A&CE, Sliema

I wrote three letters to *The Times*, on 21st July, 8th October and 4th November 2001 on how the George Cross came to Malta but they were never published, presumably because these were hand-written or else because I am a *persona non grata* to the editor. Alternatively, it could be because they did not want to bring out into the open a closely guarded secret, a serious administrative blunder, of the British authorities during the war. Something that was meant to be kept under the carpet.

The story concerns the fable that it was Lord Gort who brought the George Cross with him to Malta, when, in fact, it had been erroneously sent to RAF Hendon instead of to Southampton, from where he was due to depart for Malta in a Sunderland Flying Boat aircraft and that due to exigencies of the war of having to travel under the cover of darkness, the medal did not reach him in time and he had to leave Southampton without it, a serious breach of a Royal command!

Efforts were therefore immediately made to reach him in Gibraltar by sending it by a courier, but the courier arrived in Gibraltar the day after Lord Gort had left for Malta, and he, the courier, had therefore to follow him from Gibraltar to Malta.

The fable seems to have taken on so strongly that even a noted historian like Brian Blouet asserted on page 209 of his book *The Story of Malta* that Lord Gort brought the George Cross with him when he took over as Governor.

The secret was however blown when the courier — who carried the packet containing the George Cross which had been simply marked 'secret' though otherwise without any ground security arrangements along the way, in order to prevent any undue curiosity or suspicion — decided to reveal the whole story in his book *Cross and Controversy* many years later. The courier was FlgOff Victor Betty.

It is therefore no wonder that General Dobbie complained in his memoirs that Lord Gort refused to show him the medal, when after all, the award was made to the People of Malta for their heroism when under *his* governorship. Lord Gort did not have it with him!

Some anglophile correspondents do not accept that the British authorities committed any administrative blunder in this respect and insist that it was Lord Gort who brought the medal with him, and that the contents of Mr Betty's book is fictitious.

Flying Officer Betty was eventually promoted to Squadron Leader and when he retired he used to come to Malta twice a year, in May and November. He was made a Knight of St John of Jerusalem, Knights Hospitaller. Eventually we became very close friends and used to spend many hours chatting over a drink.

On one occasion he related to me his annoyance at having arrived in Gibraltar a day after Lord Gort had left for Malta and how he had to follow him in a Hudson aircraft named *The Spirit of Washington*.

It was a long, direct, non-stop flight from Gibraltar to Malta and when he arrived over the island it was in the middle of a night air-raid, and the pilot, FlgOff Honeman, was warned not to land and stay away. As, however, he was very short of fuel after the long haul from Gibraltar he took the risk and attempted to land. As a raid was on there was no flare path to guide him, and ack ack was exploding dangerously close to the aircraft. It was very scary. In fact Betty began to think that that was the end of the George Cross — shot down over Malta!

Luckily, however, a landing was made safely and the package containing the George Cross was handed over at Luqa to a young subaltern from the Governor's office. At first the officer did not want to sign a receipt for the package, but a firm "no signature, no George Cross" made him sign and the courier quite properly handed the receipt to the Luqa station adjutant, Flt/Lt Sugdon.

I was 18 at the time of the award of the George Cross and spent a most harrowing time during the siege and I had numerous close shaves from bombs falling close by.

Since the award was made to the People of Malta during the war it means that I was one of the awardees too. So, like the rest of the People of Malta, I feel entitled to know the true and exact story of how the medal was brought over to Malta.

I am quite sure there must be someone still alive who can confirm or otherwise how the saga actually unfolded and whether the contents of Betty's book are true or fictitious.

©*Marquis Godwin Drago d'Aragona*

Alan Keighley puts a latter day perspective on the subject

I am sure there are no documents that we can see today which would confirm or deny either story about the arrival of the George Cross in Malta.

Obviously for morale and prestige purposes using Lord Gort as the carrier would be good news. The modern term 'spin' was not current in 1942.

However, on balance I am more inclined to go with the Squadron Leader. I am relying on my memory but I think the Squadron Leader said he had it wrapped up in his pyjamas!!

Some pictures of Malta now but which give an idea of where it all happened.

Just inside the City Gates of Valetta was the Opera House, until it was bombed. Whereas the rest of the city was rebuilt after the War, the Opera House has been left derelict, as a reminder of how the islanders suffered. What was the interior is now used as a car park.

Valetta harbour, 2006.
Both ©I McKenzie

Malta and the Cheshire Regiment

The 1st Bn arrived in Malta on 21st February 1941 to boost the defence of the Island. While the Navy and Airforce did battle on the seas and in the air it was the Army which prepared the landing grounds and cleared the streets of rubble caused by the bombing, reinforced the defences and moved stores and ammunition while at times being under aerial attack. When the SS *Pampas* arrived it was the Cheshires that unloaded the precious cargo in March 1942 under awful conditions as the ship had been badly damaged and the holds were filled with oily water. The Bn also unloaded the *Penelope* (see **Copperwheat GC**) under continuous bombardment and for the efforts of these men the Regimental badge was carved on the bastion wall of the Royal Dockyard for which defence the Cheshires had been responsible from 1st April 1941 until 23rd January 1943.

Victor Magazine for Boys.

Memorials: Paintings by Robert Taylor from Aviation Art. The National Archives has many pictures and documents on Malta and of course the Museum in Valletta has much research material. In Cardiff there was a club for rest and recuperation for the Maltese merchant seamen called the George Cross Club. It was opened in September 1944. There are stamps, books and all types of souvenirs and the Maltese may write Malta GC as their address.

Sources: Alan Keighley
Derek Hollowday
Imperial War Museum
N A Hine, Regimental Secretary/Museum Curator, The Cheshire Regiment
The History of the Cheshire Regiment in the Second World War by Arthur Crookenden
Faith, Hope and Malta GC by Tony Spooner
The Ohio & Malta by Michael Pearson

Cross and Controversy Malta 1942 by Squadron Leader T.V. Betty, K.S.J., RAF
Letters in *The Times of Malta* with permission
Marquis Godwin Drago d'Aragona
Joseph Mary Wismayer
Bill Flynn
Iain McKenzie
Everyone's War, No 7 Summer 2003
The Story of Malta by Brian Blouet

Reginald Harry MALTBY, GC

Saved a child down a well, 1926, Lahore, India

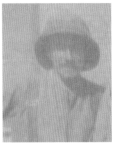

Status: 7872842 Staff Sergeant, 11th Armoured Car Company, Royal Tank Corps

The *Dewdrop*, Dover.
©R Sprules

Fear naught but to fall from thy favour dear Lord Remembered by his comrades.
©M Booker

Life dates: 24th January 1882, Fulham, South London – 17th December 1943, Dover and he is buried in Charlton Cemetery, Dover, Kent. While Reginald appears to have a CWGC headstone it was in fact not erected by them but made by a local monumental mason to the same design hence Maltby is not listed on the CWGC website.

In 1998 this new headstone was erected on Grave Ref. No 14 Row SJ. This came about as a result of the sterling efforts of Bill Green and the Royal Tank Corps and the ceremony was also attended by members of the Royal British Legion. Reginald's original memorial stated Reginald Harry Maltby, OBE (often confused with the EGM). **Obit:** *Dover Express*, December 1943

Biography: Reginald was the son of Charles and Jane Maltby. His father worked as a Refreshment Contractor. He had four brothers and a sister and his grandmother lived with the family in Fulham. By 1901 he was living in Victoria Barracks in Windsor working as a canteen waiter, and interestingly there is a Frederick Arthur Maltby also aged 19 there too, from birth records they do not appear to be brothers. Reginald married Beatrice Lubbock, the daughter of Jacob Lubbock in 1903 at All Saints and St John the Baptist Church in New Windsor and they had two children, Reginald Charles born in 1903 and Freda May in 1906.

Freda and Henry Charles Sprules' wedding in July 1938 with her father Reginald Maltby GC second from the left and her mother Beatrice Maltby seated far right. On the bride's left is her brother Reginald.
©R Sprules

We can surmise that Reginald probably trained as a motor electrician and that he subsequently underwent further specialist training on enlisting with the London Electrical Engineers (RE Territorial Force) on 7th February 1909 which had its HQ at Regency Street, Westminster. He was called up for full-time service on the 5th August 1914 and served throughout the war in the United Kingdom with the Royal Engineers as a motor engineer. (He was the 32nd most senior man (in terms of service) when he was allocated the number 562033 in 1916 — previous to this date he would have had a different number). Because he did not serve overseas he received no medals for this period. After being demobilised on 21st May 1920 it is likely that after a while in 'civvy street' the attraction of army life with the extra pay, for which he would have qualified as a skilled motor engineer, drew him back and on 11th March 1921 he enlisted in the Tank Corps.

Maltby joined the 11 Armoured Car Company (ACC) two months later. On 11th February 1922, the Company sailed for India, arriving on 4th March 1922, proceeding to Kirkee, near Poona, whilst one Section remained on detachment duty at Bombay. While he was in Kirkee he received his Territorial Efficiency Medal, named to him in the rank of Corporal, 562033. Maltby's records show him as serving with 11 ACC until 3rd October 1932 although he is shown on a seniority roll of mechanics of December 1927 as a WO2 and having returned from India on SS *California* in 1928. Reginald's final posting on the 4th October 1932 was to the 3rd Bn Royal Tank Corps which was stationed at Lydd in Kent. Here he stayed until his final discharge from the Army on 3rd August 1938 as a WO2 3RTR.

In 1939, not being recalled for service the family moved to Dover and Reginald became a publican first at the *Five Alls Inn* in Market Street, and then the *Dewdrop Inn* in Tower Hamlets Street which still stands today. He was a Freemason of two Lodges, Peace and Harmony No 199 and Military Jubilee No 2195.

Until Bill Green started researching Maltby's connection with the Royal Tank Regiment they had no knowledge of him at all, indeed he was a most neglected GC and I hope that the work Bill did to ensure that he had a headstone, his grandson's efforts and this small book, will do him justice.

Citation: *2nd July 1926*

3rd July 1926

The KING has been graciously pleased, on the occasion of His Majesty's Birthday, to approve of the Award of the Medal of the Civil Division of the Most Excellent Order of the British Empire to the undermentioned (to be dated the *5th June, 1926*):—

For Gallantry

Staff Sergeant Reginald Harry Maltby, 11th Armoured Car Company, Lahore, in recognition of the heroism he displayed in saving a child from drowning in a disused well.

Other awards: EGM (Civilian) – GC exchange. Territorial Efficiency Medal (as 562033 Corporal) awarded in November 1922. Maltby was originally recommended for an AM but this was downgraded to an EGM. He is believed to be the only serviceman to have received an EGM in the Civil Division. It was presented on 24th January 1927 by the Colonel Commandant, RTC at a parade of the 7th Indian Infantry Brigade, Razmak, NW Frontier, India and his GC was sent by post to his widow on 15th April 1948.

The story

Reginald climbed down a 40 foot well to save a little girl who had fallen down. We can only imagine her terror. He was a man of 44 and there must have been many men there who were younger than him. His courage was outstanding and it is a pity that the full story has not to date been found.

Background: *Medals and decorations to members of the Territorial Army, previously Territorial Force*

There were different criteria for the awarding of the following medals/decorations. For a fuller description please refer to the *Medal Yearbook*. In 1921, the Territorial Force became the Territorial Army.

Territorial Force Efficiency Medal — (T.F.E.M) — approved by King Edward VII on 29 May 1908. The first awards, with the head of Edward VII, were listed in Army Order 304 of December 1908. After the death of Edward the obverse was changed to the bust of King George V in 1911. It required 12 years service.

All pictures provided by Jim Lees ©

Territorial Efficiency Medal — (T.E.M.) — succeeded the T.F.E.M. (Army Order 396 of September 1921) in 1921. The first awards described as the T.E.M. appear in Army Order 51 of February 1922. Please also note change of ribbon. Those who were awarded retrospective medals would have had the current medal thus Maltby could arguably have qualified for the TFEM as by March 1921 he was in the regular army. Exact dates need to be found for this.

This is the medal Maltby was awarded.

Efficiency Medal (TA) — In 1930 the Efficiency Medal (Territorial) was introduced. The first awards were listed in Army Order 36 of February 1931 and had the crowned head of King George V. This was superseded by King George VI in circa 1936 followed by Elizabeth II in circa 1952. It was again changed to the Efficiency Medal (T. & A.V.R.) in 1969 and finally the Efficiency Medal [1982] (Territorial) in 1982. This medal consolidated the awards to other ranks within the voluntary forces

There are also two TA decorations for officers.

Territorial Decoration — (TD) — officers from 1908–1930 entitlement 20 years to 12 continuous years' commissioned service with war service counting as double.

Efficiency Decoration — (ED) — from 1930, entitlement reduced in 1949 from 20 to 12 years

Sources: Reg and Kath Sprules — grandson and granddaughter
Tony Earthy — grandson-in-law
Bill Green, *OMRS Journal*, Autumn 1998
Royal Tank Regiment
Jim Lees
Medal Yearbook

Thomas George MANWARING, GC

Mine rescue, 30th June 1949, Arthur & Edward Colliery, Forest of Dean

Status: Civilian, Miner (Haulage Man), Arthur & Edward Colliery, Forest of Dean, Gloucestershire
Life dates: 11th December 1916, Warwickshire – 7th March 2000, Forest of Dean. Thomas was cremated at the Forest of Dean Crematorium and the ashes were removed by the undertaker. **Obit:** *Daily Telegraph*, 18th March 2000

This photo shows Simmonds, Manwaring and Bradley with their wives after they had received their Edward Medals.
Courtesy Ian Pope

Biography: Thomas Manwaring worked at several pits in the Forest of Dean but retired early, partly due to the effects of his experience in 1949. He married Joan Hathaway in 1940 in the Forest of Dean and they had one daughter.

Citation: *1st November 1949*
Whitehall, November 1, 1949

The KING has been pleased to award the Edward Medal (in Silver) to Frank Bradley and the Edward Medal (in Bronze) to Oswald George Simmonds and Thomas George Manwaring in recognition of their gallantry in the following circumstances: —

On the 30th June, 1949, the Arthur and Edward Colliery, Forest of Dean, was flooded by a sudden inrush of water. Evacuation of the mine was ordered as soon as the water broke in, and the escape of the men who were underground was greatly helped by Frank Bradley, a man of 63, who took charge of the man-riding trolleys which ran up and down the long, steep main road leading to the shaft, and helped the escaping men to travel swiftly over part of their road to safety.

After many men had been helped in this way another official advised Bradley to escape at once, telling him that the rising flood would soon cut off the main shaft. Bradley, however, refused to leave the pit, saying that some of his men were still underground. He thereupon, walked back into the inner working of the mine. At this point it should be emphasised that Bradley acted deliberately and without rashness, although he knew that once he was cut off from the main shaft he would have to stay below ground for a long time and that he might never reach the surface again. As an official of the mine he must have known also that blackdamp (carbon dioxide) was given off in the mine and that the stopping of ventilation by the flood made accumulations of this suffocating gas likely. He must also have known that there was an incalculable danger to be expected from the disturbance to roof supports caused by the flood. While Bradley was helping with the evacuation another official of the mine, Oswald George Simmonds was showing great calmness in the face of danger. He went round his district ordering his men out of the pit and telling them how to reach the main shaft safely through the flooding roads.

When he was himself about to leave he heard that two men, one old and feeble, were still left in the workings. He immediately returned to help them. When he found them, they were with a third man, Thomas George Manwaring, who had voluntarily stayed back to help them. Simmonds and Manwaring, helping and sometimes carrying the old men along with them, made their way towards the main shaft, meeting Bradley on the way. At the first opportunity they telephoned to the surface and were told that the flood cut them off completely from the main shaft, but that they might be able to reach a second shaft through the workings of the mine.

Bradley, Simmonds and Manwaring set off, taking with them the other two men, of whom one was practically exhausted. The way to the second shaft was very hard, and the air in places very bad. The men had in some places to wade through torrents of water, and in others had to clamber over falls of ground. They never, however, abandoned their weaker comrades, one of whom at times was so exhausted that he had to be pushed along in a truck. Eventually, after spending nearly seven hours underground struggling through the flooded mine, the party reached the second shaft and were hauled to safety.

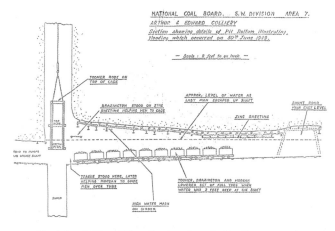

The Arthur & Edward Mine showing where the flooding occurred.

Other awards: EM (Bronze Mine) – GC exchange, Queen's Silver Jubilee Medal. George Manwaring received his exchange George Cross from the Queen in 1975 at an investiture at Buckingham Palace. He donated his Edward Medal to the Gloucester City Museum.

This award is a good example of what happened when the exchanges took place. It was decided in 1971 that only living Edward Medallists would receive the GC. Thus neither Bradley who had received the Silver version, nor Simmonds, exchanged because they had died prior to 1971. The Edward Medal was thus downgraded as those who had been awarded the EGM but died before the exchanges in 1940 had GCs presented to their next of kin — see Mahoney GC.

It seems that when these decisions were made there was insufficient consideration given to the inequity thereof and this led to a fair amount of dissatisfaction with the system. One can, years later, believe that while EGMs were mainly military awards but EMs were mainly industrial and were perhaps seen as less worthy. I find it unacceptable.

The story

As reported in *The Forester*

Floodwaters poured into the pit after new workings had accidentally breached an old shaft in the neighbouring East Slad Colliery. When the water broke through, telephone warnings were given to every part of the colliery and most of the 150 miners made for the main shaft. There they were met by a wall of water seven feet high. Some were swept off their feet; others clung to pipes and cables; all the pit ponies were drowned; the air became foul and the men became increasingly exhausted. Nevertheless they managed to struggle back towards the shaft through waist-deep swirling water which sometimes rose shoulder-high. Some reached the shaft with only their heads above water.

Crawling on top of submerged coal wagons, they made their way one by one into the cage, which took them to the surface. Only by diverting water to other parts of the pit was it possible to keep the cage in the main shaft working. The last man up rescued the pit cat, which had never seen daylight.

Tom Manwaring, haulageman, shouted "Don't worry I won't leave you" to the two men who thought they had been cut off.

Manwaring at the site where he found the two old men.

Frank Bradley, 63 year old examiner, helped to carry the exhausted men's satchels, jackets and ambulance box.

Frank Bradley who was to receive the Edward Medal in Silver.

When a count was taken on the surface, it was discovered that five men, including Manwaring, a pit haulier, were still missing. Manwaring had received orders to leave the mine, but when he heard that Albert Sims, an elderly colleague, was in difficulties, he went back to find him. He was later said by his workmates to have acted "deliberately", realising that he might never reach the surface again. He found Sims and another elderly haulage driver, Ernest Barnfield, and the three began to pick their way along the unflooded haulage road. On their way they met up with two mine supervisors, Oswald Simmonds and Frank Bradley, who had

52

remained behind to look for the missing men. Sometimes supporting and sometimes carrying their older colleagues, Manwaring, Simmonds and Bradley slowly inched their way towards the main shaft.

The Pluds shaft through which the men were rescued.

Simmonds being helped out of the Pluds shaft.

They struggled to an engine house, where they found a telephone in working order. When they called the surface with the news that they were still alive, they were told that the flood water was now 16 ft deep in the main shaft, covering the entrance to the mine workings, and that they were completely cut off. However, there was still a chance of escape if they could find their way through disused mine workings to a ventilation shaft of the old Pluds Colliery more than a mile and a half away. Bradley, Simmonds and Manwaring set off through the flooded galleries, taking with them the other two men, of whom Sims was practically exhausted and had to be carried. The way to the second shaft was very hard, the route tortuous, and the air rank and suffocating. In some places the men had to wade through torrents of water and in others had to clamber over falls of ground.

Eventually, almost seven hours after the alarm had been given, they reached the bottom of the ventilation shaft where a large bucket had been lowered to rescue them. Sims was the first to be placed in the bucket and hauled 400ft to safety. The rest of the party followed, to be greeted by their wives, who had been brought from the pit head.

HEROES OF WATERLOO
June 30, 1949: the flooding of Waterloo Pit

Men were up to their necks in water . . some short of breath clutched pit props for support and, as they paused, their mates urged them on and helped them

© *The Forester*

Background: *Arthur and Edward Mine*

This colliery was known locally as Waterloo. It opened in 1850 and closed just over a century later in 1959.

Waterloo or Arthur & Edward Mine in 1949.

Four of the men who prevented a disaster at Waterloo Pit: Cecil Brazington (pumpman), Harry Toomer (onsetter), Bert Morgan (underground fitter), and Morgan Teague (pumpman).

Four more heroes who all received the BEM.

Sources: *The Mines of the Forest of Dean* by Tony Oldham
www.lightmoor.co.uk/forestcoal/CoalA%26E.html
Ian Pope — nephew of Simmonds and who provided all the photos and who is the author of a number of books on the Forest of Dean
The Royal Forest of Dean Free Miners Association

Frederick Hamilton MARCH, GC, MBE

Attempt to thwart assassination, 19th November 1924, Cairo, Egypt

©*Teresa March*

©*Eileen Stewart*

Status: Chauffeur to Sir Lee Stack, Governor-General of the Sudan, while working for the Ministry of Public Instruction (this was probably not a permanent official appointment).

Life dates: 6th August 1891, Bowning, Yass, New South Wales, Australia – 30th October 1977, Khartoum, Sudan. While his headstone shows him to be 96 Fred was 10 years younger as his official birth certificate confirms. He is buried in Khartoum War Cemetery, Sudan, Plot 13 Row C Grave 5. This cemetery, adjoining Khartoum New Christian Cemetery, lies on the south-eastern side of Khartoum. The Australian Governement paid for his funeral.

Biography: Peter Sekuless tells Fred's story in his book and it needs only for me to precis his findings.

Frederick was the son of George Henry March and his wife Jane (Gurnett). Life was hard in the outback town of Gundaroo where drink was easy to come by but money difficult. Fred showed a remarkable practical ability at school and like so many dreamed of a better life. (Sekuless describes life in the 1890s but we know that in fact Fred was only born in 1891). Much of his life was fabricated and it is difficult to separate fact from fiction, however, we know that he left Australia for the United States, possibly as a stow-away, and then with his stated friend Bernard Cyril Freyberg (later VC) left for the UK as war broke out in 1914 in order to enlist. There they were apparently to meet up with the poet Rupert Brooke who helped them to join the Royal Naval Division.

> *The Australian War Memorial in Canberra states the following.*
> No 1580 Frederick Hamilton (Fred) March enlisted on 6th September 1915 at Goulburn NSW as No 1580 at the Divisional Signal Squadron, Anzac Mounted Divisional Headquarters and was promoted to Sergeant for motor cycle duties on 1st April 1917. He was discharged in Egypt at his own request on 6th August 1919.

I do not propose to include more of Fred's WWI exploits as much is not corroborated, suffice it to say that at the end of the war he declined to return to Australia and by 1922 was still in Cairo where he was working as a chauffeur and as a small-time intelligence agent. Hence the incident which was to change his life and for which he became a celebrity. He was well compensated for his actions and with the money bought a garage. He continued to live in Cairo and after WWII, for which no record of his having served has been found, he moved to the Sudan to work for the Ministry of Agriculture working out in the desert on water courses. He retired around 1956. Having spent so much of his life alone, though not friendless, in 1967, aged 77, he married the housekeeper of friends, Teresa Bongi. She was half Eritrean, half Italian. She helped him to curb his drinking and like many a woman before her took care of him in their modest home. As a member of the VC and GC Association and an MBE there was however, some relief from penury as he received an annuity from the Association and in addition, after much lobbying on his behalf by the Australian Returned Services League, a pension was assured and the last few years of his life were more comfortable.

There is a description of Fred having died in a mud-floored hut but it did contain a refrigerator and an air-conditioner, essential items for life in Sudan. DG Parsons says the description is misleading. Despite his claims there are no records to support Fred's claim of having been in Gallipoli, his MiD, the Croix de Guerre, nor time in the Royal Flying Corps or the Australian Army in WWII. While Fred was a keen and

54

successful motorcyclist winning a number of races Norton Villiers stated that his claim to the 100mph record could not be justified.

Citation: *5th December 1924*

St. James's Palace, S.W. 1.

5th December, 1924

The KING has been graciously pleased to approve of the Award of the Medal of the Civil Division of the Most Excellent Order of the British Empire to the undermentioned:—

For Gallantry.

Fred Hamilton March, Chauffeur to the late Major-General Sir Lee Oliver FitzMaurice Stack, G.B.E., C.M.G.

Other awards: EGM (Civilian) – GC exchange. Fred March's group of miniatures (pictured in Sekuless) are: GC, MBE (Civil), 1914–15 Star, British War Medal, Victory Medal with oak leaf, 1939–45 Star, Africa Star, Defence Medal, War Medal, Serbian Eagle, Medaille Militaire (Fr), Croix de Guerre (Fr). Additionally March received the 1953 Coronation Medal and the 1977 Queen's Silver Jubilee Medal. The only original full size medals that were donated to the Australian War Memorial were his MBE (*LG* 1st January 1957) awarded as Mechanical Field Engineer, Ministry of Agriculture, Sudan Government and his QSJM.

Fred March's group of miniatures as pictured in Sekuless and given to him by Dan Parsons. Additionally Fred had the 1977 QSJM. The fact that this is not included in the group adds further weight to the suspicion that these miniatures were collected together by Fred rather than all awarded. It is now held by the Australian War Memorial.

©*P Sekuless and Australian War Memorial*

The story

On 19th November 1924 Fred was driving Sir Lee when the car and its occupants were the victims of an assassination plot. Due to the slow-moving traffic and the general confusion of trams, cars and mule carts the assassins had just the opportunity they sought. Although wounded Fred was able to skilfully manoeuvre the car through the chaos while his passengers Stack and Campbell crouched in the back of the 8 cylinder Cadillac.

All three men had been wounded but Stack was to die two days later. His funeral was a fine affair with many dignatories attending. It must be suggested that had the passenger not been the Governor-General the award of the EGM may not have been awarded. March's presence of mind and his quick reactions saved his own life and ensured that he became an Australian legend and like all legendary figures not all the exploits attributed can be verified.

Memorials: GC Memorial in Canberra.

Background: *Sir Lee Stack*

The 1924 assassination in Cairo of Sir Oliver (Lee) Stack, the British Governor-General of Sudan and Egyptian Army Commander or Sirdar, had dire consequences for Egypt. The British ordered the expulsion of Egyptian troops from Sudan, which was at the time ruled by a condominium of Britain and Egypt.

Read about the Sudan in Volume 5.

Sources: Eileen Stewart

Fred, An Australian Hero by Peter Sekuless

Australian War Memorial

Sudannow July 1977

Cyril Arthur Joseph MARTIN, GC, MC

Bomb disposal, 1943, London

Cyril Martin with his wife Jessie, Howard
and Jocelyne about 1926.
*All pictures courtesy J Collis unless
otherwise noted.*

Jocelyne, Cyril and Jessie after the
investiture.

Churchyard of St Thomas á Becket,
South Cadbury.
©M Hebblethwaite

Status: 144910 Captain, Temporary Major, Corps of Royal Engineers Bomb Disposal Squad

Life dates: 23rd July 1897, Derby, Derbyshire – 29th November 1973, South Cadbury, Yeovil, Somerset. Cyril is buried in South Cadbury Churchyard alongside his wife who had died in 1972. **Obit:** *The Times,* 30th November 1973 and 4th December 1973

Biography: In 1901 Cyril was living with his parents Henry and Frances Ann Sealy (Griffiths) Martin at the Holy Trinity Vicarage, Derby. There were two other children, Violet and Henry Wilfred plus mother-in-law Emma Sealy Griffiths, two sister-in-laws, one of whom worked as a sick nurse and a lady's maid, a cook, a housemaid and a nursemaid. A further son Vernon, born later, was killed in a shooting accident.

Revd Henry Martin became Vicar of Crookes from 1901 to 1916 and then he moved with his family to become Rector of Oulton in Norfolk becoming the Chaplain of Mutford and Lothingland Workhouse in the town in 1922.

Cyril attended Berkdale Preparatory School in Sheffield and then became a student of Trent College from 1911–15 near Nottingham where, many years later, he was to become a Governor. In 1916 he joined the TA and was commissioned into the Royal Garrison Artillery in 1916 as a 2nd Lieutenant.

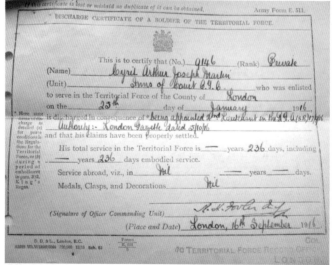

Cyril Martin's discharge certificate from the TA after 236 days dated 5th October 1916.

After demob he went up to Emmanuel College, Cambridge in 1919, obtaining his BA in Mechanical Sciences in 1922. By now he was a married man, having married Jessie Marion Cooksey on June 23rd 1920. They had two children Howard and Jocelyne. Howard was killed whilst serving on the Corvette HMS *Fleur de Lys* sunk by *U206* on 14th October 1941 in the Straits of Gibraltar. Jocelyne went on to serve in the WRENS for three years.

Then came World War II and Cyril was commissioned on 17th August 1940. He joined the Royal Engineers with No 144910 and was posted to the Ministry of Supply Directorate of Bomb Disposal in London. As each bomb was defused its fuze, detonator, clock and other useful parts were taken to HQ to be examined so that slowly the different types of mine and bomb hurled at Britain and her allies would be understood and thus the risk of death minimised. Whenever a new type of bomb or fuze was found the information was quickly circulated to teams across the UK.

Apart from wartime Cyril worked as an electrical engineer joining Crompton Parkinson in 1929 and staying with them for the rest of his working life until 1962 after which time, though semi-retired, he continued to act as a Consultant as well as becoming President of the Cromptonian Association. A good team player and a man whose intellect was respected he was Chairman of the Fractional Motors Association from 1948–1951.

In 1962 Cyril and Jessie moved down to South Cadbury. Part of the reason for this was that Henry Martin was the Vicar of North Cadbury and Violet lived locally and she played the organ in his church so there was a ready-made social group. Cyril was never idle and while still travelling to Crompton Parkinson from time to time, was active in local affairs such as becoming a church warden and a member of the British Legion as well as keeping up his extensive cider orchard and being a keen fixer of things — broken toys to farm machinery, indeed Jessie was to say that all he needed in life was "a bed and a garage". The cider apples were sold to Showerings and readers may like to read about **Bywater GC** who worked for another cider maker, Coates.

During the early 1960s the Decimal Coinage and Metric System Panel was set up of which Cyril Martin became the Chairman. He had long been concerned with British Standards and the British Chamber of Commerce and his expertise in industry enabled him to make a significant contribution. He was particularly involved in discussions on how the change-over would affect industry in all its ramifications. The globalisation of trade, the standardisation of engineering standards and the adoption of the decimal (though not necessarily the metric) system in other countries and, of course the closer ties with Europe, were strong arguments in favour of adoption. In the papers he submitted Cyril included such statistics as the shorter length of teaching time required in schools. However, it should not be thought to have been a quick decision-making process. Several years later he was still writing and debating the merits of a 10/- or £1 basis.

While Cyril is often to be found described as having "cold-blooded courage" or being "cool-headed" this belies the man in his private life where he was warm-hearted and, says his daughter, "the most kind, loving and patient of men". Patience he had in abundance and for this the nation and many individuals owe thanks.

WON GEORGE CROSS FOR SECRET DEED

Slim, dark, nerveless, he is the idol of the men who work with him.

Extract from Martin's notebook while on BD duty.

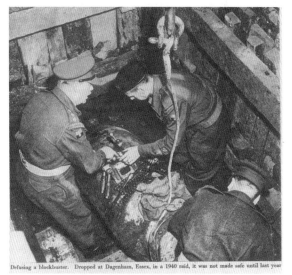

Defusing a blockbuster. Dropped at Dagenham, Essex, in a 1940 raid, it was not made safe until last year

From *John Bull*, 15th April 1950.

Citation: *11th March 1943*

The KING has been graciously pleased to approve the award of the GEORGE CROSS, in recognition of most conspicuous gallantry in carrying out hazardous work in a very brave manner, to:-

Captain (temporary Major) Cyril Arthur Joseph Martin, M.C., B.A. (144910), Corps of Royal Engineers (Worcester Park, Surrey).

Martin was the first GC to hold office in the VC & GC Association (Hon. Sec.) 1961-1970. Previously all office holders had been VCs.

Cyril Martin, approx 1971.

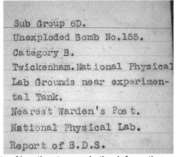

Note of location, type and other information on an unexploded bomb. The note to the right is followed by the Report made by Martin — this one was abandoned.

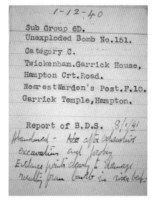

Cyril and Jessie on their 50th wedding anniversary.

Citation for MC

22nd June 1918

2/Lt Cyril Arthur Joseph Martin, RGA Special Reserve was awarded the Military Cross

For conspicuous gallantry and devotion to duty. With 2 men he extinguished a burning ammunition dump under heavy and continuous fire and while overheated ammunition was exploding close by. He showed great coolness and resource.

Cyril Martin's group and his miniatures — these are seldom seen together.
©*Martin family*

Jocelyne and her daughter Philipa, 2006.

Other awards: Military Cross (GVR 22/6/18), British War Medal, Victory Medal, Defence Medal, War Medal 1939–45 and 1953 Coronation Medal. Cyril received a 10yrs Service Medal on 1st January 1940 from Crompton Parkinson, a gold watch after 25 years and an inscribed badge after 30 years.

The story

As with so many wartime GC and other gallantry awards the Citation is short and gives very few clues as to the time, place or details of the action. Additionally this George Cross, again in common with other bomb disposals, was for multiple acts rather than one specific one though it was often the case that a particularly difficult operation was the final catalyst for recognition and award. It hardly bears repeating but the circumstances under which BD men had to work during the winter months in rain, mud, freezing conditions so that their fingers stuck to the frozen metal, and with the ever-present danger of an explosion, made heroes of each and every one of them.

Martin standing with ratings after defuzing a bomb.

The *Recommendation* for the George Cross (in the National Archives and from which the Citation was written) tells the story from the 17th January through to the 4th February 1943. Martin was by then a very experienced BD officer.

On the night of 17–18th January 1943 a number of the bombs dropped during the air raid failed to explode. There was a new marking on the 500kg bomb which dropped near Lord's cricket ground — Y — the first identification of the Y fuze. No one knew how to render the fuze safe and it was only because it was faulty that those who worked on it were not killed. The fault enabled the men to uncover the secrets of the Y fuze.

Meanwhile a large bomb had also fallen into a warehouse of the Victoria Haulage Company at Battersea which was full of essential American machine tools. Next door was a flour mill and it was imperative that it not be damaged so it was closed down while the BD team went to work.

However, instructions came from the Ministry of Supply to radiograph the bomb in order to determine if it was of the same type as the Lord's bomb and, after 12 hours of intense work by Dr JAT Dawson, Ministry of Supply and Capt B Waters RE, it was finally confirmed to be the same. But the means of rendering it safe was still not known.

While Lt RW Deans (GM) was in charge of the working party it was Major Martin, on the Directorate staff, who was called to dispose of it. Even knowing the type of fuze the bomb still presented a high risk and the TNT within it had to be removed. Martin, whose expertise was legendary, and Deans, worked carefully through the night of the 19th January until midday of the 20th removing the base plate only to find that the bomb contained solid cast TNT. They applied a high temperature steam to the explosive while at the same time keeping the fuze cold with cold water. At 8.30 the next morning the two men finally achieved their goal of emptying the bomb. It was arduous, extremely uncomfortable and dangerous work requiring a cool head and nerves of steel.

Further bombs presented equally difficult problems. When on the 2nd February a bomb in the Old Kent Road was being worked on and the head of the fuze broke off Martin again came to the rescue. Two days later Capt Carlyle (who had removed that first fuze from the Lord's bomb) was taken to hospital after suffering burns when the liquid oxygen, which was used for freezing the fuze, ignited. Martin who was present but not actually in the hole helped Carlyle to safety up a burning ladder and arranged for his immediate removal to hospital. He then quietly and with infinite patience and care refroze the fuze and was able to complete the disarming of the bomb which was in an awkward position in a shaft under a house.

Such were only three of the many actions taken to render unexploded bombs safe by Cyril Martin GC. His cool-headedness became well-known amongst his colleagues as yet again when disarming a mercury switch bomb (which relied on a dry battery) he not only gave a running commentary but quietly and purposefully cooled the fuze casing with liquid oxygen until the battery was cold enough to become inert and thus enable him to remove the fuze and render the bomb safe.

Due to the secrecy surrounding the methods used there is only mention of "new processes" and "newly developed techniques" in the *Recommendations* however Hogben and Southall in their books describe in detail the methods used. It is worth reading them for clear descriptions of the exacting procedures undertaken by Martin and all other BD men.

Memorials: There was a block in the Barracks at Chatham that was named after Cyril Martin but enquiries reveal that this is no longer standing. House at Trent College named Martin House.

Martin House at Trent College is named in his honour. It is a fine memorial.
©David Pinney

Background: *Crompton Parkinson*
Crompton Lighting is one of the oldest lighting companies in the world. It was founded in 1878 by Col Crompton. In 1927 he joined up with Frank Parkinson in Leeds to form Crompton Parkinson. In 1968 the company was taken over by Hawker Siddeley and eventually in 1999 became part of Cooper Lighting and Security Ltd though the brand still continues.

Crompton Parkinson Long Service Badge.

Crompton Parkinson Long Service Silver Medal.

Neither of these badges is exactly like the one that Martin received, perhaps there were different ones for senior members of the company.

Bomb versus mine disposals
We are familiar with bomb diposal teams but it should be remembered that while bombs dropped on land were being defused and rendered safe by members of the Army (usually Royal Engineers, either volunteers or serving soldiers) there was also another sinister weapon of Adolf Hitler, mines. They were not only dropped at sea but also in shallow water and on land by parachute. Thus Mould GC and **Syme** were mine disposal officers whereas Martin, **Barefoot**, **Wylie**, **Davies** and many others were mainly involved in the disposal of bombs. There were also RAF unexploded bomb (UXB) teams.

Each officer was allocated a rating who carried the tools but who was not supposed to be involved in the actual defuzing and rendering safe but who would be brought in to move the disarmed mine or bomb. The two men would be driven by a driver in a large fast car, often a Humber at any time of the day or night though as Ivan Southall mentions in *Softly Tread the Brave* "no one envied them and all were in awe".

Recommendations for Gallantry
All Gallantry (and indeed all Honours) awards are the result of recommendations. These are usually made by senior officers in the case of service personnel. To this end this may involve anything from a couple of letters to a score or more. Different points of view are put forward, witnesses are contacted, discussions of level of award are held and the process may take up to a year (even longer in a few cases). There are files containing these *Recommendations* in the National Archives for most GCs and some Exchanges. A few are still restricted and are not open to researchers. In some cases a person was not awarded anything at all, in others a lesser or, rarely, a higher award was made. A read of the Citation alone frequently does not tell the whole story.

For example it was first suggested that Bill McAloney GC should be recommended to the Royal Humane Society. Then the Air Force Medal was thought to be more appropriate, then after further discussion the decision was made to recommend the Empire Gallantry Medal — the EGM. Finally however, he was awarded the Albert Medal which he later exchanged for the GC.

Sources: Jocelyne Collis — daughter
Lambeth Palace Library
The Times and Sir John Smyth, VC
Designed to Kill by Major Arthur Hogben
The George Cross by Ian Bisset

John Goodbody — grandson-in-law
Softly Tread the Brave by Ivan Southall
John Bull for week ending 15th April 1950
David Pinney at Trent College

Dudley William MASON, GC

Ship's master, SS Ohio, Summer 1942, Mediterranean Sea

Dudley with his mother, 22nd September 1942.

© *Tom Rodgers 1968*

Status: Captain, Merchant Navy (Master, SS *Ohio*)

Swerford church where Dudley's parents and many members of the Cozier family are buried.

© *M Hebblethwaite*

Life dates: 7th October 1901, Surbiton, Surrey – 26th April 1987, Brockenhurst, near Lymington, Hampshire. Dudley was cremated at Bournemouth Crematorium. The service was attended by the High Commissioner of Malta GC, also present were **Cobham GC** and **Copperwheat GC**. His ashes were scattered in the garden of his home, Mill House, off Station Road, Sway. Two houses have now been built thereon. **Obit:** *The Times*, 28th April 1987

Biography: Dudley was the son of Charles John Little and Agnes Ellen (Cozier) Mason and at the time of his birth his parents were working for a local family in Long Ditton in Surrey where Dudley and his brother Charles both went to school. He left at around 14 or 15 to attend night school. When he was 19 Dudley joined the Eagle Oil Company as an apprentice.

Dudley Mason's Indenture with Eagle Oil Transport Company.

This and all pictures courtesy of P Davis unless otherwise noted.

EAGLE OIL & SHIPPING COMPANY LIMITED

16 FINSBURY CIRCUS · LONDON EC2

Telephone: LONDON WALL 1200 · Cables: EAGLOIL LONDON · Inland Telegrams: EAGLOIL LONDON TELEX

5th December, 1958

OUR REF:

TO WHOM IT MAY CONCERN

YOUR REF:

CAPTAIN DUDLEY WILLIAM MASON, G.C.

       Captain Mason was born at Surbiton, Surrey on the 7th October, 1901.

       He joined Eagle Oil as a Deck Apprentice in 1919 and after serving 4 years' Apprenticeship obtained his Second Mate's Certificate in 1924, when he was appointed Third Officer. He gained his Mate's Certificate in 1927, during which year he was appointed Second Officer. He gained his Master's Certificate in 1931 and was appointed a Chief Officer in the Fleet in May 1935. He was appointed Temporary Master in August 1941 and confirmed as a Master in 1942.

       In 1945 Captain Mason was seconded to the Petroleum Board for service in Italy and returned to the United Kingdom in May 1946, when he again took up service as a Master in the Eagle Fleet.

       He came ashore in 1951 and was appointed Marine Superintendent of Eagle Oil & Shipping Co. Ltd. in August of that year.

       He retired on the 30th September 1958.

       In 1942 Captain Mason was specially selected to command the s.s. "OHIO", which vessel Eagle Oil managed on behalf of the Ministry of War Transport, to sail in the historic Malta Convoy (Operation "Pedestal"), and for his splendid performance in command of this vessel he was honoured with the George Cross, the first to be awarded an Officer in the Merchant Navy. His courage and determined leadership on that occasion was further recognised by the award of Lloyd's War Medal for Bravery at Sea.

       Captain D. W. Mason served with distinction throughout the whole of his career with the Eagle Oil and during the six years that I have been Manager of the Eagle Oil Fleet I have had ample opportunity of recognising Captain Mason as a man of the highest integrity and undoubted ability.

       I can without hesitation recommend Captain Mason for any position in which nautical experience is required.

MARINE MANAGER

A letter of recommendation and which also acts as a CV of Dudley's time with Eagle Oil.

Dudley's second marriage to Vera de Smitt in 1948 was very successful and his kindness to her daughter Pat was such that she has always thought of him as her father. Like almost all GCs he only enjoyed telling the funny stories that had befallen him. He had a great love of his country and expected his crew to give of their best under all circumstances. In retirement Dudley and Vera moved to Sway where his favourite pastimes were his garden, his dog Dixon, cricket and reading. In 1967 when his wife died he asked Pat and her husband Leslie to come to live with him which they did and the affection that grew between the three generations culminated in Pat's son Group Captain Nigel Davis forming part of the procession at the VC and GC celebrations at Westminster Abbey in 2006.

Dudley Mason was elected a Member of this Company in November 1954 and he died in April of this year. For this Honourable Company to be presented with and asked to receive into our safe custody his George Cross is indeed a very great honour and an act of extreme generosity by his family. It not only represents the gallantry of one man but that of all who took part in "Operation Pedestal". It is with a feeling of great humility and deep pride that I as Master, receive this decoration on behalf of the Honourable Company of Master Mariners. There are no other words I can say, than: Thank you Mrs. Davis.

Extract from the Record of the Honourable Company of Master Mariners, after the gift of the GC on 27th October 1987.

Dudley Mason felt deeply that society had changed and in his will launched a tirade against "the greedy, the malicious, the lazy and the impecunious who knew nothing of work as my generation had known it."

Citation: *4th September 1942*

8th September 1942 (To be dated 4th September 1942)

The KING has been graciously pleased to award the GEORGE CROSS to Captain Dudley William Mason, Master, S.S. *Ohio*.

During the passage to Malta of an important convoy Captain Mason's ship suffered most violent onslaught. She was a focus of attack throughout and was torpedoed early one night. Although gravely damaged, her engines were kept going and the Master made a magnificent passage by hand-steering and without a compass. The ship's gunners helped to bring down one of the attacking aircraft. The vessel was hit again before morning, but though she did not sink, her engine room was wrecked. She was then towed. The unwieldy condition of the vessel and persistent enemy attacks made progress slow, and it was uncertain whether she would remain afloat. All next day progress somehow continued and the ship reached Malta after a further night at sea.

The violence of the enemy could not deter the Master from his purpose. Throughout he showed skill and courage of the highest order and it was due to his determination that, in spite of the most persistent enemy opposition, the vessel, with her valuable cargo, eventually reached Malta and was safely berthed.

Other awards: 1939–45 Star, Atlantic Star, Africa Star with clasp "North Africa 1942–1943", War Medal and Lloyd's Bravery Medal, 1953 Coronation Medal and 1977 Queen's Silver Jubilee Medal. In 1954 Dudley was elected a member of the Honourable Company of Master Mariners and his medals are part of their collection on HQS *Wellington* moored on the Thames.

Many of the crew of SS *Ohio* were decorated for their contribution to *Operation Pedestal* and include a Distinguished Service Order, five Distinguished Service Crosses and seven Distinguished Service Medals.

The story

In August 1942, the *Ohio* a 14,000-ton tanker belonging to the Texas Oil Company was chartered by the Ministry of War Transport under the nominal ownership of the British Eagle Oil Company. She was under the command of Captain Dudley Mason. There were fourteen merchant ships taking part in *Operation Pedestal* with a large escort both naval and air. The *Ohio* was carrying 1,000 tons of fuel oil while other ships carried essential foods, medicines and more fuel. Churchill was by now deeply aware of the importance of supplying Malta and of preventing it from falling into enemy hands. (Compare this to Churchill's attitude in 1940 — see Lewin's entry).

On the 10th August the convoy (Richard Woodman, in *Malta Convoys 1940–1943*, considered it more of a naval operation than a convoy in the conventional sense) passed through the Straits of Gibraltar. (Peter Smith cites a number of statements that perhaps the Operation may already have been known to the Axis command). In the early morning of the 12th August the first Italian torpedoes struck the *Ohio*. The continuous attack from both enemy aircraft and submarines for four days shattered the ship. One bomb lifted her right out of the water while another exploded in her boiler room, a Stuka crashed and exploded on her deck, her back was broken.

Although she was badly damaged, the ship's engineers kept her going and Mason with Chief Officer Douglas Gray at the helm hand-steered without a compass. Destroyers went back to look after the other crippled ships, while those that had survived the bombardment struggled on towards Malta. Soon they were within reach of the short-range Malta Spitfires, which held off subsequent attacks.

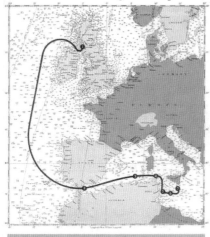

The voyage of the *Ohio* August 1943.
©*HMSO*

Three damaged ships among them *Ohio*, were however, still astern, and a great effort was being made to get them in. The *Ohio* and the *Dorset* were hit yet again and the latter sank. The destroyer *Penn* and the minesweepers *Rye* and *Ledbury* towed the *Ohio* in turn and fought off air attacks from about 11am on the 13th until the morning of the 15th. Mason and his crew were by now utterly exhausted. Twenty miles from Valetta she came to a halt. Renewed efforts to tow began again, the towing wire snapped. A new line from the the tanker's stern was attached but again it parted from the ship ahead, the *Rye*. A third tow rope and then a fourth and despite further enemy bombardment and damage finally on the morning of the 14th August the *Ohio* crept into Grand Harbour to a "tumultous reception". Dudley Mason handed his ship over to the Naval Fuelling Authority and ordered that all moveable fittings be stored ashore in case the ship should sink.

Dudley had sustained burns to his hands so he and his Chief Engineer James Wyld were flown back to Britain. No accommodation had been arranged, no reception party of any kind. They were left to find somewhere to stay and to find medical treatment. On recovery he returned to Eagle Oil and from July 1945 to May 1946, again on loan to the Ministry of War Transport, was sent to Naples to supervise the fresh water shipments into Italy.

James Wyld became the first Merchant Navy officer to be awarded the DSO.

An invitation came soon from Air Vice-Marshall Keith R Park at RAF HQ, whose fighter Squadron had given cover to the *Ohio*.

"My pilots would welcome an opportunity of seeing you and thanking you personally for bringing your ship through. Would you like to pay a visit to some of my aerodromes next Thursday 20th August departing 16.00, having tea at one of the aerodromes and having a look around them, returning with me to my house for drinks? We could then fix you up for dinner at our mess and return you to your ship or shore billet later".

We do not know if the invitation was taken up.

Captain Dudley William Mason by Terence Cuneo.
©*National Archives*

Bronze bust of DW Mason GC at the Imperial
War Museum.

Memorials: The bust in the IWM, painting at the NA , display on HMS *Wellington*.

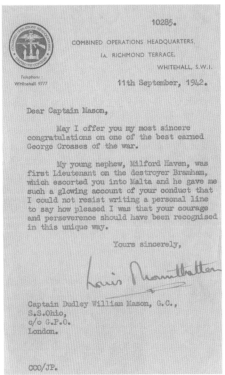

10285.

COMBINED OPERATIONS HEADQUARTERS,
1A. RICHMOND TERRACE,
WHITEHALL, S.W.I.

Telephone
WHltehall 9777

11th September, 1942.

Dear Captain Mason,

May I offer you my most sincere
congratulations on one of the best earned
George Crosses of the war.

My young nephew, Milford Haven, was
first Lieutenant on the destroyer Bramham,
which escorted you into Malta and he gave me
such a glowing account of your conduct that
I could not resist writing a personal line
to say how pleased I was that your courage
and perseverence should have been recognised
in this unique way.

Yours sincerely,

Louis Mountbatten

Captain Dudley William Mason, G.C.,
S.S.Ohio,
c/o G.P.O.
London.

CCO/JP.

Letter from Lord Louis Mountbatten.

The SS *Ohio* sinking. All was over in 7 minutes before her stern was lifted
high into the air and sunk amid a deafening noise of fittings falling inside
the ship and fire being put out. So went to the bottom the stern part of a
famous ship to find her grave beside her bow which had sunk two weeks
previously on 4th October 1946.

The crippled ship.

Background: *The Eagle Oil and Shipping Company — two famous ships*
See **D Clarke GC** who was on the *San Emiliano*
The Company was founded by Weetman Pearson who successfully challenged the American monopoly of
Mexican oil. The Eagle Fleet as it was first known "created new seaways for the flow of oil to world
markets". The two most famous ships were the *San Demetrio* and the *Ohio*.

The story of the *San Demetrio's* crew's survival after suffering attack from the *Admiral Scheer* on 5th November 1940, their subsequent abandonment into lifeboats and then the reboarding of the ship some two days later by those on No 1 Lifeboat is one of extraordinary luck and resourcefulness.

©*W Kempster and B Evans*

The ship was carrying 11,000 tons of petrol and the damage was extensive but with unbelievable determination the 16 men managed to get the engine going and they followed a course set by the North Star. Many of the men were injured and one died but there was some fresh water and limited food supplies on board. At last on the 14th they were spotted and assisted by a tug and destroyer off the coast of Ireland and eventually reached the Firth of Clyde on 19th November 1940.

Extensive repairs were carried out. She was to be attacked again in 1942 and sank with the loss of 53 men tragically after all that she and her crew had endured.

The SS *Ohio*

The importance of oil to both the Allies and the Axis forces cannot be over stated. It was thus obvious that both sides would do their best to disrupt the tankers transporting this vital commodity. The Eagle Oil and Shipping Company lost sixteen tankers. Two years after the *San Demetrio's* heroic delivery of most of her cargo the *Ohio* delivered a similar amount to Malta while being bombarded from the air and the sea. She could carry 13,000 tons of cargo, mainly petrol and was fast. The story is Mason's story. Finally in 1946 the two halves of the *Ohio* were towed out into the Mediterranean and sunk.

Sources: Pat Davis — step-daughter
Brockenhurst Royal British Legion
Mrs Dean of Sway
The Times
The Ohio & Malta by Michael Pearson
HQS *Wellington* of the Master Mariners Company
Bruce Cairns
Eagle Fleet by WE Lucas
Everyone's War, No 7 Summer 2003
Malta Convoys 1940–1943 by Richard Woodman

More Gallant Deeds of the War by Stanley Rogers
Lloyd's Medals 1836 – 1989 by Jim Gawler
Pedestal by Peter C Smith
Salute the Red Duster by AB Campbell
Under the Red Ensign by Frank Shaw
Victor, 30th June 1962
Illustrated London News, 7th January 1961
Malta Convoy — a film by the Central Office of Information

Mata DIN, GC, IOM

Earthquake rescue, 31st May – 1st June 1935, Quetta, India

Status: 10081 Lance-Naik, 4th Battalion, 19th Hyderabad Regiment, Indian Army
Life dates: 29th January 1913, Alwar District, Rajasthan, India – 29th May 1967, Gailoth Village, Alwar District
Biography: Mata enlisted on 29th January 1930 as L/Naik serving in his home country. He was promoted to Jemedar on 10th January 1942 and posted to the 8th Bn. on 15th July 1942. On 15th January 1944 he was promoted to A/Subadar and returned to his old Bn the 4th/19th Bn. which was renamed 4th Bn. Kumaon Regiment. He retired 11th July 1947 but joined the National Volunteer Force for the period March 1955 – October 1956.
Author's note: Mata Din should probably have been listed in the C-E book Volume 3.
Citation: *19th November 1935*
The KING has been graciously pleased to approve of the Award of the Medal of the Military Division of the Most Excellent Order of the British Empire to the undermentioned for services rendered in connection with the recent earthquake in Baluchistan : —

No. 10081 Lance-Naik Mata Din, 4th Battalion, 19th Hyderabad Regiment, Indian Army. On 31st May, 1935, this Non-commissioned Officer showed conspicuous devotion to duty by excavating a man who was buried in a very dangerous place (and for whose rescue three parties had already made attempts, but had left him there as there was very imminent danger of the working parties themselves being buried alive).

Burma Star.
©*Din Muhammad*

Citation for the IOM
Kangaw, Burma 13th February 1945
India Office, 21st June, 1945.
The following awards have been made in recognition of gallant and distinguished services in Burma: —
The Indian Order of Merit (Second Class).
Subadar Mata Din, G.C. (19709), 19th Hyderabad Regiment.
Other awards: EGM (Military) – GC exchange, IOM, 1953 Coronation Medal. He may have held the Burma Star seen here.

The story
Just a little more
The story of the British soldiers and civilians during the earthquake rescue and cleanup is told in the entries for **F Allen GC, J Cowley GC, A Brooks GC, E Elston GC** and **G Henshaw GC** in earlier volumes and AH Lungley GC in this book.

Devastation.

Refugees from the earthquake, the tented city.

We are now familiar with the devastation caused by earthquakes. The most fortunate part of Quetta was that there was a substantial military presence and that the area in which they were barracked was relatively little affected by the quake. Thus there was immediately a chain of command and a rescue force which was used to discipline, and which was able to effectively muster, the Indians to secure areas, to rescue the living and dispose of the dead.

The local people were displaced, traumatised and in shock. Their homes had been flattened and thousands had died or been injured. For once the British presence was a welcome one with its administrative and military skills. There were men who could set up communication links, organise food and medical stations and generally bring order to the chaos.

Background: *Indian army ranks — other than Cavalry*
Sepoy — Private
Lance-Naik — Lance-Corporal
Naik — Corporal
Havildar — Sergeant
Jemadar — junior commissioned officer in the cavalry and infantry = Cornet or Ensign
Subedar — 2nd Lieutenant

The Indian Order of Merit
Instituted by the Honourable East India Company in 1837 this award was issued in three classes with the Third Class being the lowest and the Second and First being bars for successive acts of bravery. By 1945 however, only Second and First were in existence. Kempton states that the Second was abolished in 1944 though the Citation above contradicts this.

It was first called the Order of Merit but the name was changed to Indian Order of Merit in 1902 to distinguish it from the newly instituted (Imperial) Order of Merit.

19th Hyderabad Regiment
In 1945 this regiment became the Kumaon Regiment although a request originating from the Battalion Commanders' Conference to change the name had been made in 1935 this was rejected by Army HQ at the time. Members of the Kumaonese first joined the British Indian Army in the early 19th Century. They came from the northern hills of India.
Sources: New Bodleian Library housing the former Indian Institute
http://faculty.winthrop.edu/haynese/india/medals/IOM/IOM.html
Valour & Gallantry — H.E.I.C. & Indian Army Victoria Crosses & George Crosses 1856–1946 by Chris Kempton
Din Muhammad
Tom Johnson
Thirty Seconds at Quetta by Robert Jackson

Lionel Colin (The Duke) MATTHEWS, GC, MC

Resistance to torture, August 1942 – 2nd March 1944, PoW, Sandakan, Borneo

©*Mike Curtis*

Lionel, Lorna and David Matthews when Lionel left for the railway station on embarkation leave in Melbourne in 1941. They were not to know it would be the last time they would see each other.

©*D Matthews*

Status: VX24597 Captain, 2nd Battalion, 8 Division Signals, Australian Corps of Signals, Australian Military Forces

Life dates: 15th August 1912, Stepney, South Australia – 2nd March 1944, Kuching, Sarawak. Lionel is buried in Labuan War Cemetery. Labuan is a small island in Brunei Bay, off the coast of north-west Borneo. **David Matthews** explains why.

"Dad was originally buried in Kuching in a grave which had apparently been dug before his trial ended. He was given a full military funeral with a select band of Australian officers and a few troops in attendance, as well as Japanese officers in full dress and wearing their decorations. A most unusual occurrence. My mother received a letter dated 18th November 1946, from the Directorate of War Graves Services in Melbourne informing her that Dad's remains had been reburied in the Labuan War Cemetery, Plot J. Row B, Grave No. 15. The letter also explained that the maintenance of war cemeteries would soon be taken over by the Imperial War Graves Commission which has maintained the cemeteries to this day.

I imagine the bodies of other Commonwealth servicemen buried in Kuching were reburied in Labuan about the same time as my father's. I know that parties of natives with Australian officers had picked up the bodies of men who died on the death marches from Sandakan to Ranau soon after the war ended and these were buried at Labuan."

Biography: Lionel was the third child of Edgar Roy and Anne Elizabeth (Jeffery) Matthews. His father was a plumber at the time of his birth. Educated first at East Adelaide Public and then Norwood High schools Lionel's first job was as a salesman in a shop. He was a keen sea-scouter and an excellent swimmer and life-saver. He married Myrtle (Lorna) Lane, on 26th December 1935 in Kensington, South Australia. The couple had one son David.

David Matthews says

"*I am the only child of the marriage, the war saw to that, and Mum and I remained in Melbourne until Dad went overseas in early 1941 to Malaya. We had lived in the Hawthorn district of Melbourne (an inner suburb) as Dad worked as a wallpaper salesman for a firm in the city. Mum brought me to Adelaide when he left and we lived with her mother and some of Mum's siblings.*"

In addition to his work with the Scouts Lionel gave of his time to work voluntarily at Melbourne Pentridge Gaol during 1937–1938. He trained as a signalman in the Citizen Naval Forces then enlisted in the Militia on 11th April 1939 being commissioned in January 1940 in the Army School of Signals. On 10th July he transferred to the 8th Div Signals, Australian Army **. In February 1941 he embarked for Singapore where he became attached to the 2/10th Field Regiment of Artillery until 30th April 1941. After suffering from appendicitis in late 1941 he was promoted to Captain in January 1942 while operations against the Japanese from mid-January onwards, starting with air raids backed up by ground defences on the Malay Peninsula, were taking place. On 16th February he was reported missing in action and taken as a PoW to Changi Camp. On the 8th July he embarked at Singapore with B Force for Borneo, though it was not generally known at the time and only on the 29th March 1943 was he reported as a PoW in Borneo.

**This was at that time the Australian Imperial Force but for simplicity will be referred to as the Australian Army.*

Citation: *28th November 1947*
The KING has been graciously pleased, on the advice of His Majesty's Australian Ministers, to approve the Posthumous award of the GEORGE CROSS, in recognition of gallant and distinguished services whilst a prisoner-of-war in Japanese hands (prior to September, 1945), to:-
    Captain Lionel Colin Matthews, M.C. (VX 24597), Australian Military Forces.

Citation for the Military Cross
8th January 1946
War Office, 10th January, 1946.
AUSTRALIAN MILITARY FORCES.
The KING has been graciously pleased to approve the following awards in recognition of gallant and distinguished services in Malaya in 1942 : —
The Military Cross.
Captain Lionel Colin Matthews (VX 24597).

    During operations at GEMAS this officer succeeded in maintaining cable communications between his Brigade headquarters and units under heavy artillery and mortar fire and aerial bombardment, displaying a high standard of courage, energy and ability in doing so. Later during the operations in Singapore Island Captain Matthews succeeded in laying a cable over ground strongly partrolled by the enemy and then restoring communications between his Divisional Headquarters and the Heaquarters of a brigade at a critical period.

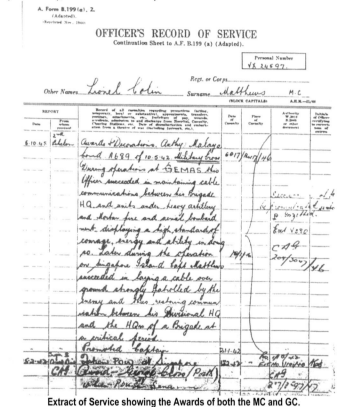

Extract of Service showing the Awards of both the MC and GC.

Other awards: Military Cross, 1939–45 Star, Pacific Star, Defence Medal, War Medal 1939–45 and Australian Service Medal. Due to a post-war error the Australian Central Army Records Office did not recognise Capt Matthew's eligibility for the Defence Medal until 1983. That year, at the Corps Day parade of the Royal Australian Corps of Signals, Third Military District, David Matthews was presented with his father's Defence Medal by Major General Taylor.

©*D Matthews*

Matthews' Military Cross was presented to David by the Governor-General, William McKell on 20th November 1947. He subsequently received his father's George Cross from the Governor of South Australia, Sir Willoughby Norrie on 4th October 1949.

The story

(The Commonwealth of Australia Gazette, 11th December 1947)

Captain Matthews was a prisoner of war held by the Japanese in Sandakan, Borneo, between August 1942 and March 1944. During this period he directed personally an underground intelligence organisation and arranged through native contacts for the delivery into the camp of sorely needed medical supplies, food and money, factors which not only kept up the morale and courage of the prisoners but which undoubtedly saved the lives of many. He was instrumental in arranging a radio link with the outside world and was able to send weekly news bulletins to the civil internees on Berhala Island. He was also responsible for arranging the delivery to a secret rendezvous of firearms for future use. Although a prisoner of war, Captain Matthews was appointed to command the North British Armed Constabulary and at great danger organised that body, together with the local native population in Sandakan into readiness for a rising against the Japanese. He gained contact with guerrilla forces in the Philippines and successfully organised escape parties. He continued these activities at the greatest peril to himself until arrested. Captain Matthews, although subjected to brutal torture, beatings and starvation, steadfastly refused to make admissions to implicate or endanger of the lives of his associates. His conduct at all times was that of a very brave and courageous gentleman and he worthily upheld the highest traditions of an Australian officer. Captain Matthews was executed by the Japanese on 2nd March 1944 and even at the time of his execution defied the Japanese.

Lionel Matthews before the war.
© Both D Matthews

Lionel in Malaya. The expression on his face tells us what a serious buisness he was involved in. This photo was sent home to his wife and small son.

Matthews was captured, along with most of the 8th Division, at the fall of Singapore on 15th February 1942. He was known as 'The Duke' by those with whom he served in the Signals. He was moved along with several thousand British and Australian PoWs from Changi prison in Singapore to a work camp at Sandakan in British North Borneo in July 1942. He was the first to be approached by a local man, Majinal, a Malay, who told him of his group's activities. This group consisted of a most diverse range of people from doctors and store owners to farm labourers, all with contacts and skills necessary for the assistance of internees and PoWs. There is not space here to detail all the activities and I recommend Silver's book listed below.

Once here, the men were forced to work on constructing an airfield. Matthews became a key player in a variety of underground activities. He organised and equipped the disbanded force called the British North Borneo Armed Constabulary in preparation for possible Allied landings in the area. He also helped to organise several escape parties, which he could have joined at any time, but remained behind in order to continue to organise similar schemes for others.

In July 1943, however, a Chinese member of the organisation was betrayed to the Japanese, he was tortured and gave Matthews and his colleagues away.

A diary (this has since been refuted by Silver — page 314) was apparently found belonging to Lt RG Wells in which there was mention of a radio. The searches began until it was found. Matthews was implicated and he and Wells along with Sgt Stevens and Cpls McMillan and Roffey suffered a regime of brutality and torture.

Matthews consistently refused to tell the Japanese anything. At the trial, although the court records that all five pleaded guilty, Wells contradicted this.

> (**Author's note:** In *Kill the Prisoners* by Wall there is also mention of LAC Matthews — this is not Lionel).
>
> Peter Lee, whose diary forms the bulk of the book, states that "*A Japanese spy had fallen out with local people friendly to the Australians and reported the fact that the Australians possessed a wireless in the Camp*". This wireless was to form the major exhibit at Matthews' trial when a charge of "insurrection, endeavouring to obtain arms and possessing arms to assist an invading force — the PYTHON activities — the massacre of Japanese seamen by escaped prisoners — and they believed an Allied air-borne invasion of Sandakan was imminent using the airfield the prisoners were building".

In all 22 Australians were involved, one died before the trial was complete, one was acquitted, one received six months imprisonment and the remainder sentences ranging from 1½ to 12 years' penal servitude. Matthews and eight local North Borneans were executed on 2nd March 1944 — the natives were certainly shot but there is no conclusive evidence of how Lionel met his end. While Lt Wells had also been sentenced to die permission was given by the Southern Army Chief in Saigon for only one European to be killed (even this is questioned and it may have been a deliberate mistake by the typographer), thus Matthews as the senior officer paid the price. His grave was dug by fellow Australians and grotesquely they had already been given instructions before the trial was over. Silver quotes his last words.

"Keep your chins up boys. What the Japs do to me doesn't matter. They can't win".

The conditions for the men left behind at Sandakan greatly worsened, and they were routinely beaten, starved and overworked by the Japanese.

In February 1945 the Japanese, anticipating Allied landings in Borneo, decided to force the remaining PoWs, more than 1000 of them, to take part in the 'Death Marches to Ranau'. Only 260 PoWs reached the destination of Ranau, 160 miles inland from Sandakan. Of these 260 PoWs, only 6 survived to see the end of the war. These 6 only survived due to escaping and living with tribesmen in the jungle.

MATTHEWS, Captain, LIONEL, COLIN, G C, M C, VX24597. A.I.F. 8 Div. Sigs. Australian Corps of Signals. 2nd March 1944. Age 31. Son of Edgar Roy Matthews and Anne Elizabeth Matthews; husband of Myrtle Matthews, of Marryatville, South Australia. J. D. 13. The following particulars are given in the London Gazette of 25th November, 1947: The King has been graciously pleased, on the advice of His Majesty's Australian Ministers, to approve the posthumous award of the George Cross, in recognition of gallant and distinguished services whilst a prisoner of war in Japanese hands.

Testimonies of witnesses to Matthews' conduct forming part of the Recommendation of an award for courage and devotion to duty.

These were taken from, among others, RG Wells, AG Weynton, JP Taylor, A W Weston and R W Ewin. They gave evidence of Matthews' determination to continue all his clandestine activities and that he was the "prime mover in an underground movement to overthrow Japanese control at Sandakan". Even after his arrest and four months of torture, while being moved to Kuching in Sarawak by steamer he was planning and thus inspiring his co-prisoners. His total unselfishness and his dignified demeanour were invaluable to those around him. For in those most difficult of circumstances he endeavoured to maintain morale — an essential element for survival.

We can ask what was it that drove him and it is worth comparing him with others who were similarly imbued with such determination and spirit. In Volume 4 the Hong Kong Five and in Volume 5 the story of **D Kinne GC** and of H Madden GC in this book are but some of the men who had within them some extraordinary strength of character. Can we ever know why or what it was?

Matthews Place, Gowrie, Canberra.
© *Ken Marshall*

Memorials: WWII Book of Remembrance at the Royal Memorial Chapel, Sandhurst. GC Memorial Canberra and in Melbourne at the School of Signals' Simpson Barracks there is a studio portrait by Robert Anderson. The *Lionel Matthews Merit Award* was established on 1st January 1966 (prior to that date a Lionel Matthews Scholarship valued at $100 had been awarded annually) for presentation to other ranks of the Corps for achievement on School of Signals' courses, in his honour. There is also a copy set of his medals in the foyer of the School. In Gowrie, Canberra there is a Matthews Close named in his memory. Only years later were memorials erected in both North Borneo and Australia to all those who died in Sandakan.

I have been questioned as to why Matthews name should be in the Book of Remembrance at Sandhurst. The archivist Dr AR Morton gave me this reply.

The Book of Remembrance you refer to contains the names of all British <u>and</u> Commonwealth officers who died in the Second World War, regardless of whether or not they trained at RMC Sandhurst.

A different type of memorial

There must have been many stories of the heroism of East Adelaide old scholars during the war, but that of **Captain Lionel Matthews** was singled out to be published in *The Children's Hour* in 1948.

This is a story of supreme courage and unswerving devotion to duty. It is the story of a soldier who was a prisoner of war with the Japanese during the last war. He was determined to fight for his country even though a prisoner. He knew only too well the price of his resistance, yet he was resolved to resist, and did resist, unto death.

His way was not one impulsive act. It was a series of acts deliberately planned. The certain penalty of discovery was execution following torture. For the sake of Australia and the security of you and me he accepted that risk.

He was betrayed. He was tortured. He was put to death by the Japanese.

He died as he had lived, a loyal and gallant soldier, with a smile on his lips in the face of the firing squad.

...

Then Singapore fell, and the dark and depressing curtain of captivity cut us off from Australia. But Japanese restraint did not deter nor depress Lionel Matthews. He had made up his mind that, come what may, he would do his best for Australia. Such was his cheerful assurance to me as he left Changi Gaol in July, 1942, for an unknown destination. We now know that it was Sandakan in British North Borneo; a locality associated with one of the worst tragedies (a death march) and one of the most gallant deeds of the war.

Shortly afterwards I was moved to Formosa and to us, late in 1943, came Governor Smith of the British North Borneo Company. He told us of an Australian, one Captain Matthews, who had supplied them through miles of jungles and across a stretch of water with continuous news of the outside world. This entailed not only the risky business of operating a listening set, but the organisation of a chain of native carriers through the Japanese controlled areas. These natives had been the North Borneo Constabulary until taken into captivity; but they remained loyal. Governor Smith made Matthews the Chief of Police. To these natives he became Tuan Matthews.

We heard no more until we were more in contact with the civilised world. Then we heard that Matthews was dead, that his work had been betrayed to his captors, and that he had paid the supreme penalty.

Sandakan is a port in British North Borneo, now Sabah. It is surrounded by jungle which concealed malaria and other tropical diseases fatal to the white man. Its inhabitants consisted of Chinese, Malays, Sikhs, and Dusuns, any of which would be capable of the highest loyalty or the deepest treachery. The whole area was guarded and patrolled by Japanese soldiers. It took a very stout heart even to think of resistance in such conditions.

Matthews was Intelligence Officer of the prisoners. As such he did the most extraordinary things. He established contact with Europeans outside the gaol and had medical supplies smuggled in. He procured parts for a wireless receiver and established a listening post. This news he distributed throughout the camp and as far afield as Berhale Island. He made contact with Philippine guerillas and arranged escape parties and through them he had arms and ammunition secreted near the camp. He carefully laid plans for an insurrection when help from the outside world became available. These were extraordinary things for two reasons. Firstly, they could only be done with the greatest secrecy and at the gravest risk to himself. Secondly, and this is the most marvellous point of the story, he could have escaped himself but elected to stay and continue his dangerous task.

His end was brought about by the treachery of a coloured foreman. This man betrayed to the Japanese his coloured companions who were working for Matthews. Under torture Matthews' work was revealed by the foreman to the Japanese. The terrible sequel was then inevitable.

We all revere brave men. The contemplation of their actions is a spur to us. We derive from them an inspiration to serve our country as nobly as we are able.

Australia has been blessed with many brave and noble men. Among the greatest of these is Captain Lionel Matthews. He was awarded, posthumously, the George Cross for his bravery.

The glory that is his shines through the melancholy tragedy of Sandakan. If we can sense that glory and its inspiration, his work will not have been in vain.

©*Colonel J.H.T. THYER, C.B.E, D.S.O*

Background: *POW or PoW* (used throughout this series) = Prisoner of War — plural of Prisoners of War is *PoWs* which could of course be read as Prisoner of Wars

Pentridge Gaol

The gaol started life in 1850 as a stockade in the area now called Coburg and is part of Melbourne. The prisoners were mainly employed in hard labour breaking up the rock, called bluestone. Gradually the prison population grew and by 1870 there were 650 male and female prisoners and 100 staff. When Melbourne Gaol closed in 1926 all executions were carried out at Pentridge, the last being in 1967. It was not really until the 1950s that life in prison became more acceptable and the realisation that prisoners also needed to be rehabilitated and educated rather than just punished. By 1970 there were over 1000 inmates. The end of the prison's life began in 1997 and by 1999 the site was sold. The developers moved in.

British PoWs in Sandakan — I have included this story because Lionel represented many people and his fate was not unique and I am very grateful for all who share these painful memories.

From **Steve Mockridge**

My father was LAC Leslie HG Mockridge, RAF. He was part of the Malayan retreat to Java where he was captured by the Japanese. Returned to Changi Camp, Singapore he was one of 824 British PoWs sent to Sabah, North Borneo. They arrived at Jesselton on 9th October 1942 and them moved to Sandakan in April 1943 by which time Captain Lionel Matthews from the Australian Camp was establishing and organizing a local underground movement. A radio receiver had also been built.

The British PoWs were kept at the airstrip away from the Australian Camp at Sandakan. In the period before the underground was betrayed and the receiver discovered Australian PoWs secretly passed news gained from the radio to the British whilst both groups worked on the airstrip. At this time British and Australian PoWs were forbidden to mix or communicate with each other.

On 14th August 1943 British PoWs were moved to a separate compound at the Sandakan Camp. The British unaware of the betrayal, the arrest and receiver discovery had no idea why the news messages had stopped. A group of other ranks (probably RAF) decided to draw straws. The loser was to fake illness and hopefully be removed to the Australian camp 'hospital' to discover why the news had stopped.

My father drew the short straw. He held back all bodily waste functions for some days until he became ill enough to be removed from the British Camp. Unfortunately for him appendicitis was diagnosed. He was taken to the Civil hospital. Unsure of the consequences of owning up to the situation he went through with the ordeal. His appendix was removed under local anaesthetic by a Japanese doctor on 16th October 1943.

It was during this period and just after that my father came into contact with Capt Matthews and other Australian PoWs arrested for their underground/radio involvement. In the short period my father became close to Captain Matthews. They both had a love of scouting and this earned each other's trust.

So close, my father became part of Captain Matthews incredible escape plan. The plan was for Capt. Matthews, Lt Rod Wells (the radio builder) and my father to escape from their prison, make their way to the airfield, steal a plane (flown by my father!) and fly to freedom. When my father pointed out to Matthews that he was an RAF electrician and not a pilot Matthews responded that he was in the RAF and that was good enough for him. Father believed that Matthews and Wells knew they were to face execution and therefore were prepared to take a last chance.

The plan to escape was never put into practice because all those arrested, PoWs and locals, were sent to Kuching for trial on 25th October 1943. There was a shock too for my father and his nursing orderly LAC T. Wilson when they were told that they had been 'contaminated' by Matthews and the others. They were too dangerous to return to Sandakan Camp and they too would be shipped with them.

They were transported on the SS *Subuk*. My father and the others arrived in Kuching on 6th November. My father steadfastly refused to tell anyone what happened aboard this vessel. All I know is that it was a horror journey in very rough seas. My father did once, without giving details, tell me of a journey where he and others were tied to the ships rails in a storm and how they fought for life. I can only guess it was this journey.

Leslie Mockridge (right) with his best friend Leslie Barnes killed by the Japanese at Ranau 12th June 1945.

When they arrived at Kuching everyone including Matthews was taken away with the exception of my father and Wilson. They were again told they were 'contaminated' and were therefore too dangerous to be put into the British other ranks compound at Kuching and would therefore have to be put in with the officers. What a punishment! The irony being that the British other ranks had already built their own radio. My father never saw Capt. Matthews again.

Captain Lionel Matthews was executed along with 8 locals on 2nd March 1944. Lt Rod Wells survived because of an administrative error on his execution documentation. On the day of Captain Matthews' execution a lone piper played in Kuching Camp.

Sadly nursing orderly LAC Wilson passed away at Kuching on 14th August 1945. Tragically the group containing Capt. Matthews and my father was the last to leave Sandakan. Of the 2400 left behind only 6 Australian escapees survived. The remainder either died at Sandakan, on the death marches to Ranau or at Labuan.

Throughout his life my father held the Australians he met in captivity in the very highest respect and as a boy I remember him telling me Captain Lionel Matthews '*was the bravest man I ever knew*'.

My father's best friend LAC Les Barnes suvived the death marches but is thought to have been executed at Ranau Jungle Camp One. His crime — he was too ill to continue. Dad and his nursing orderly were with Matthews and other Aussies who were the last to be removed from Sandakan. Therefore of the British PoWs no one suvived after Dad left.

Dad passed way on 4th September 2000. His younger brother (80) has only just told me the marks all over my father's body were not a childhood disease as I was told but cigarette burn scars from torture. All these men were heroes.

Please appreciate my father never told his story fully and what he told his family was very fragmented. The jigsaw of his captivity will never be complete.

©S Mockridge

ANNEX A TO
CORPS MEMORANDUM NO 12

THE LIONEL MATTHEWS MERIT AWARD

Aim

1. The Lionel Matthews Merit Award was established on 1 January 1966 for presentation to other ranks of the Corps for achievement on School of Signals' courses, in honour of Captain Lionel Matthews GC, MC.

8. The award takes the form of a medallion depicting the Corps Badge on the obverse side and Inscribed with the words *LIONEL MATTHEWS MERIT AWARD*. The reverse side shows a laurel wreath and space for the presentation inscription. The presentation inscription will show the serial number and abbreviated title of the course, student's regimental number and name. The date, recipient's rank and name shall be placed on an Honour Board, donated by 8th Divisional Signals Association, on display in the foyer of the School of Signals.

9. The award shall only be made to an outstanding student on courses conducted at the School of Signals.

10. Factors taken into account when making the awards are to include:

    a. examination results

    b. practical work

    c. conduct, and

    d. the general contribution by the student to the course as a whole.

11. The number of medallions awarded in any one year, January to December, will be governed by an expenditure limit of $100.

12. The Award is to be administered as follows:

    a. The Commanding Officer, School of Signals, or an officer delegated by him is to select the recipients of the award. The award is to be restricted to other rank members only.

    b. The award will be financed by RA Sigs General Purpose Fund as follows:

        (1) The School of Signals is to maintain a stock of award medallions. The medallions are accountable. Replenishment of stock is to be requested by the School as required from the Corps Shop.

        (2) Claims for reimbursement of expenses incurred by the School of Signals such as engraving, etc. are to be submitted to the Corps Committee Treasurer by 31 Jan and 31 Jul each year.

        (3) A consolidated list of recipients of the award is to be included with the claim.

    c. Names of recipients are to be notified to the Director of Signals — Army on the normal Course Report forwarded by the School of Signals at the conclusion of courses.

PYTHON — a British-led party which reported on enemy shipping and other movements to GHQ. It was led by Gort Chester who had first-hand knowledge of Borneo and who had been recruited by MI6 and had been a member of SOE. It was secret and small comprising only 6 men, two British and four Australian. Together they formed *Operation Python*.

Gemas — this small town was divided by the Gemencheh Bridge which was destroyed in order to stop the Japanese invasion from the larger town of Tampin. The original town was on the Negeri-Sembilan side of the border with Johore. On 14th January 1942, "B" Company of the 2/30th Battalion, launched an ambush against the Japanese in the hope of preventing them from advancing further south. As the advancing Japanese soldiers passed by the ambush site, the bridge was blown. The battle following the ambush, and a further battle closer to Gemas, lasted two days. It ended with the Australian withdrawal through Gemas to Fort Rose Estate

Sources: David Matthews — son

Steve Mockridge

An Old Soldier Remembers a Wartime Atrocity, by Thomas Fuller, *International Herald Tribune*

http://home.vicnet.net.au/ ~ rasigsau/mem_chap_12.HTM

Sandakan — A Conspiracy of Silence by Lynette Silver. This is an exceptionally well-researched book.

They Dared Mightily by L Wigmore

Lt Col Neil Smith

Colonel JHT Thyer, C.B.E, D.S.O.

Kill the Prisoners by Don Wall, containing the war diaries of Peter Lee, CBE

Graham Donley of the Australian Army Museum

Alexander Henry MAXWELL-HYSLOP, GC

Fire aboard HMS Devonshire, 26th July 1929, eastern Mediterranean

Alexander with his sons Alexander (Sandy) and Robin and his beloved dogs.

©M Hebblethwaite

Status: Lieutenant-Commander, HMS *Devonshire*, Royal Navy

Life dates: 25th May 1895, Woolwich – 28th August 1978, Par, Cornwall. Alexander is buried in the churchyard of Saints Ciricius and Julitta, Luxulyan, with his wife. **Obit:** *The Times*, 1st September 1978

Biography: Alexander was the second son of Colonel Robert Maxwell Hyslop (RMH) RE and his wife Emily Clara Brock who was the sister of Admiral of the Fleet Sir Osmond de Beauvoir Brock GCB, KCVO. His father was a descendent of John Maxwell of Terraughty and the Hyslop family of Lotus. (In 1923 Alexander's brother Robert unilaterally hyphenated the name by Deed Poll, this was not a particularly popular move with the family.) While RMH was in command at Dover Castle the family lived there and after prep school Alexander (AHMH) entered Osborne Naval School in 1907, moving on to Dartmouth Naval College in 1910, passing out in 1912. He went to sea as a Midshipman in 1913. His first ship was HMS *Centurion*. In 1919 he transferred to the Royal Naval Air Station at Polegate in Sussex as he had volunteered for an unspecified 'dangerous' posting. He found that he had first to qualify as a balloon pilot before training for an airship. Here he served on four airships of the Submarine Scout class, SS1, SS10, SS12 and SS14.

The ships and airships on which Alexander served are engraved on to a silver cigarette case.

AHMH's service manual with his signature and to the right the list of ships and airships noting that here he lists SS14 but not SS12 as to the left.

Courtesy R Maxwell-Hyslop

Sea Scout SS1.

Adrian Paull, courtesy FAA Museum

On 15th July 1915 Alexander wrote to his mother of a lucky escape in one of the airships. "*The Commander and I were out flying, he piloting, and we had just turned over the sea when we got a very bad down bump, and hit the water at about 50mph. The bottom part of the fuselage crumpled up and our propellor smashed, so we lost all control of the ship. The water rushed in up to my armpits. Then she rose to about 400 feet and the wire suspension, holding the car to the gasbag started to snap. However we got her down to the water before they all went and floated along about half submerged"...*

Fortunately a torpedo boat saw them and coming to their rescue the pilot jumped aboard only for the airship to start rising again with AHMH hanging on. But for the quick action of the pilot, who jumped back and hung on to the undercarriage, AHMH would have risen up thousands of feet and landing up in Belgium.

Alexander was a very fit, athletic young man and during WWI when he knocked out the heavy-weight champion of the Grand Fleet as a light heavy-weight he became the heavy-weight champion.

After an episode in which he *"incurred their Lordships' displeasure"* when he bombed a U-boat when ordered not to, though he did not receive the order owing to a faulty radio, he asked to be transferred somewhere where he would NOT incur any displeasure when bombing the enemy! The Captain of his new ship HMS *Africa* ordered him to write a formal statement of his treatment detailing the complaint and to sign it whereupon he sent his own covering letter to the Rear-Admiral who passed it on to Admiral Sir John Jellicoe Commander of the Grand Fleet, who sent it on to the Admiralty. AHMH's reputation was restored. He had come to the notice of important men in the Navy and he duly received a note *"Their Lordships have been pleased to withdraw their Displeasure"*.

From 1916–1917 AHMH served on HMS *Repulse* and HMS *Revenge* and then in 1919 he underwent the Long Gunnery Course passing out with Maximum Seniority. He was then appointed Gunnery Officer on HMS *Ceres* and in this capacitry designed and fired the barrage of 6" shells which held back the Turkish Army under Attaturk at Smyrna. In 1922 and 1923 he led the Royal Navy Rugby Team's forwards, and his younger brother Jack led them in the English team.

Alexander, now AHM-H, married Cecelia Joan Bayly in 1927 and they had two sons Alexander Bayly (Sandy)(1929) and Robert John (1931), though he has always been called Robin.

Alexander was further promoted and by 1929, he was a Lieutenant Commander serving as Gunnery Officer on board HMS *Devonshire* — the story of which is told below.

His first command was the sloop HMS *Laburnham* on the New Zealand station in the Pacific in 1933. He told the story of how when he was two watchkeepers down he told the Governor-General that although his Medical Officer was a keen and competent sailor he was not allowed by the Admiralty to grant him a Harbour Watchkeepers Certificate.

"I am His Majesty's representative here in New Zealand," said the Governor General. *"I can therefore, override, in His Majesty's name, ANY order to you from the Admiralty. So, tomorrow I shall write, sign, seal and deliver to you an Order requiring you to grant a Harbour Watchkeeping Certificate to the Surgeon Lt Page!"*

Surgeon Lt Page became the only one of his kind with the Certificate and ended his days as Surgeon Rear-Admiral Page.

AHM-H returned to the United Kingdom in 1935. Following his promotion to Commander, he commanded the RN Barracks in Alexandria, then attended courses at Greenwich before assuming command of the Boys' Training Establishment, HMS *Impregnable*, where, in 1938, he was promoted to Captain. This was a happy time for his family who were living in Ivybridge as he was able to be at home with them — almost the only time in the boys' childhood — as for so many children of seamen.

Returning to sea in 1939, he took command of the delapidated cruiser HMS *Durban* with a crew of reservists and they proceeded to Hong Kong where he bacame ill and had to return home to recover. The German invasion of Norway saw him appointed RN Liaison Officer to the British 5 Corps based at Aadelsnes which witnessed horrific air assaults. By 1941 he was Captain of Destroyers at Devonport but then came three years on Arctic duties as he took command of HMS *Cumberland* in January 1942.

HMS *Cumberland*.
©*R Maxwell-Hyslop*

Arctic conditions on HMS *Cumberland*.
©*R Maxwell-Hyslop*

She was a high free-board ship with both 8x8" and 8x4" guns, was extremely seaworthy and carried two Walrus amphibian aircraft for reconnaisance (see McClymont for picture of a Walrus). Her task was distant support of the Arctic convoys to Murmansk and Archangel where his duty was to place his ship between the convoy and the German warships which could easily have outgunned him. However, when he took command AHM-H found that the pipes and guns had not been ice-protected which destabilised the ship when covered in ice and made life for the crew rather uncomfortable.

On one return run, in desperate arctic conditions, there was only ship's biscuit and dried reindeer meat to eat. Among his duties AHM-H conveyed Sir Stafford Cripps to and from Russia in his capacity as British Ambassador. With that came an entitlement to an additional food and drink allowance. However, Cripps was a vegetarian and abstainer — this last resulting in a net profit. When the vegetarian food ran out AHM-H ordered the Master-at-Arms to seek out the 12 filthiest pairs of underpants. From these he chose the 6 worst, burning the rest and issuing clean ones to all now deprived. The 6 chosen pairs were wrapped round 6 footballs, covered in mustard-and-cress seeds then sprinkled with water by the Paymaster-Commander. Within a very short time in the steamy heat of the boiler-room a fine crop soon grew and, as it was shaved off each day, Cripps was presented with a salad of mustard-and-cress and gulls' eggs (previously collected on Jan Mayan Island).

Arctic 1942.

AHM-H with his crew on HMS _Cumberland_.

Before disembarkation AHM-H asked Cripps what arrangments had been made between Churchill and Stalin about the Government of Poland after the war.

"I couldn't possibly tell you, Captain", expostulated Cripps, "those are state secrets". Then he unfroze and asked, "Alec, do tell me how your steward produced those wonderful salads in the Arctic?"

"I couldn't possible tell you Ambassador" came the reply, "HMS _Cumberland_ has her own secrets, too!"

Capt Maxwell-Hyslop on the right with HM King George VI.
Courtesy R Maxwell-Hyslop

In 1944 Captain Maxwell-Hyslop assumed command of the battleship, HMS _Nelson_, which was involved in the bombardment of the Normandy landing area's fortifications. In the later part of 1944, he was ADC to King George VI. His last post was as Commander of the Naval Officers' Selection station, HMS _Raleigh_ at Torpoint with about 2000 potential oficers for Hostility Only commissions under training.

In 1946 Alexander was invalided out due to the recurrance of the duodenal ulcers which had caused him to leave Hong Kong. He and Cecily retired to Prideaux House, north of St Blazey in Cornwall. They kept their schooner Alkelda in Fowey harbour and he was for a while Vice Commodore of Fowey Yacht Club. For many years he was the Chief Warden of the county's Civil Defence. Still fit until his eighties, he shot with friends and ploughed at least 5 acres annually at Prideaux until his death in 1978.

Ross McWhirter (see also page G91), who was once a Walrus pilot on HMS _Cumberland_, never forgot his old Captain and was influential in persuading HM the Queen to convert the Albert Medal into the George Cross. As AHM-H was the senior living holder of the AM and, though reluctant to part with that medal, he agreed to go along with the majority. His citation was read out as the paradigm Citation at the start of the exchange Ceremony.
Thanks to Sir Robin Maxwell-Hyslop

Citation: *19th November 1929*
Admiralty, 11th November, 1929

The KING has been graciously pleased to approve of the award of the Albert Medal to Lieutenant-Commander Alexander Henry Maxwell-Hyslop, R.N., and No. Po./21038 Marine Albert Edward Streams for gallantry in saving life at sea.

The following is the account of the services in respect of which the decorations have been conferred:—

H.M.S. *Devonshire* was carrying out full calibre firing on 26th July, 1929, when at the first salvo there was a heavy explosion which blew off the roof of one of the turrets. Marine Streams was the only man in the gun house who was not either killed instantly or fatally injured. He was seriously shaken by the explosion and instinctively climbed to the top of the side plating to escape but, on arriving at the top he looked back and saw the conditions inside the turret, and deliberately climbed back into it amidst the smoke and fumes notwithstanding the grave risk of further explosions. He then helped to evacuate the one remaining man of the right gun's crew, and took charge and played a major part in evacuating the crew of the Fire Control cabinet. When all the wounded were out he collapsed. His bravery, initiative and devotion to duty were beyond praise.

Lieutenant-Commander Maxwell-Hyslop was in the fore control when the explosion occurred, and immediately proceeded to the turret and climbed inside. He made a general examination of the turret, and descended the gun well through most dangerous conditions of fumes and smoke, necessitating the use of a life line, remaining in the turret until the emergency was over, directing arrangements for the safety of the magazine, and supervising the evacuation of the wounded. He was fully aware of the danger to himself from the results of cordite fumes, and the grave risk of further explosions.

At the time this officer and man entered the turret the fire produced by the explosion was still burning and it was impossible to estimate the real state of affairs due to the heavy smoke. They both were fully aware that there were other cordite charges in the hoist and handling room below which might ignite at any moment with almost certain fatal results to themselves, and they deliberately endangered their own lives to save the lives of others.

Maxwell-Hyslop, back right with his wife holding the bouquet.

Maxwell-Hyslop's miniatures at the Fleet Air Arm Museum, they are not on display.
Photo by M Hebblethwaite, courtesy FAA Museum

Other awards: AM (Bronze Sea) – GC exchange. 1914–15 Star, British War Medal, Victory Medal, 1939–45 Star, Atlantic Star, Africa Star, War Medal 1939–45 with Mention in Dispatches oak leaf (28/11/44), 1935 King's Silver Jubilee Medal and 1977 Queen's Silver Jubilee Medal which is not in the group of miniatures nor is the 1953 Coronation Medal. While commanding HMS *Cumberland* AHM-H was offered an OBE, he declined, saying that the Albert was quite enough.

Capt. A.H. Maxwell-Hyslop AM (GC) RN *Name brought to Admiralty Notice for Norwegian Ops Service to Army.* (*LG* 20.10.40).

Capt. A H Maxwell-Hyslop AM RN awarded MiD HMS *Nelson* for *Operation Neptune* off the coast of Normandy. (*LG* 28.11.44).

Maxwell-Hyslop's Albert Medal was presented to HMS *Excellent* where it is on display at the Museum on Whale Island. His George Cross, was generously presented to the Speaker of the House of Commons by his son, Sir Robin J Maxwell-Hyslop. When he was an MP it was pointed out to him by a young girl who was visiting the House that there was no George Cross in the collection of Gallantry awards.

The story

On 26th July 1929 the newly-commissioned heavy cruiser HMS *Devonshire* was carrying out gunnery trials in the eastern Mediterranean. It was armed with four turrets each bearing two 8" guns whose shells each weighed 232 lbs. Traditionally in the Royal Navy the third turret was always manned by Royal Marines rather than sailors.

During the trial the No 1 gun hung-fired (that is its propellant charge of cordite failed to explode) but, as three other 8" guns had fired correctly, No 1's breech-control operator did not immediately realise that his gun had not fired, and therefore moved the breech-control lever to the 'open' position, and the breech-block rotated until the interrupted thread was fully clear and then started to withdraw.

Too late, the lever was moved to the 'close' position, the breech-block moved forward and had just started to re-engage with the interrupted thread again when the smouldering cordite charge in the gun exploded, blew the breech-block out, and the flame blew back into the turret, igniting the ready-use cordite charges.

The resulting explosion blew the top off the turret, killed an officer and eleven marines outright and injured all the others (five fatally)* though Marine Albert Edward Streams managed to climb onto the edge of the turret. But he then looked back into the smoke and flame and deliberately climbed back into the inferno.

The Gunnery Officer, Lt Cdr Maxwell-Hyslop, rushed down from the Gunnery Control, climbed into X turret and made a general examination of the turret. He descended the gun well through most dangerous conditions of fumes and smoke, necessitating the use of a life line, remaining in the turret until the emergency was over, directing arrangements for the safety of the magazine, and supervising the evacuation of the wounded assisted by Streams(AM)**. **Cobham** (EGM) and **Niven** (EGM) rigged and brought into the turret a fire-hose to get the fire under control.
©*R Maxell-Hyslop*

* See Stream's diary below for list of those who died — he includes 18 men by name.
** Whereas the other three men went on to exchange for the George Cross, Streams did not live to do so.

Guns firing on HMS *Nelson* off Normandy.
©*R Maxwell-Hyslop*

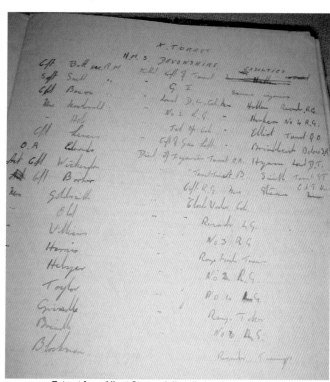

Extract from Albert Streams' diary listing those who died.
©*Streams family and courtesy Lt Col D Oakley*

From **John Hole**

My Great-uncle (my paternal granddad's elder brother) was Marine William George Hole RM — one of the six killed outright in the accident (out of 18 deaths in total).

Will Easton remembers that before the dead could be buried at the Aegean port of Volos in Greece the crew "first had to buy a plot of land and then build a low wall around our comrades"

Memorials: While there is no specific memorial to Maxwell-Hyslop there is a memorial at Volos to those who died on the *Devonshire*.

Background: *Marine Albert Streams AM*
Citation for the Albert Medal

Marine Streams was the only man in the gunhouse who was not either killed instantly or fatally injured. He was seriously shaken by the explosion and instinctively climbed to the top of the side plating to escape, but on arriving at the top he looked back and saw the conditions in the turret, and deliberately climbed back into it amidst the smoke and fumes, notwithstanding the grave risk of further explosions. He then helped to evacuate the one remaining man of the right gun's crew, and took charge and played a major part in evacuating the crew of the Fire Control Cabinet. When all were out he collapsed. His bravery, initiative and devotion to duty were beyond praise.

At the time this man entered the turret the fire produced by the explosion was still burning, and it was impossible to estimate the real state of affairs due to the heavy smoke. He was fully aware that there were other cordite charges in the hoist and handling room below, which might ignite at any moment, with almost certain fatal results to himself and he deliberately endangered his own life to save the lives of others.

Extract of a letter to Albert Streams from AHM-H.
©R Maxwell-Hyslop, courtesy Streams' family and D Oakley.

Derek Oakley has researched Streams extensively with the aid of significant material from the family including his diary, photographs and official documents.

Marine Streams joined the Royal Marines in 1920. He had already served in the Territorial Army for nearly a year. In 1929 he was serving as a Marine in HMS *Devonshire*. After the tragedy in the turret he became Lt Cdr Maxwell-Hyslop's Attendant, known as a WRA (Wardroom Attendant). They remained in touch and close friends.

Albert Streams went on to serve in the Royal Marines for a further 14 years, mostly at sea as either a Marine Officers Attendant (MOA) or a Wardroom Attendant. He was due for pension soon after World War II broke out, but was signed on for the duration. By this time he was MOA to Captain, later Lt Colonel 'Bertie' Lumsden, who subsequently became CO of 41 Royal Marine Commando. On his final 48 hours leave in mid-June 1943, before embarking for the Middle East, he saw his family for the last time, including seeing his newly-born, second daughter, Patricia for the only time. Albert Streams, now aged 40, was killed in action during 41 Commando's landings in Sicily on 10th July 1943 and was subsequently buried in the Syracuse War Cemetery, Plot III, Row B 5.

Sources: Sir Robin Maxwell Hyslop — son
Captain Derek Oakley MBE, Royal Marines, Publications Editor of the Royal Marines Historical Society.
John Hole
www.aht.ndirect.co.uk/airships/ss/index.html
Will Easton, in *Navy News*, Royal Naval Association March 1996
Fleet Air Arm Museum and Jan Keohane

Phillip Robert Stephen MAY, GC

Shipboard rescue, 20th June 1947, Hay Wharf, Malta

Phillip and Dorothy's (Dee) engagement photograph, February 1946.

Phillip and Dee's wedding, 29th June 1946.
All photos ©D May

Phillip with his father and son Stephen in 1974.

Status: CSP/R 225814, Leading Seaman, HM Cable Ship *St Margarets*, Royal Navy

Life dates: 6th August 1922, Canterbury, Kent – 14th December 1994, Thanet, Kent. **Obit:** *The Times*, 30th January, 1995. The obituary has the incorrect date of 15th. Phillip was cremated at Thanet Crematorium and his ashes were scattered in the Garden of Remembrance.

492	*Sixth August 1922.* 16 St Peters Street U.D.	*Philip Stephen Robert*	*Boy*	*Frederick Arthur May*	*Jessie May late Baillie formerly Sayer*

Extract from Phillip's birth certificate to confirm his given names. There are many instances of name and spelling changes between birth and death amongst the people in these books as there are in the population at large.

Biography: Phillip (his preferred spelling) was the son of Frederick Arthur and Jessie (Sayer) May and he had one sister Gloria. Frederick served in the Royal Navy and was awarded the DSM (*LG* 3.03.1944). He retired to Malta where Phillip was to meet up with him when the *St Margarets* was on its return from Greece.

Phillip attended Simon Langton Grammar School in Canterbury from the Autumn term of 1934 after completing his primary education at the Wesleyan Methodist Primary School. In 1935 he joined the Naval League Cadets and then from 1938–39 worked as an apprentice electrical engineer in Canterbury. His yearning to go to sea was fulfilled in 1940 when he joined the Port Line MV *Port Hunter* as Deck Boy and sailed round the world stopping off at ports and harbours that had until then just been a dream. On his return he joined the Royal Navy as T124 Seaman specialising in degaussing mines.

During the next few years he was to serve on a number of ships sailing all the oceans of the world. There was cable laying, repair work to pipelines and underwater clearing. Then in 1947 after being Chief Petty Officer on HMS *Bullfinch* he reverted to Leading Seaman on HMS St *Margarets*. She was to undertake the extremely dangerous task of clearing mines in the Mediterranean. He was demobbed in September 1947.

Stephen and Julia.

On 29th June 1946 Phillip married Dorothy Steed and they had four children, Stephen, Julia, Vincent and Virginia. Dorothy acquired the nickname Dee from her American colleagues when she was working for Lockheed on the Royal Saudi Airforce base in Jeddah, Saudi Arabia.

Vincent and Virginia.

Returning to civilian life Phillip went back to his first training in electrical engineering and while he was to "take any job that was going" he worked on electrical engineering projects in many countries in Africa, Asia and the Middle East where he was to work for 8 years. In all he spent nearly 20 years working abroad.

But the call of the sea was greater and when he retired in 1980 he and Dee bought a 1909 wooden ketch, restored her and sailed to far away places once more, living aboard until she was destroyed by fire. In 1987 he finally came ashore in England.

Phillip was a Brother of the St Augustine Chapter, Canterbury. He wrote *Beyond the Five Points*, a record of Freemason VCs and GCs but unfortunately died before he was able to complete it. His wife Dee gave the manuscript to Richard Cowley of Monkshood Books to edit and finally to publish. It is a fitting memorial to its author though a number of GCs are omitted, such as **Jolly GC**, and throughout this series their Lodges are mentioned unless the family have specifically asked for this information to be withheld.

He was, says Dee "at his best in a crisis and could turn his hand to anything". Their life was full of fun.

An unusual photo of a GC. Phillip servicing the family's scuba diving gear in Jeddah in 1965.

Phillip and workmen on the ferry crossing the Arawimi River in Zaire in 1978.

Citation: *21st November 1947*
Whitehall, S.W.1.
25th November, 1947
The KING has been graciously pleased to approve the award of the Albert Medal for gallantry in saving life at sea to: —

Leading Seaman Phillip Robert Stevens (*sic*) May, CSP/R.225814.

H.M. Cable Ship *St. Margarets* was lying at Hay Wharf, Malta on 20th June 1947 when a Chief Petty Officer, entering No. 2 cable tank, was overcome by gas. The First Lieutenant, the boatswain, and four ratings entered the tank to rescue him and were themselves all overcome.

Leading Seaman May then entered the tank, and, in a series of rescues, secured a line with a timber hitch round each of the seven men, so enabling them to be hauled on deck. He did this by taking deep breaths, and holding them. Speed was essential, and to have waited for apparatus would have been fatal. He made six separate attempts and although the first victim of the gas died later, he was able to save the lives of all those who had followed him.

After his third venture, Leading Seaman May was himself so exhausted by the fumes and exertion that a ship-mate offered to relieve him, but he himself was overcome and required to be rescued. May therefore continued his gallant work single-handed until the task was completed. Seven men owe their lives to his selfless bravery and determination. (**Author's note:** only six survived.)

Other awards: AM (Bronze Sea) – GC exchange. 1939–45 Star, Atlantic Star, Africa Star, Burma Star, Italy Star, War Medal 1939–45, 1953 Coronation Medal, 1977 Queen's Silver Jubilee Medal & 1992 Malta Commemoration Medal – not illustrated here. The Albert Medal was presented on 10th February 1948.

Phillip May with Odette Sansom.

Unusually Phillip retained both the Albert Medal and his GC. Note the spelling of his middle name.

May Road, Daget's Wood, Chatham, Kent.
©*M Hebblethwaite*

Memorials: May is listed on the honours board at his old school, Simon Langton School. There is a road named after him in Chatham.
Background: *degaussing* — neutralising the magnetic field
Sources: Dee May — wife
Dr Matthew Baxter
Beyond the Five Points by Phillip RS May GC
Hell's Corner 1940 by HRP Boorman

William Simpson (Bill) McALONEY, GC, OBE

Air-crash rescue, 31st August 1937, Hamilton, Victoria, Australia

©Syd Cauveren

©McAloney family

Status: 2239 AC1, (Flight Fitter), No 1 Squadron, Royal Australian Air Force

Life dates: 12th May 1910, Adelaide, South Australia – 31st August 1995, Melbourne. Both Bill and his wife Dorrie were cremated and their ashes interred at Cheltenham Cemetery, Melbourne. There is a plaque for Bill and Dorrie together with a rose bush *in memoriam*. **Obit:** *The Times*, 11th September 1995

Biography: William Simpson McAloney was the 2nd of 6 children and the eldest son to William Samuel and Mary Ann (Murphy) McAloney. He attended Threbarton School and the Adelaide School of Mines. From there he joined the South Australian Tractor Company in 1928 and worked as a salesman for it for the next three years. In 1931 he bought a garage and engineering workshop and in 1935 married Dora (Dorrie) Winifred Johnson, a young farmer's daughter. As for many others small town life during the Depression was hard, the family fell on bad times and bankruptcy became an inevitablity. Bill decided to join the RAAF. This provided a way out of their financial difficulties. Dorrie, who disliked the outback, longed to live in the city with its shops and movies and she envisaged a better life for their children than her own had been.

Bill enlisted into the Royal Australian Air Force on 1st July 1936 at Laverton and trained not only as a fitter but also qualified as an air gunner and later studied navigation, being commissioned before the Second World War, during which he saw action in Dutch New Guinea. But leaving his home town of Adelaide and moving to Melbourne without family or friends was not easy.

The couple had seven children, 3 boys and 4 girls. Their second son, John died in 1991 while refereeing a rugby match in Canberra where he was stationed. He was a career soldier with the army, having attained the rank of Colonel. He was awarded the Military Cross while on duty in Vietnam.

Paul McAloney recalled his father's aptitudes.

"I can only add that my father was a very knowledgeable and intelligent man. Most of this I believe was all self-taught as he used to read most nights until early in the morning. He also had a photographic memory and if you were having a discussion about any subject he could quote dates and timings as if they only happened yesterday. I can remember on one occasion two Jehovah Witnesses came to our door and they were amazed when he started quoting verses out of the Bible to them. We were also quite amazed as he wasn't really a religous person. He achieved a great deal without any formal education, and this was due to his intelligence and also to his knowledge of anything mechanical which served him well in the Airforce. He could dismantle any engine and assemble it again almost with his eyes closed."

Bill McAloney remembers his father.

"My Father was very strict in the upbringing of his seven children. In my case, I believe he was responsible for my sense of honesty in my application to life. He was a perfectionist in everything that he approached and did. As a person who had very little education, it is a credit to him that he reached such a high rank in the RAAF. It was not until adulthood that I began to appreciate his dry sense of humour. My Mother did say that she thought the rescue attempt and the consequences at Hamilton seemed to change his personality and behavior".

Bill McAloney Snr could be charming to people outside his home but it has been acknowledged by all his surviving children that he denied them any love nor did he interact with them in any way. There were harsh punishments for quite small misdemeanours. How much of this was due to the failings he saw in himself as a result of not saving the pilot's life and his early business ventures it is difficult to judge. After the Hamilton accident he suffered what was described as a "nervous breakdown". Unfortunately his wife and children became the victims of his anger, frustation and obsession with perfection and money (after his father died he had taken on the financial responsibility of supporting his elderly mother and some of his younger siblings). All the children left home as soon as possible and some were denied the chance to finish school.

Bill and Dorrie with their seven children on Bill's 80th birthday in 1990. L-R Paul, Jude, Bill, Glen, John, Rae and Anne.

Bill with his son Bill, grandson Greg and great-grandson Ryan in 1994.

Both pictures McAloney family

One of Bill's daughters-in-law remembers.

"Personally, I found him a very charming man with a dry sense of humour which appealed to me. Our three children, always enjoyed his visits and remember him with affection. His own children perhaps saw him differently as he was a very strict father but life moves on and we took both him and Dorrie on a great holiday to Cairns in the mid 80's which we all greatly enjoyed."

After the war McAloney remained with the RAAF and retired as an Honorary Group Captain in 1967 having been discharged on 9th December 1966 with the rank of Wing Commander. (This type of promotion is well-established and affects a person's pension rights). His final posting was at the Aircraft Research and Development Unit. While working with the RAAF in the 1960s as an Engineer Officer he became closely associated with Qantas often inspecting engines that had failed with the aim of ascertaining whether modifications should be made, and with Qantas staff, drew up policy on the economics thereof.

In 1966 Bill was appointed OBE for his services with the Australian Aircraft Research and Development Unit within the RAAF. The award took particular note of the valuable work he had done to introduce the French Mirage fighter into service with the RAAF. A number of the aircraft were subsequently built under licence in Australia.

Bill and Dorrie lived in the suburb of Sandringham in Melbourne and he was a very active Brother of two Lodges in Victoria achieving high office in the Grand Lodge.

Bill on the right with the crew of their ill-fated Demon A1-31 two weeks before the accident.

Courtesy W McAloney and Syd Cauveren

Citation: *18th February 1938*

Whitehall, February 4, 1938

His Majesty The KING has been graciously pleased to award the Albert Medal to Aircraftman William Simpson McAloney, Royal Australian Air Force, for conspicuous gallantry in attempting to rescue an officer from the burning wreckage of an aircraft at Hamilton, Victoria, on the 31st August, 1937.

Despite the fact that the aircraft was ablaze from nose to rudder, Aircraftman McAloney dashed into the flames and continued his efforts at rescue until pulled away in an unconscious condition, having received severe burns which necessitated his removal to hospital.

Citation for the OBE

1st January 1966
O.B.E.

To be Ordinary Officers of the Military Division of the said Most Excellent Order:

Wing Commander William Simpson McAloney, A.M. (03600), Royal Australian Air Force.

Bill presenting the Albert Medal to Point Crook where it is now displayed in a cabinet.

Other awards: AM (Bronze Land) – GC exchange. OBE, 1939–45 Star, General Service Medal 1918–62 with clasp 'Malaya' and 1977 Queen's Silver Jubilee Medal. The original Recommendation dated 6th September 1937 was for the Medal of the Order of the British Empire — the EGM — three days after that for the Air Force Medal which had been submitted by Squadron Leader AM Charlesworth which had been rejected. Finally he was recommended for the Albert Medal. His had been an unprecedented case and the authorities did not really know which award was appropriate. The investiture by Lord Huntingfield took place on 30th May 1938 at Parliament House.

Bill's AM is now at the RAAF Museum at Point Crook, the presentation of which took place at the same time as a restored Hawker Demon A1-8 was handed over to the Museum on 3rd February 1987. Bill was the only member of the RAAF to receive either the Albert Medal. He is also remembered at the Victorian Air Forces' Centre in Melbourne.

The story

Taken from an interview with **Sydney Cauveren** for *Transit* with permission.

It was while serving as an aero-engine fitter in the Royal Australian Air Force that William McAloney was awarded his Albert Medal in 1937 when he tried to pull the two-man crew of a crashed aircraft to safety, at the cost of severe burns to himself. The plane, a Hawker Demon fighter, was one of three from No 1 Squadron which had unofficially flown in to the Hamilton Royal Show, Victoria. The first plane took off at 1515hrs with the second following on behind. It crashed on the runway and burst into flames. One can only imagine the terrified and shocked reactions of the crowd.

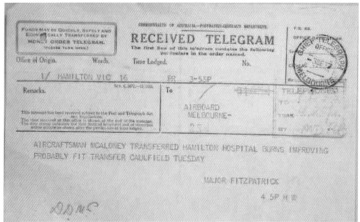

One of the telegrams to the Air Board regarding McAloney's hospitalisation. He was first taken to the private Kleore hospital. There were a number of telegrams and letters advising a transfer to a public hospital as soon as possible and then further to the Repatriation Hospital in Caulfield, Melbourne when he was able to undertake the journey.

In spite of the fact that flames spread from nose to tail of the aircraft in a very short time, McAloney repeatedly tried to get into the aircraft's twin cockpits, in an attempt to release the crew from their harnesses and drag them clear. Combusting high octane fuel quickly transformed the entire wreckage into an inferno and McAloney was badly burnt. Eventually he fell unconscious from the aircraft and was pulled from the scene and taken to hospital to have his severe injuries treated.

Despite his efforts, the Demon's pilot, Flying Officer KM McKenzie, and the observer/air gunner, Sergeant Norm Torrens-Witherow, died in the conflagration.

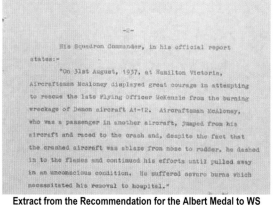

-2-

His Squadron Commander, in his official report states:-

"On 31st August, 1937, at Hamilton Victoria, Aircraftman McAloney displayed great courage in attempting to rescue the late Flying Officer McKenzie from the burning wreckage of Demon aircraft A1-12. Aircraftman McAloney, who was a passenger in another aircraft, jumped from his aircraft and raced to the crash and, despite the fact that the crashed aircraft was ablaze from nose to rudder, he dashed in to the flames and continued his efforts until pulled away in an unconscious condition. He suffered severe burns which necessitated his removal to hospital."

Extract from the Recommendation for the Albert Medal to WS McAloney.

All courtesy of the Australian National Archives

Telegram from the Military and Official Secretary to the Air Board conveying congratulations to McAloney.

WgCdr Mark Lax, RAAF Air Power Studies Centre, described the crash.
As with all air accidents, extensive investigations were and are still made into the cause of any crash. Additionally an inquest into the deaths takes place should there be fatalities.

There were three aircraft at the Hamilton show, one had taken off and the second was close behind but while attempting a climbing turn in the hot air with a 'sluggish' machine it stalled at only 200 feet and fell to earth in front of the crowd. McAloney was in the third plane with his Flg Off Joe Godsell when this occurred and while all dressed up in warm flying clothing managed to jump out and run the 1/4 mile to the wreck. Desperately trying to extricate the pilot from his cockpit he was overcome with fumes and his life was saved by members of the crowd.

The Air Accidents Investigation Committee in their Report No 182 A found there to have been pilot error. McKenzie was relatively inexperienced and did not follow correct procedure and was not fully conversant with local weather and airfield conditions. Above all he did not take pay due care and attention.
Memorials: Canberra, Australia and a photo at Point Crook.
Background: *Hawker Demon*
The Hawker Demon fighter was a two-seater variant of the Hart light-bomber (which first flew in 1928) and which the Air Ministry intended should be able to intercept the Hart until the Hawker Fury considered to be the ultimate biplane, came into service. In all 234 Demons were built but they did not remain in use for long as they were declared obsolete in 1939 though some were used for second-line operations for a while during WWII. **Lax** explains that the engine was slow to take off and climb and did not really attain speed until cruising at around 160 knots.

They were equipped with a single rear Lewis gun (see **Barraclough GC**) and two Vickers guns in the front (see **Hardy GC** and **Jones GC**) and were powered by Rolls Royce Kestrel engines flying up to 182mph.

At home, 1974.
©*S Cauveren*

Bill in the reclining chair he received from his family for his 80th birthday.
©*McAloney family*

Sources: William Stuart and Lynette McAloney — son and daughter-in-law
Paul McAloney — son
Glenice Adams — daughter
Rae Woolfe — daughter
Anne McCleod — daughter
Judith Bell — daughter
Sydney Cauveren
Dean Norman, ADF-Serials *Newsletter*, 2004
WgCdr Mark Lax, RAAF Air Power Studies Centre
Beyond the Five Points by Phillip RS May GC
Ivor Smith
The Third Brother by C.D. Coulthard-Clark

Thomas (Tommy) McAVOY, GC

Putting out fire, 15th March 1939, Jinsafut Camp, Palestine

A Cameron Highlander, 1927.

Tommy in the 1970s.

Status: 2926326 Private, 1st Battalion, The Green Howards (Alexandra, Princess of Wales's Own Yorkshire Regiment)

Life dates: 11th December 1909, Glasgow, Scotland – 20th May 1977, Stobhill Hospital, Glasgow. The funeral service was held on 24th May 1977 in the Church of the Immaculate Heart of Mary on Broomfield Road in Glasgow, Scotland followed by a cremation at Maryhill Crematorium. Representatives of Tommy's old regiments, the GPO and the Sheriff's Court attended and the VC & GC Association was represented by Mr John Carmichael VC and Lt Cdr Horace Taylor GC MBE. Such was the respect he commanded amongst old and young solders and civilians alike. **Obit:** *The Times*, 24th May, 1977

Biography: Tommy was the son of John and Margaret (Kelly) McAvoy. His father, who had married in March 1896, was a labourer on the quays in Glasgow. When Tommy was 18 he enlisted in the Queen's Own Cameron Highlanders on 30th September 1927. After seven years service, he returned to Glasgow in March 1935 when he transferred on to the Reserve. Two years later he joined the Green Howards on 19th October 1937 for their operational tour in Palestine.

On 3rd June 1939 he married Helen O'Connor in Glasgow while still recuperating after the events in Palestine but soon returned to his old regiment, The Green Howards, until a further transfer to the Duke of Wellington's (see **Kempster GC**) then on 24th November 1942 to the Durham Light Infantry, finally being discharged on 1st June 1946 though remaining on the Reserve.

Tommy then took up a position with what was then known as the GPO — the General Post Office — now Royal Mail. However, his last job was as an usher at the Sheriff's Court. When the *Glasgow Herald* described the mugging of Tommy late in his life they mentioned that he had with him his "certificates for the George Cross and another bravery award ..." his most precious possessions, carried with him always. A proud old soldier but never a vain one.

Citation: *25th July 1939*
St. James's Palace, S.W.1.
The KING has been graciously pleased to approve of the award of the Medal of the Military Division of the Most Excellent Order of the British Empire to the undermentioned:—
For Gallantry.
No. 2926326 Private Thomas McAvoy, 1st Battalion, The Green Howards (Alexandra, Princess of Wales's Own Yorkshire Regiment).

At Jinsafut Camp, Palestine, on the 15th March, 1939, a truck in the centre of the mechanical transport caught fire. Private McAvoy was amongst those endeavouring to put out the flames of the burning truck, working beside the near-side petrol tank, which was alight.

To relieve the pressure in the petrol tank, and to save a possible explosion, he took up a pick-axe and pierced the petrol tank, without any thought for his own safety, though he must have been fully aware of the appalling risk he was taking. The jet of burning petrol, which immediately rushed out, caused him to be badly burnt.

©*The Green Howards Museum*

Other awards: EGM (Military) – GC exchange   General Service Medal 1918–62 with 'Palestine' clasp, 1939–45 Star, Africa Star with '8th Army' clasp, Italy Star, Defence Medal, War Medal 1939–45 with oak leaf. Interestingly although Tommy died in April 1977 there is no QSJM. 1953 Coronation Medal. His original group of miniatures is at the Green Howards Museum. He was invested with the EGM on the 25th July 1939 by HRH The Princess Royal at Catterick and with his GC on 9th July 1946. Tommy sold his medals to an old friend.

The story
See 4388625 Corporal **T Atkinson GC** who was also awarded the EGM in this action. Two men were decorated with the BEM. They were 4382938 Sergeant (Acting Company Sergeant-Major) John Brindle and 4387078 Private Thomas Fowler of the Green Howards.

For Meritorious Service.
No. 4382938 Sergeant (Acting Company Sergeant-Major) John William Brindle, 1st Battalion, The Green Howards (Alexandra Princess of Wales's Own Yorkshire Regiment).

At Jinsafut Camp, Palestine, on the 15th March, 1939, a truck in the centre of the mechanical -transport caught fire, and the petrol tank eventually exploded. The force of the explosion not only spread burning petrol over a large area, but blew many men over. Of these, two were lying in burning petrol, and had their clothes alight. Without hesitation, Company Sergeant-Major Brindle went straight to Private Watson, pulled him out, and extinguished the flames on his clothes, despite the intense heat and danger.
No. 4387078 Private Thomas William Fowler, 1st Battalion, The Green Howards (Alexandra, Princess of Wales's Own Yorkshire Regiment).

At Jinsafut Camp, Palestine, on the 15th March, 1939, a truck in the centre of the mechanical transport caught fire, and the petrol tank eventually exploded. The force of the explosion not only spread over a large area, but blew many men over. Of these, two were lying in burning petrol, and had their clothes alight. Without hesitation, Private Fowler went straight to Lance-Corporal Izard, and extinguished the flames on his clothes, despite the intense heat and danger.

Background: *Why Palestine?*
As we are now, in 2006, very aware, the Palestine situation is an ever-present source of discord and disharmony. While many may say that the troubles stem from antiquity in modern times the Balfour Declaration (the letter below) can perhaps be said to be at the root. Even as I write this Prime Minister Tony Blair has called on the US President George W Bush to recognise that the key to Middle Eastern peace is the Palestine/Israel situation. The Middle East is seen to include countries as far apart geographically as Lebanon and Iran and with Iraq in its present state of turmoil an early solution is essential though far from easy to achieve.

Foreign Office
November 2nd, 1917

Dear Lord Rothschild,

I have much pleasure in conveying to you, on behalf of His Majesty's Government, the following declaration of sympathy with Jewish Zionist aspirations which has been submitted to, and approved by, the Cabinet.

"His Majesty's Government view with favour the establishment in Palestine of a national home for the Jewish people, and will use their best endeavours to facilitate the achievement of this object, it being clearly understood that nothing shall be done which may prejudice the civil and religious rights of existing non-Jewish communities in Palestine, or the rights and political status enjoyed by Jews in any other country."

I should be grateful if you would bring this declaration to the knowledge of the Zionist Federation.
Yours sincerely,

Arthur James Balfour

Thus came about a reason for Arabs to revolt and for the British Government to send troops to quell the riots. Israel Cohen, a distinguished journalist, was on the Executive of the English Zionist Federation. He comments that while the Declaration *"fell far short of those proposed by Zionist leaders the enthusiasm that its publication aroused throughout the world exceeded all expectations. The vast crowd that swarmed into the London Opera House on December 2nd 1917 to celebrate the event by a public demonstration was so great that an overflow meeting had to be held at Kingsway Theatre"*.

In 1920 the Supreme Council of the Peace Conference resolved that the Declaration should be incorporated into the Treaty of Peace with Turkey and the Mandate for Palestine should be allotted to Great Britain. Military rule could then later be replaced by a civil administration. After the first Arab riots in the Spring of 1920 however, British policy became the subject of controversy mainly in connection with the alleged promise of independence to the Arabs in Palestine. Churchill repudiated this in 1921 but the critics did not go away.

Starting in 1936 and lasting for three years the Arab Rebellion was seen by many Britons as a waste of their tax payers' money and lobbied for the withdrawal of troops before any more of their soldiers were killed — the same argument has been put forward during the 21st Century with regard to the deployment in Iraq in particular. So when the 1st Bn Green Howards were dispatched to Palestine, arriving in October 1938 and basing themselves in the Jinsafut Camp, they were in many ways operating in circumstances not all that far removed from 2006. Some of the arguments may have been different and certainly British public opinion was less informed and thus less censorious.

The Zionist Bank.
©LJ Cohen estate

Sources: The Green Howards Museum
Beyond their duty by Roger Chapman
A Jewish Pilgrimage by Israel Cohen

John McCABE, GC

Industrial accident, 2nd April 1940, Royal Ordnance Factory, Irvine, Scotland

©Norman Kiff

Status: Assistant Foreman, Royal Ordnance Factory, Irvine
Life dates: 18th July 1896, Irvine – 2nd April 1940, Irvine, Ayrshire, Scotland. John is buried in Shewlton Cemetery with his father, mother and sister, Grave Reference A326. Note the incorrect OBE after John's name. The funeral took place at St Mary's Church, Irvine on 5th April 1940. **Obit:** *Irvine Herald*, 5th April 1940
Biography: John was the only son of John and Margaret (McGrath) McCabe. His father was described as a Hammerman at the time of his birth and a shipyard foreman on his son's death certificate. John had a sister Margaret, neither of whom married.

The above tells little of John McCabe's life and I am deeply indebted to the Library and Information Services of North Ayrshire for rediscovering him for me. Of all the GCs the finding of John McCabe has given me the most satisfaction.

It was indeed a prodigal moment when I spoke to the son of the foreman with whom John had worked. John has never had a photograph printed in any book on the GCs, yet in his home town he is honoured but not for the GC of which no one knew. Of such discoveries are a researcher's life made meaningful.

IRVINE MEADOW XI
1927–28

Back row—J. Hay, D. McQueen, J. Kerr, J. Duncan, J. Semple, R. Faulds, A. Currie, J. Bowman, D. Butcher. Middle row—J. McCabe (Assistant Trainer), John Mitchell, J. Parker, J. Samson, W. Maxwell, F. Campbell, L. Wallace, M. Sim, D. Strain, A. Gowie, W. Brown, James Mitchell (Secretary), S. Murray, A. Campbell (Trainer). Front row—D. Cairns, D. Watson, T. Burgoyne, S. Donnelly, J. McCulloch, R. F. Longmuir (President), W. Strain, W. Johnstone, H. Shedden, J. Ross, J. Devlin.
Ayrshire Intermediate Cup   Western Intermediate League Cup   Stirling Trophy   Scottish Intermediate Consolation Cup

Courtesy John Woods of the Irvine Herald

"He was ever ready to lend his organising ability to any deserving cause and his work in connection with the annual treats to the old men of the town will long be remembered." Thus read the obituary of John McCabe, EGM. *"He worked tirelessly for both young and old, but it was his sporting interests which "brought him into greatest prominence."*

John was associated with the Scottish Junior Footbal League Club, Meadow XI, then trained the team during which time they were highly successful. Though there is mention of John playing football no record of this has been found however, it is thought that he was more of an athlete. This was often the route to becoming a trainer/coach according to John Woods, the Sports Editor of the *Irvine Herald*.

"Training in those days largely consisted of lapping the track and the players only saw a ball on match days." Notice that all the coach carried in those days was a towel and a bottle of water.

Nevertheless John McCabe was a most successful trainer of this Junior Club — Junior in this context simply means semi-professional for fully-grown adults (not wee boys). Meadow was one of the most successful Junior teams in Scotland from 1940 to 1980 but fell on hard times though, says Woods "they are on their way back now!"

IRVINE MEADOW XI SPECIAL FINANCIAL COMMITTEE
Back row—W. McGuire, R. Alexander, R. Scott, R. Balmer, R. Mitchell, A. McKelvie.
Front row—J. McCabe, J. Kerr (Chairman), J. D. Mitchell (Secretary), J. Purdon
(Treasurer).
Cup—Calder Glen Trophy.

Courtesy John Woods of the Irvine Herald

John founded the Irvine Carpet Bowling League but was "*above all a young man with a most engaging personality and he was popular with all who knew him. With his many interests his place will be difficult to fill and his loss will be much felt by the community in which he filled so unique a position*".
Citation: *31st May 1940*
Author's note: I have included all three Citations for this action, though only McCabe's award was exchanged being the only one for Gallantry, as together they tell the story. Also due to the nature of secrecy at the time there was little publicity in the press.
St. James's Palace, S.W.1.
31st May, 1940.
The KING has been graciously pleased to approve of the posthumous Award of the Medal of the Civil Division of the Most Excellent Order of the British Empire, for Gallantry, to the late:—
John McCabe, Assistant Foreman, Royal Ordnance Factory.

The late John McCabe tragically lost his life through his exemplary devotion to duty on the 2nd April, when an explosion took place in the Factory. From the time that it was noticed that there were unusual conditions in the plant, he did all that was possible to get conditions normal. When this was unavailing and a fire was seen in one of the vessels, he attempted to use the mechanism which empties the contents of the vessel to a drowning pit. By this time the fire had spread to other vessels, and, after warning their men to escape, Messrs. Asquith and McLelland tried to use the appliance which is worked from outside the house for emptying all the vessels in the house, McCabe himself proceeding to work the same appliance within the building. While he was in the act of doing this, the explosion happened and he was instantly killed.

The KING has been graciously pleased to give orders for the following appointment to the Most Excellent Order of the British Empire:—
To be an Additional Member of the Civil Division of the said Most Excellent Order: —
Thomas Leach Asquith, Esq., Chemist, Royal Ordnance Factory.

When a serious explosion took place in the Factory on the 2nd April, Mr. T. L. Asquith was in general charge of operations. He proceeded immediately to the scene of the trouble and took control. He had just issued instructions for the operation of the drowning device and warned men not needed for its operation to escape, when the explosion occurred. He was blown by the explosion up the side of the mound, but recovered consciousness after a few seconds; he immediately resumed control of the situation and worked most efficiently until more senior help arrived. He showed a quick appreciation of the circumstances, initiative and quiet courage.

The KING has also been graciously pleased to approve of the following Award:—
The Medal of the Civil Division of the Most Excellent Order of the British Empire, for Meritorious Service:—
Hugh McLelland, Charge Hand, Royal Ordnance Factory.

On the occasion of the explosion which took place in the Factory on the 2nd April, McLelland remained with and helped McCabe and Asquith in all that they did, and had, in accordance with the latter's instructions, just operated the lever on the outside of the house to empty all the vessels in the house when the explosion took place. He was blown by the explosion through the entrance in the traverse and was seriously injured.

Other awards: EGM (Civilian) – GC exchange. The EGM was presented to John's sister on 2nd July 1940 on the same day as Hugh McLelland and Thomas Asquith received their awards.

John McCabe's GC was one of only four exchanges of posthumous EGMs — those which had been awarded since the beginning of WWII were the only ones eligible and the awards were presented to their next of kin. The other three were **Jolly GC**, HJ Miller GC and JNA Low GC.

The story

It had been almost impossible to find out anything about John McCabe and the story of his bravery is dismissed in the announcement in *The Times* of 22nd June 1940 with the comment, ".. *an assistant foreman Mr John McCabe, who lost his life through his devotion to duty has been posthumously awarded the medal of the Order of the British Empire, Civil Division, for Gallantry.*"

Additionally Herbert Morrison the Minister of Supply commented that for "*those key workers whose daily job is the handling of explosives we have a specially warm regard*".

It has also long been thought that the incident took place in Waltham Abbey, in fact it took place at Irvine not as is sometimes assumed at Ardeer, nearby in Scotland. The area is now Irvine Industrial Estate.

However, thanks to the Mrs J McColl, Norman Kiff and John Woods who have unearthed the story we know that 3 men were killed and five seriously injured. There was an Official Report and a Court of Inquiry set up.

The explosion was heard for miles around and the smoke and flames shot out of the buildings. Glass was shattered by the blast in windows both in the factory and in nearby homes and shops. Debris rained down and all that was left was a large crater, dirty and black and smoking. Fortunately the explosion occurred during tea-break so instead of there being 20 men in the section there were only a very unfortunate few.

Norman Kiff whose father was the Foreman at the Royal Ordnance Factory in Irvine told me the story.

His father Jack, an acidman, had been working at the Powder Mills in Waltham Abbey (see **O'Hagen GC**) when, on account of his specialist skills, he was asked to transfer to Irvine in 1936. He and his brother had been told by their boss "we think you should take the job there is going to be a war".

On arrival Jack found that the factory was being built by Wimpey and that many of the workers were Germans whose technology was being used to build the TNT plant. When he questioned one of the men as to what he did when back home the man replied that in Germany he was a "storm trooper".

As Jack was a key worker, along with the policemen and fire fighters, he had a tied house about a quarter of a mile from the factory and at the time of the explosion was back home for his break. Norman remembers sitting round the table for tea when they heard the huge explosion and the cloud of soot coming down the chimney. His father left for the factory immediately. So great was the power of the blast that a huge dragline had been blown right over the security fence.

The factory was in fact never bombed by the Germans and Norman puts this down to the fact that the buildings were well camouflaged and had flat rooves. There were three barrage ballooons called locally Huey, Dewy and Louie after the Disney characters. One day one of these broke free and the cables wrapped around the Kiff's chimney and took it out to sea. The balloon had to be shot down. The house remains without a chimney.

After the war the plant was used for the dismantling of bombs from all over Europe. The TNT and cordite was burnt. The boxes in which the ordnance was shipped were eagerly sought by the townsfolk to make huts in their backyards. Some are still standing.

One of the plaques in the Memorial garden in Irvine which has recently been renovated by the Irvine Royal Academy and the Irvine Rotary Club. In fact only seven of the men listed were killed at the Royal Ordnance Factory.

The list above includes a girl, Mary Manderson, who was in the ATS and who was driving a car across a level crossing at Heatherhouse with a high-ranking passenger on board when a train ploughed through the car killing them both.

Norman Kiff remembers that on the side of her car were the words "Broadway Trust Co Ltd", an investment company. No doubt it been requisitioned?

The other person on the list who was not an employee was Thomas McCulley. He died on the beaches of Dunkirk and was a member of the Argyll and Sutherland Highlanders.

John Woods of the Irvine Herald

Memorials: There is an impressive Memorial Garden in Irvine to those from the town who lost their lives during the two World Wars. It includes not only servicemen and women but also civilians.

Dedication of the War Memorial in Irvine at the factory.
Courtesy N Kiff

Background: *Irvine*

Norman Kiff has provided all these photographs. The Germans built the factory in 1936–37, returned to Germany and many then returned to the PoW camp just outside the town between 1944–45. The factory was never bombed and Norman puts this down to the fact that the flat rooves made it a difficult target to identify. He has some of the badges from the PoWs including some from Italian soldiers who had fought in the desert under Rommel. Some of the prisoners — who were allowed out of the prison for short periods — later stayed and married local girls. The Irvine factory closed in 1954–55.

There is a story he told me about an Irishman who was caught by the policeman on duty with a cigarette in his pocket. The Irishman incensed put a curse on the policeman's sons saying they would die before they were 21. Neither made their 21st birthday and both died of the same infection.

The factory canteen.
Note the flat roof which was typical of the majority of the buildings.

The contraband hut. All cigarettes and matches had to be handed in before entering the gates.

The old boiler-house.

The half house which was used as an ARP station during the war and later was given to the Head Plumber. Next door is Norman Kiff's mother's house minus chimney!

Sources: Richard James
Ardrossan • Saltcoats Herald
The Irvine Herald
J McColl of North Ayrshire Council
John Woods
Norman Kiff
Joe Houston
The History of Irvine Meadow XI FC by James F. Delury
History of Irvine by John Strawhorn

John McCABE, GC

Mine rescue, 9th July 1918, Stanrigg Colliery, Airdrie, Lanarkshire, Scotland

Annie and John McCabe with his sister-in-law Elizabeth.
Courtesy A McCabe

©A McCabe

...

And one there was that day who played a hero's part,
Nor thought of his own danger as he rushed back in the dark
To warn his gallant comrades of their impending fate;
And by his gallant conduct sixty men made their escape.

...

JG McKay

Status: Drawer, Stanrigg Colliery, Airdrie, Lanarkshire, Scotland
Life dates: 6th December 1901, Longriggend, Lanarkshire – 29th January 1974, Caldercruix, Lanarkshire, Scotland. John is buried in St Joseph's Cemetery, Airdrie.

Biography: John's father, Joseph, was a coalminer and he and his wife Mary (McCue) had 8 children in all. Sons, James, Thomas, John, Joseph, Peter, Archie and daughters Morran and Catherine. Young James died in the Great War in 1915 aged 17.

The children attended the local school and John left at 14 to go down the pit joining his brothers Tommy and Joseph. Their home was a tied cottage with no running water. After his heroic deed John was offered a scholarship to the University of his choice but he declined. His father asked if his brother Joseph could have it but was informed that it had to be used for "*the boy that done the deed*".

John went back down the pit with his brother shortly after the disaster as there was no other alternative work at that time in the area.

John was an excellent athlete and a keen footballer and played for Workington Town in the old English 2nd Division whilst continuing to work in the pits.

John as the best man at his brother Archie's wedding to Mary with Elizabeth Carroll as best maid.
©McCabe family, courtesy A McCabe

He later married Annie Dowdalls and had two sons, Joseph and John and a daughter, Mary. Tragically his son John died of pneumonia at an early age and Joseph died aged 40 of a heart attack, with Mary the only surviving child.

John came from a close-knit, loyal family and he and Annie continued this tradition. He was a "good livin' man" says his nephew **Archie**, "doing much work for the Catholic charitable organisation St Vincent de Paul" within Saint Patrick's Roman Catholic Church, Longriggend.

His daughter **Mary** remembers the fatal day, "it had been an Indian summer," she said, "with weeks of very heavy rainfall which had destabilised the earth".

Citation: *13th June 1919*

Whitehall, 11th June, 1919

Also to John McCabe, a drawer at the Stanrigg Colliery, Airdrie, aged 17.

On the 9th July, 1918, there was an inrush of moss into the workings. McCabe, with two other drawers and three miners, was at the bottom of number 3 shaft when they were told that the moss had broken in. The two other boys and the three men at once ascended the shaft and escaped. McCabe, however, knowing that there were men at the face who might be cut off, returned for a quarter of a mile and warned the men. He and the men he had warned were ultimately collected and raised by another shaft. When he returned to the face, McCabe did not know where the break had occurred, or whether the moss might not at any moment fill the workings through which he returned, as in fact it soon afterwards did. He faced a grave and unknown danger, which might have been fatal, in order to enable others to escape.

The pocket watch below was presented to John and the inscription on the inside reads:

Presented by the trustees of the Carnegie Hero Fund
TO
John McCabe, Airdrie
for the heroism in saving human life 9th July 1918.

Other awards: EM (Bronze Mine) – GC exchange. John was one of 10 men to receive the Edward Medal on 13th June 1919, he was the only one to live to exchange his medal for the GC the investiture for which took place on 27th February 1973. He was also awarded a silver watch of the Carnegie Hero Fund. The George Cross was sold a number of times, lastly by Spinks on 6th November 1996.

This rare picture shows the symbols of the Carnegie Hero Fund Trust on the watch.
Both pictures ©A McCabe

The story

Of all those involved in the disaster at Stanrigg one name stands out above all the rest and that is John McCabe. The seventeen-year old drawer is credited with saving the lives of 58 men. He was fortunate to live but chose not to tell the tale.

There were three shafts of which only the upcast and downcast were in any way connected to ventilation, the third was for the transporting of material, equipment and men. There were three seams, Humph, Splint and Virgin with the last being the deepest at 126 feet and its upper leaf was known as the 'Sour Milk'.

NARRATIVE OF THE ACCIDENT.

On the day of the accident the two firemen, as was their custom, came to the surface to have their breakfast between 10 and 10.30, and whilst they were at breakfast a bottomer at No. 3 shaft named James Rafferty came to the surface and informed them there was something wrong, as the ventilating current was "coming out very strong." They descended the No. 3 shaft at once, and William McCracken, who was fireman in the Humph Seam, was proceeding inbye when at about 90 yards from No. 3 shaft he met liquid moss moving along the haulage road in the Virgin Seam and pushing a hutch before it towards the shaft. Edward McCracken went to his section of the workings—the "Sour Milk"—and was able to proceed to the Wee Stone Mine leading to the machine section (*see* plan) before he met moss flowing towards him. He collected the men in that part of the workings and took them to No. 2 shaft, up which, after steam had been raised to work the winding engine there, they were drawn to the surface.

The inflow of the moss, by filling up the two roads by which the persons working in the Humph Seam could have escaped, had cut off and entombed 19 men and boys and prevented the rescue parties getting to them from the Virgin Seam. The 58 men and boys working in the other parts of the mine were rescued and got safely to the surface.

From an *Inrush of Moss*, 9th July 1918.

There was little difference of opinion amongst the rescue team and those who held the Inquiry as to the chance of rescue of the entombed men or of the recovery of their bodies. It was considered that the inrush of moss and additional flooding up to 9 feet, made the chance of survival impossible. With the possibility of another inrush of moss it was considered to be too great a risk to take. Many years later of course opinions changed but it is worth remembering that the War was not yet over and millions had died with devastating effects on families.

John McCabe along with 57 other men bore witness to the events and today there are many people alive who are alive due to his foresight and courage. It was the courage of youth, but also the character of the boy who had been brought up to think of others, his two brothers being among those he went to warn.

The Geology

One of the witnesses, *R W Dron*, Mining Engineer described the geology of the area for a greater understanding of the cause of the disaster.

"When the ice (of the last glacial period) came, the channels of the rivers became filled up, and, subsequently, the whole area was covered with a deposit of glacial debris. This debris consists frequently of sand and gravel, but the greater part of it is stiff, plastic clay mixed with stones and boulders — boulder clay. The sand and gravels were laid down as glacial moraines. The boulder clay appears to have been laid down under the ice. It extends in a sheet over most of the lowlands. As the glaciers melted away, the boulder clay was traversed by streams of water.

We thus find that at places the whole of the boulder clay has been washed away so sand and gravel is lying on the adjacent strata. The retreating ice must have left the surface with very irregular contours with numerous depressions which would be filled with water.

Some became lochs ... while others became filled up with vegetation. These hollows form the peat mosses ...

The areas and depths appear to be quite irregular and depend entirely on the varying conditions which were present when the ice melted.

...

In areas where soft undrained moss is found, the only safe rule is to assume it has been proven that the underlying boulder clay has been washed away. In these areas the depth of the moss should be proven just as the depth of water be proven if the workings were coming under a loch.

The fact that the surface is growing heather gives a deceptive appearance of security.

It is obvious that a considerable number of bores would be required ... to confirm the depth of the moss within the basin."

Thus, he concluded that insufficient information had been available as to the depth of the moss. In future where workings were to be under undrained moss measurements should be taken and operations conducted according to the results thereof.

At the Inquiry Mr Walker did not find any person responsible for the accident and made recommendations as to changing working practices. He also commended John McCabe for his bravery. This was reiterated a week later by Sheriff Lee at the Fatal Accident Inquiry.

Memorials:

The momument and (below) the relief sculpture on the back of the main stone. Set around are blocks carved with the initials of all those who died.

©A McCabe

There are a number of memorials to the 19 men who died. 11 are still entombed in the earth they worked in. Larry O'Hare in his book *The Stanrigg Pit Disaster* quotes Wilfred Owen's poem *Miners* which it is believed was inspired by the Stanrigg disaster. There is also a song, really a ballad, entitled *Stanrigg Pit Disaster* composed by Gunner Jas G McKay, RGA.

After much wrangling a monument to the 19 miners who died was built in 1998. A ceremony was held at the Park Pit Open Cast Site on 9th July, 80 years afterwards and, for the many who would have remembered it, many years too late.

It is unfortunate that all the books and websites relating to the Stanrigg Disaster say that McCabe received the George Medal — he did *not*, he received the George Cross.

Background: *Stanrigg Colliery as it is today*

This is the land that now covers Stanrigg where large pipes were inserted into the ground in the hope that the men could escape. However, the moss had already taken over the area and the bodies are still interred.

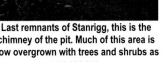

Last remnants of Stanrigg, this is the chimney of the pit. Much of this area is now overgrown with trees and shrubs as you can see.
Anne-Marie McCabe

On top of the hill stands this sign to Stanrigg and the surrounding villages from whence the miners came.

The Stanrigg Pit Disaster Memorial.
©*A McCabe*

Sources: Archie McCabe — nephew — Joseph's son
Mary Morris — daughter
The Stanrigg Pit Disaster by Larry O'Hare
Report on the Causes and Circumstances Attending the Accident at Stanrigg & Arbuckle Colliery, Lanarkshire by W Walker CBE
Gunner Jas G McKay, RGA
www.geocities.com/droughan123/stanrigg_pitt_disaster.html with details of each of the deceased
Anne-Marie McCabe — great-niece

William Henry Debonnaire (Mac, Bill) McCARTHY, GC

Life-saving, 1943, at Benghazi, Libya

Mac at Christmas 1942.

Mac in Gibraltar Docks.
All pictures ©McCarthy family

Mac and his bride Violet (Vi) on their wedding day, 16th June 1945.

Status: Coxswain, HMS *Nile*, Royal Navy

Life dates: 2nd April 1911, Kensington, London – 21st July 1978, Portsmouth, Hampshire. It is perhaps appropriate that Mac was cremated at Porchester on 27th July 1978 exactly thirty-five years to the day that *The London Gazette* first reported his act of gallantry. There is an entry in the Book of Remembrance which reads:

Courageous in life, dearly loved, ever remembered.

Obit: *Daily Telegraph* 16th August 1978

Biography: William Henry Debonnaire was the only son of William and Alice Mary (Carley) McCarthy. His father was working as a butcher's assistant at the time of his birth but died when William was 2 years old. His mother remarried and took William to live in Camberwell with her new husband and two stepsons. In 1917 Alice's second husband died and most sadly three years later she herself died. The three boys were then looked after by family but after a short while they were split up and were finally admitted to the care of Dr Barnardo's.

Mac, as the *Victor Ludorum* the top athletics award he won while at Watts.
Information from Reg Trew

Mac with a friend. He was a keen swimmer and could continue to smoke in the water.
Photos from McCarthy family

Mac, Vi, Carolyn and Jackie in 1956 in Gibraltar just before leaving to do salvage work in the Suez Canal.

William's daughter **Carolyn Lawson** told me his story.

Bill, the name by which he was known by his brothers and friends and then later Mac, spoke little of his childhood but when he did he showed appreciation for what Dr Barnardo's had done for him. Clearly the training he received in his youth stood him in good stead in later life and had a profound effect on the kind of man he became.

William attended Watts Naval Training School in Elmham, (near Dereham) Norfolk. Life here included being woken at six a.m. by a bugle, sleeping in a dormitory, cold showers and a hard working very organised day which would have involved lots of physical activity. The education provided was a general one as well as specialised subjects relevant to a future career in the Navy. (see **Alf Lowe GC** who also trained at Watts).

McCarthy's record of service includes the following promotions and ships.

1927 — joined the RN as a Boy 2nd Class and given the nickname Mac which stayed with him all his life

1930 — Able Seaman

1936 — Leading Seaman

1937 — recommended for a warrant

1939 — Boatswain

01.43 — HMS *Nile* at Alexandria

07.45 – 04.46 — HMS *Victory* at Portsmouth

07.48 — Pembroke Dock (naval store and fuel depot — HMS *Drake*)

15.08.49 – 05.50 — HMS *Bulawayo*, a supply ship

01.10.51 — Lieutenant

07.01.52 – 05.53 — Master Rigger HMS *Victory* at Portsmouth. During which time he was praised by the Captain of the Dockyard in the following words: "I have always been impressed with the efficiency and the cheerful and co-operative outlook of the Officers and men of your Department".

15.01.54 – 01.56 — HMS *Rooke* at Gibraltar and he served in the Suez campaign specialising in salvage work.

01.57 — HMS *Angelo* at Malta as Lieutenant Commander with special duties

His last appointment was at HMS *Dryad* where he served as a Staff Officer. Here he was described as handling the welfare of the Ratings in a sympathetic yet firm way, "an outstanding success. I am most grateful for his services." wrote his Commanding Officer.

02.04.61 — retired

During his time in the Royal Navy he travelled all over the world and took a great interest in all the places he visited, keeping notes on the geography and history of the various countries he visited along with photo albums. He gained qualifications in Gunnery, Diving and Salvage work and specialised in salvage work. His Naval records describe him as "*zealous, reliable, diligent, conscientious, exceptionally able and loyal*".

During the war he continued to travel extensively and in 1943 found himself in Benghazi.

Mac knew his wife-to-be Violet Glover throughout the war but they chose to wait till the end of the war before marrying in London in June 1945. They had a daughter, Carolyn, in 1946 and a second daughter, Jackie, was born in 1948.

In 1961 when Mac retired he and his wife decided to stay in Portsmouth initially because the two girls were then settled at grammar school in Portsmouth then later after their daughters had grown up and left home remained happily where they were. Mac became a grandfather in 1971 and liked to spend time with his granddaughter. He also loved his garden and spent many hours tending it. Another hobby of his was needlework which he had taken up many years before during long sea voyages.

He worked as a securities agent/debt councillor and later for the civil service before retiring completely at the age of 65. Sadly his retirement was not a long one. His wife was taken ill with cancer the following year and he turned his hand to caring for her most attentively and took on a domestic role, a role not previously required of him. On 21st July 1978 he suffered a sudden and fatal heart attack and died the same day. He had been out that morning, eaten lunch and had a nap in his armchair when he died.

Mac was a very modest man who hardly ever spoke of his act of bravery to anyone. Always kind , always calm and patient with his children and granddaughter he is remembered with much love and affection by all his remaining family. A grandson was born in 1979 and both his grandchildren, daughters and sons-in-law hold his memory very dear.

© C Lawson

Citation: *23rd July 1943*

ADMIRALTY. Whitehall, 27th July, 1943

The KING has been graciously pleased to give orders for the following appointments to the Distinguished Service Order and to approve the following Rewards and Awards: *for gallantry in saving life at sea.*

The Albert Medal.

Mr. William Henry Debonnaire McCarthy, Boatswain, Royal Navy.

Mr. McCarthy dived into a tempestuous sea from the Mole at Benghazi to save some Indian seamen who had been thrown into the sea from a raft. When a line was thrown he swam with it to the Indians, caught hold of one of them and successfully brought him ashore. He then returned to the rescue of another. There was grave danger that Mr. McCarthy would be dashed against the rocks by the gale and the high sea.

Other awards: AM (Bronze Sea) – GC Exchange. 1939–45 Star, Atlantic Star, Africa Star with clasp 'North Africa 1942-43', Burma Star, War Medal 1939-45, Naval GSM 1915-62 with clasp 'Near East' and QSJM. The AM was presented 18th May 1945.

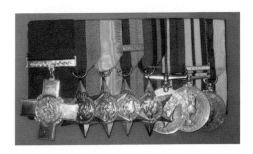

Jackie (centre) with her sister Carolyn and Carolyn's daughter Alison presenting the medals to the IWM in 1982 with the then Director of the Museum.

After the death of his wife William McCarthy's medal group passed into the hands of his two daughters. In 1982 they decided to loan them to the Imperial War Museum where they are on permanent display in the Victoria and George Cross gallery.

Background: *Dr Barnado's Homes and today*

In 1867 Thomas Barnardo set up a school for poor children in the East End but so shocked was he by the conditions in which some of the children were living and sleeping rough that he opened his first Home in 1870 for destitute boys. Girls were catered for soon after in the Girls Village Home in Barkingside. However much he thought the Homes could do for the children he firmly believed that a family was the best place for a child to be brought up and built up a network of foster parents.

Thomas Barnardo died in 1905. By then the charity ran 96 Homes caring for more than 8,500 children. Residential care emphasised children's physical and moral welfare rather than their emotional wellbeing. Some homes housed hundreds of children and sometimes staff were harsh and distant. Many adults who grew up in the homes look back with affection and believe the charity was a true family. Others remember loneliness, bullying and even abuse.

From the 1970s onwards, Barnardo's, as it had now become, continued to expand its work in fostering and adoption. Family centres were set up in communities to support families in deprived areas. The charity set out to help families facing problems such as unemployment, poor health, bad housing and poverty with the aim of defusing the stress and tension that might lead to family breakdown and child abuse.

Bardardo's also support young carers, a particularly overlooked group of people. These are often quite young children who take care of a parent at home. The charity works to enable the families to stay together.

Despite their best efforts however, in *Handle with Care. An Investigation into the care system* Harriet Sergeant almost destroys any faith we may have had in the Care System in the 21st Century, either the public or the private sectors. The Social Services and Local Authorities are failing our most vulnerable children. It is no longer the practise to send young boys of 13 to the Navy as it was with McCarthy and Low. Yet Sergeant finds that those who are admitted into the Armed Forces are more likely to find fulfilment and thus avoid the downward spiral of poverty, unemployment and crime into which so large a proportion of Care Leavers fall.

We read with profound humility and admiration of such men as McCarthy, Low and **Kent GC.** They were lucky to have been born when there was still a system of care, and most importantly of advice and help, to enable them to find their place in society and in so doing they found honour and dignity and their names will live on.

HMS Nile

HMS *Nile* was the Naval HQ at Ras el Tin Point in Alexandria Naval Base throughout WW2. Almost all Royal Navy personnel serving in the Eastern Mediterranean, other than those serving in ships, were borne on the books of HMS *Nile*. These included locations such as Tobruk, Mersa Mutruh, Port Tewfik, Cyprus and probably Benghazi.

Sources: Imperial War Museum, London

www.barnardos.org.uk

Alison Creamer — granddaughter

JN Houterman

Carolyn Lawson — daughter

Lawrie Phillips

Handle with Care. An Investigation into the care system by Harriet Sergeant

Shore Establishments of the Royal Navy by Lt-Cdr Ben Warlow

John MacKintosh McCLYMONT, GC

Fire rescue, 18th January 1940, 18 Balloon Centre, Bishopbriggs, Glasgow

Extract from the Registrar of Births showing the spelling of his and of his mother's name.
©Registrar General for Scotland

Status: 874574 Corporal, City of Glasgow Auxiliary Air Force, 18 Balloon Centre, RAF (The AAF was embodied into the RAF on 24th Aug 1939)

Life dates: 15th October 1903, Glasgow – 10th June 1996, Hamilton, Ontario. He was cremated and interred at Bethesda United Church Cemetery, Ancaster, Ontario . Note that on his headstone his second name is MacIntosh.

Biography: John was the son of Hugh and Annie Eliza (McIntosh) McClymont. Again note that in the Register of Births there is a difference in spelling in his mother's maiden name and his own second name. His father was a farm grieve.

John MacKintosh McClymont left School at fourteen and emigrated to Canada in 1923, returning to Scotland to do forestry work in 1932 and sometime thereafter he joined the Auxiliary Air Force (AAF). He was called up in 1939 to No 18 Balloon Centre, Glasgow and sent to a balloon site of No 947 (Balloon Barrage) Sqdn. He qualified as a driver and quickly reclassified from Aircraftman Class 2 to Aircraftman Class 1 and then Leading Aircraftman and on 15th January 1940 was transferred to No 950 (BB) Sqdn formed at Bishopbriggs and promoted to Corporal. Shortly after the Sqdn transferred to Scapa Flow.

About 1940 McClymont moved to No 967 (BB) Sqdn based at Ardrossan having qualified as a Motor Transport Mechanic. It is thought that as he had received burns to his hands that was probably the reason why he was discharged from the RAF on medical grounds on the 25th February 1942. He returned to Hamilton, Ontario, Canada in 1949 to take up forestry again, his wife, Alice Jane Irwin (McLay) joined him in 1950. He then took a job with International Harvester Company as a security officer, retiring in 1968.

Among his interests were photography, model engineering, snooker and gardening.

Note here a further change in the spelling of John's middle name.
Courtesy Tom Johnson ©Terry MacDonald

McCLYMONT, John M. - At McMaster Medical Center, on Monday, June 10, 1996, John M. McClymont, husband of the late Alice Jane McLay, in his 93rd year. Mr. McClymont was a member of the George Cross Society and a former security officer with International Harvester and the Federal Building. Friends may call at the DODSWORTH AND BROWN Funeral Home, ANCASTER CHAPEL, 378 Wilson Street East, on Tuesday, 7-9 p.m. Service in the Chapel on Wednesday at 1 p.m. Interment, Bethesda Cemetery. If desired, memorial gifts may be made to the charity of your choice.

Notice of John McClymont's death.
Courtesy Tom Johnson.

Citation: *19th July 1940*

The KING has been graciously pleased to approve the following Awards: —

The Medal of the Military Division of the Most Excellent Order of the British Empire, for Gallantry:—

874574 Corporal John McIntosh (*sic*) McClymont, Auxiliary Air Force.

On the 18th January, 1940, an aircraft, with two occupants, crashed during a snowstorm and immediately caught fire. Several individuals ran to the scene and Corporal McClymont, who was one of the party, helped in extricating one of the airmen from the cabin. As the flames were increasing in intensity and ammunition and Very lights were continually exploding, all ranks were ordered to stand away from the aircraft. Corporal McClymont heard the order but considered it did not prevent a single-handed attempt being made to rescue the second occupant and remained behind for this purpose.

An officer returned shortly to help him and, together, they succeeded in extricating the airman just before the petrol tank exploded. During the second operation, whilst Corporal McClymont was holding back part of the cabin, he received injuries to his hands. He displayed great courage in the face of extreme danger and had the second airman been alive would undoubtedly have saved him from being burnt to death. Both occupants had, however, been killed instantaneously when the aircraft crashed.

Other awards: EGM (Military) – GC exchange. Defence medal, War Medal 1939–45, 1953 Coronation Medal and 1977 Queen's Silver Jubilee Medal. The EGM was presented on 23rd September 1941 at Buckingham Palace. The group was later presented to the RAF Museum, Hendon but it is not on display.

The story

Enquiries revealed that the aircraft was a Fleet Air Arm Walrus amphibian (serial P5648) catapulted from the cruiser HMS *Norfolk* of the Home Fleet, *en route* to Lee-on-Solent, Hants. The pilot Lt Edward Pope and his passenger Leading Airman John Baxter had no opportunity to climb from the blazing wreck.

While the immediate reaction of the men was to run out to affect a rescue it was almost immediately obvious that there was nothing to be done and the danger was extreme. Had McClymont considered for a minute he would have realised that the men he was trying to save were already dead. In times of such great stress adrenalin takes over and perhaps common sense is a casualty.

So great was his surprise when he heard that he had been awarded the EGM when questioned all John would say was: "A few of the lads and the Flight Lieutenant (F C Hornsby-Smith) ran over and managed to get two bodies out."

A Walrus just after being catapulted from a ship.
© Fleet Air Arm Museum

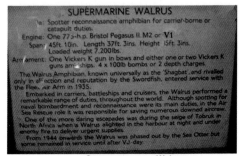

Some notes on a Walrus.
© Fleet air Arm Museum

Historian **Len Bacon** has done considerable research for me into the events of that day and this is what he found out.
Serial number 874574 indicates that at the age of 35 John volunteered into No. 947 (City of Glasgow) Balloon Squadron of the Auxiliary Air Force (AAF).

Early in 1939 that Squadron and two others 945 and 946 were established with individual temporary headquarters in the area of the City of Glasgow. The necessary recruitment for them commenced with posters, advertisements and balloon displays; this was aimed at local men between the ages of 30 to 50 years.

I find that John was the 74th man to sign up as an Aircraftman Second Class and he was soon required twice a week and on Sundays to attend for lectures and drill in the operation of Barrage Balloons. For that he would receive uniform and be paid six shillings (30p) a week.

While this was going on the construction of the 18 Balloon Centre (Bishopbriggs) was taking place and it is thought that it was late in 1939 before it was fully operational.

On Thursday 24th August 1939 the AAF Squadrons, men and officers were embodied into the Royal Air Force and were to serve full time.

As an RAF (Aux) John and colleagues would undergo Trades Tests for Balloon Operator or Rigger and if they passed they would become Aircraftman First Class. I feel that John's marks were high and he was possibly also seen to be a leader of men as he soon became a temporary or acting Corporal; something which he was to lose after his brave action at the plane crash as from his injuries he was unable to carry out NCOs' duties. It is thought that he would not have had any RAF training dealing with an aircraft fire or the rescue of crew.

While the flying of the Glasgow Barrage of Balloons had started by the late summer, by the 1st October 1939 only 24 were flying. It should be noted that each balloon was flown from a required location at which a self-contained Site was established. The number of such Sites was to increase to 79 by October 1940.

However, on the Thursday 18th January 1940 the day of the plane crash some 31 Balloons were flying. The question was; "*Did the Walrus P5648 hit the cable of a balloon which could cause it to crash?*"
Unfortunately my records of such RAF incidents only start in May 1940.

Early in 1940 No. 950 and later 960 Squadrons were formed at No 18 Balloon Centre and then sent to No. 20 Balloon Centre at Lyness in Orkney and the first Barrage there was deployed in February 1940; that could have been John's next posting.

As his trade was changed to Driver it could be suffixed with 'MT' (Motor Transport) or 'W' (Winch) the latter would mean he was still in a Balloon Crew.

As we know John was medically discharged in 1942.

The Royal Navy part

There are three key questions relating to the incident which I put to Len.

Why was Walrus P5648 on HMS Norfolk catapulted off the ship during a snowstorm?

Why were there only two in the aircraft which normally had a complement of 3 or 4?

Why did the plane take off so soon after the ship had left port on its way to Lee-on-Solent?

In the record books at the FAA Museum where the names of Pope and Baxter are listed there is no indication of answers to these questions however, Len has put together the following facts and his considered explanation. Of course this is partly a surmise.

- The Walrus crashed and immediately burst into flames (remembering that it was full of fuel) North of Glasgow.
- The fact that there were only two occupants on a wintry day in January 1940 with the loss of two lives suggests to me that it was not a normal flying operation.
- The Pilot was Lieutenant (Air) Edward Frank Pope. His age is unknown. He was the son of Ada Pope, of Honiton, Devon. (He is thought to have been of Canadian Nationality.)
- The passenger was Leading Airman FX/76321 John Baxter, aged 25, the son of Andrew and Susan Baxter, and husband of Elizabeth Gardner Baxter of Mossend, Bellshill, North Lanarkshire. (His trade would be either Air Frames or Engines.)
- Both were from HMS *Norfolk* a Cruiser of the Home Fleet.

Since the outbreak of the War the Home Fleet had assembled in Scarpa Flow where in October HMS *Royal Oak* was sunk by torpedoes with the death of 833 personnel at the same time HMS *Norfolk* had received torpedo damage which was later repaired in Belfast.

With such large numbers of casualties it is likely that the morale in the Home Fleet was very low and home leave was unlikely, but is very possible that two crew members of the *Norfolk* had other ideas. It is known that HMS *Norfolk* could carry two Walrus amphibians and without putting the ship to risk one could evidently be used for a personal reason.

Lt. Pope after obtaining permission could 'borrow' P5648 for a private flight to his home area and a flight plan to RN Airfield Lee-on-Solent was obviously submitted with the reason for it being recorded as an 'Exercise'. This was normal practice in the Services and he would be received at all airfields in an emergency.

No doubt John Baxter got to hear of this trip, he worked on the aircraft and it is possible he was either offered or asked for a lift to the mainland.

(Imagine then that perhaps John Baxter had only been married a short time and his wife was living with his parents and for some good reason he might have requested compassionate home leave which would have been agreed.)

Here the question arises. *Was Lt. Pope heading for a landing to drop off John Baxter, were they off course or was it because of the bad weather?*

At that time 2.5 miles West of Girvan in Renfrewshire there was an RAF Station Abbotsinch (today the BAA Glasgow International Airport) and the Fleet Air Arm were there during 1939–1940. To land there Baxter was only 21 miles from his home.

Some information received by me several years ago relates that adjacent to RAF Bishopbriggs there was a Flying Control Building together with a landing area. Have done some research but to date nothing found, however, it could have been the actual site of the plane crash and have been the landing area Pope was looking for. It is obvious that the bad visibility made it very difficult over Glasgow which was now exacerbated by 31 Barrage Balloons; to hit one of the half inch thick cables connected to them would result in a crash.

The 1939–40 winter was a very bad one. Records for January 1940 state on the 17th, '*Thames freezes for the first time since 1888 as a cold wave strikes Europe*' whilst on the 27th, '*The worst storm of the Century sweeps the country.*'

In conclusion I feel that Lieutenant Pope was a thoughtful and caring man to put his career on the line by helping one of his men to get to his home.

©*Len Bacon 29th September 2006*

Background: *Very lights* — flares fired into the air for illumination from a Very pistol, they are usually coloured

farm grieve — manager or bailiff on a farm in Scotland

Sources: John Blatherwick

The George Cross by Ian Bisset

John Hamlin

Airmail, RAF Assn Journal, Summer 1986

www.fleetairarmarchive.net/Aircraft/Walrus.htm and the Fleet Air Arm Museum where you can see a Walrus.

Tom Johnson

The Canadians in Britain 1939–1944 by the Ministry of National Defence. This book gives an idea of the importance Canada attached to the role played by her citizens during WWII.

Len Bacon

Andrew Cormack at RAF Hendon

Terry MacDonald

Thomas William McCORMACK, GC

Industrial rescue, 27th November 1908, Jarrow Dry Dock, Co Durham

Status: Dry Dock worker, Jarrow Shipbuilders, Co. Durham
Life dates: 23rd February 1886, Jarrow, Co Durham – 6th March 1973, Jarrow, Co. Durham. Thomas was buried in Jarrow Cemetery in Section 5 Grave Number 632 after a funeral on 9th March 1971 joining his wife Emily who died 25th March 1961. There is an additional person in the grave which was unpurchased, Ellen Liddle, died 16th December 1943. There is no headstone.
Biography: Thomas was the son of Michael and Elizabeth McCormack. His father worked in the shipyards as a riveter. There were at least 4 siblings. In 1901 Thomas was working as a cement labourer but by 1908 while still employed in the shipyards was working as a painter. He married Emily and had a son and three daughters.

Citation: *23rd July 1909*

The KING was pleased, on Thursday, the 22nd of July, at Buckingham Palace, to present to Arthur Eccleshall, an employee of the London and North-Western Railway Company; to George Henry Smith, of Woburn Sands, Bedfordshire; to James Kennedy Chapman and Thomas McCormack, both of Jarrow; and to James Vivian Reed, lately Second Mate of the steamship *Afonwen*, of Cardiff, the Albert Medals of the Second Class, which have been conferred upon them by His Majesty for gallantry in saving or endeavouring to save life, as detailed below:

James Kennedy Chapman and Thomas McCormack

On the 27th November, 1908, workmen were engaged painting the inside of an iron tank in the stokehold of a steamer lying in dry dock at Jarrow.

Owing to the fact that very strong fumes were given off by the anti-corrosive paint or solution used the men were working in relays, each squad of three men being relieved after 10 or 15 minutes had elapsed. A workman named Graham was overcome by the fumes, and the chargeman, Archibald Wilson, sacrificed his life in endeavouring to save Graham.

Thomas McCormack, who had already been affected by the fumes while at work in the tank, went to Wilson's assistance, but was himself rendered insensible, and was rescued by James Kennedy Chapman, Works Manager at the Dock, who, having pulled McCormack out, re-entered the tank and endeavoured to save Graham, but was himself overcome by the fumes. The rescue of Chapman and Graham was eventually effected from the top of the tank.

Archibald Wilson's Citation (note the later date)
Whitehall, February 26, 1910.
The KING has been pleased to allow Mrs. Isabella Wilson, now residing at South Shields, to receive the Albert Medal of the Second Class which, but for his untimely death, would have been awarded to her late husband, Mr. Archibald Wilson, in recognition of his gallantry in endeavouring to save life as detailed below:—

On the 27th November, 1908, workmen were engaged painting the inside of an iron tank in the stokehold of a steamer lying in dry dock at Jarrow.

Owing to the fact that very strong fumes were given off by the anti-corrosive paint or solution used the men were working in relays, each squad of three men being relieved after 10 or 15 minutes had elapsed.

A workman named Graham was overcome by the fumes, and the chargeman, Archibald Wilson, sacrificed his life in endeavouring to save Graham.

Thomas McCormack, who had already been affected by the fumes while at work in the tank, went to Wilson's assistance, but was himself rendered insensible, and was rescued by James Kennedy Chapman, Works Manager at the Dock, who, having pulled McCormack out, re-entered the tank and endeavoured to save Graham, but was himself overcome by the fumes.

The rescue of Chapman and Graham was eventually effected from the top of the tank. The award of the Albert Medal of the Second Class to Mr. Chapman and Mr. McCormack was notified in the *London Gazette* of the 23rd July, 1909.

THE JARROW DOCK RESCUE
HEROES HONOURED BY THE KING.

Among the recipients of the Albert medal (second class) at the investiture held by the King at Buckingham Palace yesterday were Jas. Kennedy Chapman and Thos. McCormack, who, in November last, jumped into a tank on a steamer lying in Jarrow dry dock to the rescue of a man who had been overcome by fumes. Archibald Wilson, who also jumped into the tank, was himself overcome, and died, and the King has directed that his medal should be handed to the widow.

Announcement of the investiture on 22nd July 1909.
Courtesy S Wilson

Other awards: AM (Bronze Land) – GC exchange. Only McCormack lived to exchange his medal for the GC. Thomas McCormack was the first recipient of the Carnegie Hero Fund Medallion. He received it in December 1908.

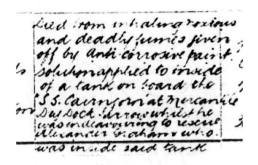

Archibald Wilson's death certificate.

Background: *Archibald Wilson AM*

Thanks to Archibald's great-granddaughter I am able to include a fascinating family story. Wilson received a posthumous Albert Medal which was handed to his wife. He may have died saving his step-son.

The lengthy cause of death of Archibald Wilson given on his death certificate:

Died from inhaling noxious and deadly fumes given off by anti-corrosive paint solution applied to inside of a tank on board the SS Cairngorm at Mercantile Dry Dock, Jarrow whilst he was endeavouring to rescue Alexander Graham who was inside said tank.

Archibald Wilson (born 15th October 1867) was the eldest child of eight to Stafford Wilson (a shoemaker born in Greenock, Scotland to parents of Irish and Scottish descent) and Margaret Benner (who was born in Ireland, before the whole family migrated to England). Archibald's original profession was that of Glassmaker. On the 25th December 1895 he married Isabella Graham. If you have a look at the death certificate, Archibald died whilst trying to save the life of Alexander Graham (this is the only document I have which states this). Alexander Graham was Isabella's son who was born on 6th February 1887. There is no name of father on the birth certificate. So Archibald saved the life of his stepson (who is recorded as nephew on the 1901 census). From what I can gather from family information, Alexander didn't realise Isabella was his mother till 1893. Alexander went on to marry and died in 1927.

Archibald and Isabella had a further seven children, between 1896 and 1906, including my grandfather Stafford. Unfortunately although the three youngest children, Stafford, Isabella and Sarah lived into the 1990's by the time I started to ask about the family they could neither remember very much nor want to. As I mention earlier, I'd been told about the incident in Jarrow and the medal when I was eleven, (1986) but it took me until this year (2006) to find solid facts. Isabella, Archibald's widow lived till 16th January 1931, and, from what I can gather, was a very formidable lady. Both Archibald and Isabella are buried at Harton Cemetery in South Shields.

I'm afraid there isn't much more I can tell you. I'm the youngest of Stafford's grandchildren and all his children bar one are now dead, and I'm afraid no one has much more information. I have no idea where the medal is now, but as Archibald's eldest son died in WWI, I'm guessing that his second son, Robert Graham Wilson, inherited it. Here's an interesting fact, Robert Graham Wilson's son, Robert Wilson was an astrophysicist, who designed the precursor to the Hubble telescope and was knighted for his works.

Jarrow shipyards and the Jarrow March

The town is located approximately eight miles from the mouth of the south bank of the river Tyne. Until the development of the coalfields and industry, in particular shipbuilding Jarrow was a small town. Its most famous son is the Venerable Bede who translated the Gospel of St John into Old English and introduced the Gregorian Calendar.

In 1852 Charles Palmer established the Palmers Shipbuilding and Iron Company Ltd, thus began the era of Jarrow as a shipbuilding centre. This was in part thanks to the armour-plating technique developed by the company. In all about 1000 ships were built at the yard. Ellen Wilkinson however states, "the history of a town is not that of its famous men only, but the story of the tenacity if its unknown fighters in the struggle for existence".

By 1907 Jarrow offered secure employment with a range of cultural and educational opportunites. But then came the slump in ship-building. However, times changed and by 1914 with the inevitability of war there was again a demand for ships for both the Royal and Merchant Navies. Repairs too were soon to be required for those ships damaged by German torpedoes. Men enlisted and women were employed in jobs they had never thought to perform. Orders kept coming in until 1929 when the tide turned and by 1932 the town was "*stagnant. There was no work ... and the unemployment rate was over 80%*".

With unemployment came poverty and a growing dissatisfaction with Government and so the idea was sown — to march to London arriving for the opening of Parliament to rouse public knowledge of the desperate plight of the men, women and children of the North-East.

200 healthy men took part in the Jarrow March, or Crusade, which began on Sunday 4th October 1936. They marched from Jarrow to London and on the way they were provided with food and shelter and decent boots. All that was provided by the Council was leather and nails and a waterproof groundsheet. A bus carried cooking equipment, kit and blankets. Throughout the March the men were aided by people from the towns through which they passed. They received medical and dental treatment, food, clothing and accommodation. It took a month to complete and by then the whole nation knew of their endeavours to bring the plight of the unemployed to the notice of the Government. Though they were small in number they came to represent the suffering and injustices that were the lot of the working-class.

Sources: Sharron Wilson — great-granddaughter of Archibald Wilson
South Shields Gazette
Jarrow Bereavement Services

Carnegie Dunfermline & Hero Fund Trusts
The Town That Was Murdered by Ellen Wilkinson

William Neil (Mac) McKECHNIE, GC

Air-crash rescue, 20th June 1929, Cranwell, Lincolnshire

McKechnie in December 1929 at RAF Cranwell.
©RAF Cranwell

WN McKechnie with his wings.
Courtesy D McKechnie

Neil and Mary's wedding day 17th August 1935 at St Michael's, Inveresk.

Status: 26144 Flight Cadet, 106 Squadron, Royal Air Force

Life dates: 22th August 1907, Kasauli, India – 30th August 1944, Pokarber, Germany. Neil was flying Lancaster III serial JB593 at the time. Built by the parent company, this Lancaster had operated almost continuously since being accepted by 106 Squadron on 6th November 1943, a brief spell of five days spent undergoing service in early June being its only respite. When lost, it had flown 638.05 hours. Six others died in the same crash. **Obit:** *The Times* 18th August 1945

Madam,

I am directed to refer to the letter from this Department dated 29th October last, concerning your husband Group Captain William Neil McKechnie, G C., Royal Air Force, and to express sincere regret for the oversight which occurred in omitting further details of the loss of the aircraft in which your husband was flying.

The captured German records also stated that the aircraft was shot down by night-fighter at 1.20 hours on the 30th August, 1944, near Pokarber, 4 kilometres east of Bradenburg, and exploded on impact with the ground.

I am, Madam,
Your obedient Servant,

WH Andrews

for Director of Personal Services.

Mrs. W.N.McKechnie,
9 West Holmes Gardens,
Musselburg,
Midlothian.

Letter from the Air Ministry to Mrs McKechnie confirming her husband's death in an air crash over land.
Courtesy D McKechnie

He flew to danger with the new boys

'Bitter blow'

"His huge enthusiasm for 'ops' and readiness to fly on every possible occasion was an inspiration to every member of the squadron. He was particularly admired for the way in which he always insisted on operating with new or inexperienced crews.

"His loss will be a bitter blow and his spirit will long be remembered with the utmost respect.

"Metheringham will be a monument to his thoroughness and foresight."

As a group captain there was no call for Neil McKechnie to fly operationally. But he could never have been happy not sharing all the dangers of the men he commanded.

McKechnie was the pilot of 106 Squadron's Lancaster III serial JB593 (codes ZN-T) on a raid on Konigsberg. He took off at 2030 from Metheringham.
Extracts from the newspaper as an obituary.

Biography: Neil was the elder son of Lt.Col. William Ernest and his wife Marion Alice McKechnie. William Snr was with the Indian Medical Service. Neil (as he was known) entered the Perse School in Cambridge as a boarder in School House in 13th January 1921 in Form IIId but left at the end of the summer term in 1923. His brother JK McKechnie arrived and left at the same time. As the school was the target of an incendiary device during the war most of the records were destroyed including anything further on the McKechnie brothers though a small note has been found reading, *Parents left Cambridge* and the boys left the school.

Neil married Mary Roma Doig, of Musselburgh, Midlothian (since 1974 East Lothian) the daughter of Robert Doig a professional golfer who taught in Marienbad, Austria and also in Italy from where Roma gained her name. The couple had two children Fiona and David, who was born only a few months before his father died.

Neil's training began at Halton and he passed on to Cranwell where he not only shone in his chosen career but also on the rugby and hockey pitches. Neil's Assessment of Ability is always Superior, including such subjects as Naval Organisation, General History, Carpentry and Rigging, but, in Airmanship, Drill and Physical Training he is Exceptional with marks over 91% (would that today be the equivalent of A******?)

He is described as *"An attractive character with a high idea of duty ... His fine character permeates his flying"*. We can understand the loss felt by Metheringham from the quote in the newspaper above.

At the outbreak of WWII Neil served in the Middle East until 1942 when he returned to England, and commanded heavy bomber stations. In his position as a Group Captain he no longer needed to fly but he not only enjoyed it but knew that his presence boosted morale as he shared the dangers with his men. He was strict with himself yet always kind to others. He was described as "just such a good chap" and it is believed that he died doing what he loved best — flying.

Author's note: It has been queried that a Group Captain would be a bomber station commander but all the documents I have seen support this. He was a man of talent, experience and resource with a deep sense of loyalty and responsibility.

Christine Doig White, Roma's cousin who knew the family well described Neil as a "big tall man, quiet and very handsome in his uniform."

Rugby XV, RAF College, Cranwell, December 1929. McKechnie is seated second from the left.
©RAF Cranwell

Neil McKechnie's record at RAF Cranwell as number 465.

12.01.28 joined the college as an ex-aircraft apprentice from the Air Apprentice School, Halton with further comment; *rugger XV, cricket XI, batting and good fielder. Should do well.*

06.09.29 promoted to Cadet Sergeant

13.12.29 passed out as Sgt with Order of Merit — 10 (highest mark) & EGM

14.12.29 commissioned in the RAF

13.01.30 posted to RAF Calshot — Air Force List Feb '30*

14.06.31 Flying Officer

14.06.35 Flight Lieutenant

1936 — 1937 served in India, North West Frontier

01.08.38 Squadron Leader

30.09.40 AM Casualty List No 47

01.12.40 T/Wing Commander as No 26144

10.04.41 no longer seconded for Special Duties

25.02.43 Wing Commander (WS)

01.07.43 T/Group Captain

30.08.44 death (Air Operations Europe)

Neil's cufflinks which were recovered after the War from the German Authorities by the British Army of Occupation and returned to Mary.
©*D McKechnie*

* **Walter Anderson GC** is in the same list as a Flg Off.

From the *Journal of the Royal Air Force College* by G.W.B. Spring 1930.

We all offer our sincere congratulations to F/Cadet Sergt McKechnie on the award of this signal honour, both to himself and the College, and all those who know him will grant that the deed was worthy of the man.

It is an honour to the Service, for I think I am right in saying that not only is this the first Military Award made to a Cadet of the Royal Air Force, but also to any Cadet of the other services.

It is interesting to compare this with "Mac's" own modest account given at a Court of Inquiry:—

"On June the 20th at about 1000 hours I was flying a D.H.9A and had landed on the Bristol Aerodrome when I saw the D.H.9A piloted by Flight Cadet Giles on my right—he having come in to land after me. He at once took off again, but almost immediately crashed. After a few seconds the machine burst into flames. I went across to the crash. Flight Cadet Giles was clear of the machine when I got there. His clothing was on fire and I helped to put out the flames. After about ten minutes the ambulance arrived and took charge of him."

There is, then, not the slightest doubt that, but for the timely assistance of McKechnie, Giles would have lost his life.

It seems to the writer that the action was typical of the man, for, during his two years at Cranwell, he has made his mark. He has been awarded his Colours for rugger, boxing, swimming, cricket, and hockey. Surely this is a great record in itself.

Unassuming, keen, an exemplary student, a good pilot, and a great sportsman. It is a combination of epithets and qualities which augurs well for the future. We shall follow his career as an officer with interest, and in anticipation of fresh laurels.

Extract from the *Journal* with Mac's account of the Action.

A de Haviland DH9A training plane in which Mac would have done his training.
Both ©*RAF Cranwell*

Neil McKechnie spent his whole working life in the service of the RAF. From his medal group and service record we know that he served in India in the North West Frontier and also in Africa. At the time of his death he was the Station Commander of Metheringham and of 106 Squadron of Lancaster Bombers.

After the news that Neil's plane had crashed the Base Commander paid a moving Tribute to Group Captain WN McKechnie.

He did not confine his activities to administration and welfare. A magnificent leader, and a courageous pilot, he believed that it was his duty to set an equally high example in operations.

He often flew with a young crew, giving them confidence and boosting morale. His wife too took a deep interest in the Squadron and the Station of which they were both so proud.

Citation: *18th October 1929*

St. James's Palace, S.W. 1

The KING has been graciously pleased to approve of the Award of the Medal of the Military Division of the Most Excellent Order of the British Empire to the undermentioned: —

For Gallantry.

Flight Cadet William Neil McKechnie, Royal Air Force.

On the 20th June, 1929, an aeroplane piloted by Flight Cadet C. J. Giles crashed on landing at Cranwell Aerodrome and burst into flames. The pilot was stunned but managed to release his safety belt and fall out of the machine in a dazed condition. Flight Cadet McKechnie, who had landed in another aeroplane about the same time some two hundred yards away, left his machine and ran at full speed towards the scene of the accident.

The petrol had spread over an area of about ten yards diameter in full blaze, with Giles lying in it, semi-conscious. McKechnie, without hesitation, ran into the flames and pulled out Giles, who was badly burned about the legs and face, with his Sidcot suit and clothes actually burning. After dragging him clear of the flames, during the process of which he was scorched and superficially burned, McKechnie proceeded to extinguish the flames of Giles' burning clothing.

By this time, the machine was in full blaze, with the petrol spreading along the ground so that without McKechnie's assistance, there is no doubt Giles would have been burned to death, as he was quite incapable of moving himself. Ultimately the machine was entirely destroyed by fire and the ground for some distance around was completely burned up by the spread of the ignited petrol.

Other awards: EGM (Military) – GC exchange, Indian General Service Medal with 'NorthWest Frontier' Clasp 1936–1937, 1939–45 Star, Africa Star, Defence Medal and 1939–45 War Medal.

©Perse School in Cambridge

©D McKechnie

Memorials: Runnymede Memorial, Surrey; Panel 200. Neil McKechnie is commemorated on the Roll of Honour at the Perse School in Cambridge. In August 2006 the 55,000 who served in Bomber Command and who gave their lives were honoured in a service of dedication in Lincoln Cathedral. There has long been comment that no medal was awarded for them and the Memorial only goes some way to redress this injustice.

The Ledger Stone in Lincoln.
Courtesy Frank Haslam

Background: *Sidcot suit*

This flying all-in-one suit could be electrically wired for warmth. There were a number of versions and that below is the 1941 issue. It was developed by Frederick Sidney Cotton who was an Australian inventor, aviation and photography pioneer, responsible for developing and promoting an early colour film process, and largely responsible for the development of photographic reconnaissance before and during World War II.

A Sidcot suit.
©Aviation clothing

However, it was Cotton's experience of high level and low-temperature flying that led him to develop the Sidcot suit, a flying suit later used by the RAF. He had found that when he flew in his oily overalls he did not feel the cold and asked his tailor to make up a suit which consisted of layers which would trap a layer of warm air next to his body. It had a lining of thin fur and air-proof silk together with fur cuffs and neck. Lewin GC earlier in this book appears to be wearing one. They were much sought-after by pilots.

Sources: *www.adastron.com/lockheed/electra/sidcotton.htm*
Jennie Wallis of Old Perseans
Christine Doig White — cousin
David McKechnie — son
RJM Pugh
Mary Guy of RAF College Cranwell
Journal of the Royal Sir Force College
RAF Bomber Command Losses of the Second World War by WR Chorley
Frank Haslam
Aviation Clothing

Thomas Patrick (Tommy) McTEAGUE, GC, DCM

Sea rescue, 10th December 1928, off Leysdown, Sheerness, Kent

Tommy standing with his brother Edward.
©*T McTeague*

Status: 346415 Corporal, Royal Air Force (Armament and Gunnery School)

Life dates: 2nd October 1893, Belfast – 28th February 1961, Belfast whilst staying with his sister. The funeral service was held at Holy Cross Church, Ardoyne, Belfast and he is buried in Milltown, Grave Ref VA 320 B. Tommy's sister and other members of the family are buried in this grave and although he was the first (on 2nd March 1961) there is no headstone for him The grave was purchased by the RAF.

The stone of Tommy's sister Sara.
©*M Hebblethwaite*

> McTEAGUE—February 28, 1961, Thomas Patrick (George Cross), beloved brother of Sarah Notaro.— R.I.P. On his soul, sweet Jesus, have mercy. Funeral on to-day (Thursday) after 9 a.m Mass in the Sacred Heart Church, Oldpark Road, to Milltown Cemetery. Deeply regretted by his sorrowing Sister, Brother-in-law and Family. St. Anthony, intercede for him. Sarah and John Notaro, 13 Etna Drive.

Funeral notice in the *Irish News and Belfast Morning News.*

Biography: Tommy was the son of Thomas Patrick and Elizabeth (Quinn) McTeague who married on 8th September 1883. There were eight children. All the children attended St Anthony's Public Elementary School, Millfield, Belfast. Three of the younger boys, Edward, Thomas and John joined the British Army at the outbreak of WWI. John was killed on 16th August 1917 in Flanders — he was 19. Tommy served with the 2nd Royal Irish Rifles entering as Private No 8722 on 19th September 1914.

After demob Tommy joined the RAF and served under Lord Tedder and Bomber Harris in the Far East and Middle East. He was an air-gunner in twin engine bi-planes. He told the story of leaning out and dropping small 5lb bombs by hand on the insurgents there. When he returned to Belfast he was stationed at RAF Aldergrove.

Tommy married Minnie Donnelly and they had two sons, Tom and Ernest and two daughters, Kathleen and Jean. His duty in Belfast at the beginning of WWII was as a Recruiting Sergeant successfully recruiting many young people from both Northern Ireland and the Republic, the latter being neutral in the conflict.

Author's note: Walter Anderson GC with whom Tommy was awarded the GC was from the Republic.

Tommy was posted to Abingdon as a Warrant Officer and it was while he was here that his nephew Thomas met up with him. He too had joined the RAF and was trained at Cosford and then posted to Burma with Bomber Command.

Citation: *12th April 1929*

The KING has been graciously pleased to approve of the award of the Medal of the Military Division of the Most Excellent Order of the British Empire to the undermentioned :—

For Gallantry.

115 Flying Officer Walter Anderson, Royal Air Force.

346415 Corporal Thomas Patrick McTeague, D.C.M., Royal Air Force.

Pilot Officer H. A. Constantine while flying an aeroplane off Leysdown on December 10th, 1928, crashed into the sea, about 200 yards from the shore. Corporal McTeague and Flying Officer Anderson immediately entered the sea from the shore and swam to his assistance. The weather was bitterly cold; an on-shore wind was blowing and the sea was fairly rough. Constantine, fully clothed and suffering from injuries and shock, commenced to swim ashore, but was in a state of collapse when the first swimmer (McTeague) reached him. McTeague, though exhausted himself, supported him until the arrival of Anderson, and Constantine was then brought to safety (this involving swimming for a distance of about 100 yards) by their combined efforts.

The extremely prompt and timely action of Anderson and McTeague, and the gallantry and persistence they displayed, undoubtedly saved the life of Constantine.

Tommy as Flight Sergeant in the centre with his young recruits.
Courtesy TP McTeague

Distinquished Conduct Medal (DCM) Citation *26th January, 1918*
8722 L./Cpl. T. P. McTeague, R. Ir. Rif. (Belfast).

For conspicuous gallantry and devotion to duty. During an attack he displayed the greatest dash and initiative, and by his determination in rushing forward when any signs of resistance were offered he put to flight and captured at least two parties of the enemy. After reaching the objective he carried an important message back to battalion headquarters, and whilst crossing the enemy barrage he was wounded. He delivered his message safely, however, returned at once to his company, and remained on duty doing excellent and gallant work for the remainder of the operation. He refused to have his wound dressed until afterwards.

Other awards: EGM (Military) – GC exchange, Distinguished Conduct Medal, 1914 Star, British War Medal, Victory Medal and 1953 Coronation Medal.

The story

The story is told in the entry for **Anderson GC** in Volume 1, Book A.

Anderson & McTeague rescued Pilot Officer HA Constantine, later Air Chief Marshal Sir Hugh Constantine KBE CB DSO.

Memorials: The story was reported in *Aeroplane* of 17 April 1929.

Sources: David Fell

Thomas McTeague — nephew

Ernest (Mac) McTeague — son

The Dam Busters by Paul Brickhill

Irish News and Belfast Morning News

Albert John MEADOWS, GC

Industrial rescue, 18th September 1931, Camden Town, London

© The RLC Museum and courtesy of David Owen

© The RLC Museum and courtesy of David Owen

Status: Assistant Store Keeper, The distillery of W.A. Gilbey Ltd., Camden Town, London

Life dates: 6th June 1904, St Pancras, London – 19th March 1988, Selsey, West Sussex. Albert was cremated at Chichester Crematorium and his ashes were scattered in the Garden of Remembrance. **Obit:** *The Times*, 25th March 1988

Biography: Albert was the son of John Edwin and Elizabeth Jane (Gosling) Meadows. His father was working as a wine merchant's porter at the time of his birth. He attended the local school and went to work for WA Gilbey.

Albert Meadows served with the Royal Army Ordnance Corps during the Second World War, and was demobbed with the rank of Sergeant. After the war he returned to WA Gilbey where in all he worked for 47 years. He lived his retirement in Sussex where he was a member of the Bognor Regis Art Society. He was a cheerful and optimistic sort of man. His wife whose name was Laura Phyllis predeceased him. There were no children.

Citation: *29th December 1931*

Whitehall, December 10, 1931

His Majesty The KING has been graciously pleased to award the Edward Medal to Harold Henry Hostler and Albert John Meadows in recognition of their gallantry in the following circumstances: —

On the 18th September, 1931, John Gale, an employee at the distillery of Messrs. W. A. Gilbey, Limited, Camden Town, who was cleaning out with a hosepipe the residue in an empty cherry brandy vat, was discovered unconscious in the vat by his mate, Frederick Wormald, having apparently been gassed by the carbon dioxide generated by the fermentation of the residue. Wormald went down the ladder and tried unsuccessfully to get Gale out. He then called Leonard Wright, one of the firm's analysts, and went down a second time, but was slightly gassed and had to be assisted out by Wright. Wright then went down himself but was overcome by the gas and became unconscious in the bottom of the vat. In the meantime, the Manager had sent for assistance, and Harold Hostler, a vatter, arrived on the scene and immediately entered the vat. He succeeded in dragging Wright to a sitting position near the foot of the ladder, but feeling himself being overcome by the fumes he was forced to come out of the vat. He made a second attempt with a wet cloth round his mouth and at a third attempt with a rope round his body he succeeded in getting Gale to the foot of the ladder and part of the way up, when he was overcome by the gas and Gale slipped from his grasp. Hostler himself was drawn up by the rope.

Albert Meadows (assistant store keeper) then volunteered to go into the vat, and at the second attempt, with a wet cloth round his mouth and a rope round his body, he succeeded in rescuing Wright. Although partially affected, he made a third but unsuccessful attempt to rescue Gale. He then asked for a length of rubber gas piping and placing it in his mouth to breathe through and taking a looped rope with him, he went down a fourth time. He managed to place the rope round Gale and he and Gale were both drawn up from the vat. Wright and Gale recovered consciousness after an hour.

Both Hostler and Meadows displayed great courage and resource in their attempts to rescue the two men. Both were aware of the risks they were incurring, as two of the rescuers had already been overcome by the gas, and both took precautions calculated to render their attempts at rescue successful. They showed great persistence in facing deliberately what was a considerable risk. Hostler entered the vat three times and Meadows four times, and the periods occupied by their attempts at rescue were ten to fifteen minutes, and fifteen to twenty minutes, respectively.

Other awards: EM (Bronze Industry) – GC exchange. Meadows' EM is now in the RLC Museum collection at Deepcut. 1977 Queen's Silver Jubilee Medal. The investiture for the GC took place on 27th February 1973.

The vatter, Hostler was also awarded the Edward Medal for his heroism but did not live to exchange in 1971.

Background: *Edward Medal*
On 3rd December 1909 the scope of the Edward Medal was extended from the original warrant of 13th July 1907. It was henceforth to include heroic acts performed by those working in industry as well as mines and quarries. There were also two classes silver and bronze. The Mine medal was paid for by a fund set up by a group of philanthropists of which the leader was a mine owner called A. Hewlett.

WA Gilbey and gin
Though probably best known for their gin the Company traded predominantly as wine and spirit merchants. The first shop was opened in Edinburgh in 1857. In 1962 Gilbeys joined three other merchants to form International Distillers and Vintners Ltd (IDV).

Gin Lane **by William Hogarth.**

Gin appears to have originated in Holland where a spirit distilled from grain, flavoured with juniper berries was made in the 17thC. It was given the name genever, from the French for juniper. By 1714 the spirit, which had quickly travelled across the North Sea, was called Gin in England. The famous Hogarth engraving *Gin Lane* (1751) of the drunk mother with her baby falling backwards, possibly also drunk, over the stairrail, portrays the disastrous effects of cheap spirits on the population. The Gin Act of 1736 was passed to curb sales but a riot broke out and the Act failed. Thereafter the price of wine with its lower alcohol content was dropped and thus made more accessible to the poor who were thuis encouraged away from the more potent spirit with its debilitating effects.

The most popular variety of gin today is the high-proof London Dry Gin. However, it is the United States that is the largest consumer thereof though there are new brands coming on to the market from time to time as with Broker's Gin.

Sources: David Owen at RLC
Caroline Ragless of the Bognor Regis Arts Society
The Complete Imbiber, Gilbey Centenary Exhibition 1957
Ruth Mariner
Brian Cane
A Dawson of Brokers

Brokers Gin, the newest variety of London Dry Gin.
©A Dawson

Dr Arthur Douglas MERRIMAN, GC, OBE

Bomb disposal, 11th September 1940, Regent Street, London

The badly eroded headstone of Arthur and his wife Ivy.
©M Hebblethwaite

Status: Part-time Experimental Officer, Directorate of Scientific Research, Ministry of Supply (Bomb Disposal)

Life dates: 25th November 1892, South Manchester – 4th November 1972, Streatham, London. Arthur is buried in Streatham Park Cemetery, London, Grave 60174, Square 33. **Obit:** *The Times*, 8th November 1972, *Metallurgist and Materials Technologists*, January 1973

Biography: In the 1901 Census Arthur was living with his parents Harry and Elizabeth and his sister Jessie at his grandfather's home in Manchester. His grandfather, William, a widower, was a baker's clerk and his father at that time a warehouseman in the cotton industry. Arthur attended the Central High School, Manchester and the Universities of Cambridge, Durham and Lille in France.

Arthur Merriman served in the RAOC during WWI only entering France on 3rd April 1918. (*LG*, 1918: Army Ordnance Dept. T/Lt AD Merriman to be Actg. Captain).

After WWI Arthur worked as a teacher and academic including the post of Principal of the County Technical School, Wallsend-on-Tyne from 1926–38. He went from there as the Administrative Secretary to the Faculty of Artchitects and Surveyors but was called to serve as Assistant Director Bomb Disposal (Technical) with C-in-C, Middle East with the Directorate of Scientific Research, Ministry of Supply early in 1939. He became the Joint Secretary of the Unexploded Bomb Committee and as such *"was forever out and about wherever new bombs or fuzes were to be found or there was new equipment to be tested"*, (Hogben).

The London Gazette of 3rd January 1941 lists Arthur Douglas Merriman GC DFC** MA (118185) to be 2/Lt (without pay & allowances) from 17th December 1940 and is granted the unpaid Acting rank of Lieut-Col. He was the senior member of a group of scientists and engineers dealing with bomb disposal problems. He is sometimes credited as having developed "Freddie" (see Moxey GC for details) but this is incorrect. From 1941–44 he was Scientific Advisor to the Commander-in-Chief, Middle East, and in 1944 was appointed to a special Intelligence assignment in Russia and Germany in his capacity as Superintendent of the Armament Design Department at Fort Halstead in Kent.

Merriman left the service in 1945 with the rank of Colonel, Royal Engineers, and then became the Principal Scientific Officer (Technical Intelligence) at the Armaments Design Department, Ministry of Supply. He was a prolific writer and published 16 books on such diverse subjects as *The Night Sky* (for Scouts) and *A concise encyclopaedia of metallurgy* and many academic papers. He augmented his Engineering qualifications by becoming a Fellow of the Corporation of Certified Secretaries. In 1948 Merriman was appointed to the first full-time post of Registrar-Secretary of the Institution of Metallurgists, which he held until 1957. Of this appointment it was said that "he comes to us at the height of a distinguished scientific and military career". The April 1948 edition of *The Iron and Coal Trades Review* comments that an arrangement whereby one person acted as the joint Secretary of both the Iron and Steel Institute and the Institution of Metallurgists came to an end Dr Merriman's appointment to his new position.

In 1967 he became Master of the Worshipful Company of Tinplate Workers.

** The DFC (the Distinguished Flying Cross) is incorrect and should be DSc, ie a Doctor of Science. This error is repeated in his OBE Citation.

Citation: *3rd December 1940*

The King has been graciously pleased to approve the award of the GEORGE CROSS to:-

Arthur Douglas Merriman, Part-time Experimental Officer, Directorate of Scientific Research, Ministry of Supply.

For conspicuous bravery in connection with bomb disposal.

Citation for the OBE — he was one of over 40 such recipients on this day.

4th January 1944

St. James's Palace, S.W.1

6th January, 1944.

The KING has been graciously pleased to give orders for the following promotions in, and appointments to, the Most Excellent Order of the British Empire, in recognition of gallant and distinguished services in the Middle East: —

To be Additional Officers of the Military Division of the said Most Excellent Order: —

Major (temporary Lieutenant-Colonel) Arthur Douglas Merriman, G.C., D.F.C. (118185), Corps of Royal Engineers (London, S.W.16).

Other awards: OBE, Victory Medal, British War Medal, 1953 Coronation Medal.

Academic and professional qualifications and Fellowships: MA (Cantab), MEd (Dunelm), DSc (Lille), FCS, AIMechE, FRMS, FRAS, DL, London, 1955. Honorary Doctorate from the University of Surrey.

The story

On 11th September 1940 Arthur Merriman with Capt Kennedy and the Chairman of the Unexploded Bomb Committee, Dr HJ Gough used a newly designed device called a steam steriliser. In Regent Street the perfect opportunity presented itself for testing as a bomb lay ticking away. Starting at 2pm it was not until nearly four hours later that the equipment appeared to be working properly. With the three men taking cover behind sandbags the bomb exploded and the lesson learned was that no amount of practice was the equivalent of work on a 'real-life' situation with a live bomb.

Background: *Abbreviations for academic and professional qualifications and fellowships*

MA (Cantab) — Master of Arts, Cambridge, though the subject taken may in fact be a science

MEd (Dunelm) — Master of Education, Durham

DSc (Lille) — Doctor of Science, Lille University, France

FCS — Fellow of the Chemical Society

AIMechE — Associate of the Institute of Mechanical Engineers

FRMS — Fellow of the Royal Microscopical Society

FRAS — Fellow of the Royal Astronomical Society

DL — Deputy Lieutenant — Deputy Lieutenants are appointed by the Lord-Lieutenant, subject only to Her Majesty not disapproving of the granting of the commission.

The qualifications for Deputy Lieutenants as set out in the Lieutenancies Act mean that a person may be appointed a Deputy Lieutenant if:

(a) He or she is shown to have rendered appropriate service: such service includes service as a member of, or in a civil capacity in connection with, the Armed Forces, and other suitable public service; and

(b) He or she has a place of residence in, or within seven miles from the boundary of the County.

Sources: *The Times*

The Institute of Materials, Minerals & Mining (IOM³), which was created from the merger of The Institute of Materials (IOM) and The Institution of Mining and Metallurgy (IMM), and the Bulletins thereof.

Designed to Kill by Major Arthur Hogben

Michael Henderson-Begg, C.C., Clerk to the Tin Plate Workers Company

For those interested in the Institutes mentioned:

The Road to Progress with Safety by Ernest Loynes

A History of the Institution of Mining Engineers, 1889–1989 by Geo R Strong

The Professionals. The Institution of Mining and Metallurgy by AJ Wilson

Alfred MILES, GC

Shipboard rescue, 1st December 1940, Methil Old Dock, Fife

Alfred Miles with his daughter Daphne.
Courtesy Daphne and Mary Stubbersfield

©*M Hebblethwaite*

Status: P/23965 Able Seaman, HMS *Saltash*, Royal Navy
Life dates: 12th June 1899, Marylebone, London – 27th May 1989, Gillingham, Kent. Alfred is buried in Woodlands Cemetery Section CJ, Grave 85 **Obit:** *Daily Telegraph, The Times*, 8th June 1989

2	Jane Miles	Head	Wid		69	Retired Charwoman		♀		do	St Georges
	Florie do	Daur	S		15	Tailor's Errand Girl	Worker			do	do
	James do	Son		12		School				do	Marylebone
	Annie do	Daur			5	do				do	do
	Alfred do	Son		2		do				do	do

Biography: Alfred was the son of Annie Louisa Miles who was in service so he lived with his grandmother not far away. The 1901 Census provides interesting information and reveals a lot about society at the time. If we were to believe it Alfred's mother would have been 67 when he was born. We know that in fact Jane Miles was his grandmother we also know from his birth certificate that he was born in June 1899 and therefore not quite 2 on 31st March 1901 when the Census was taken nor could he have been 'at school'. He lived in Paddington and he used to talk to his own children of playing in the streets around Duke Street. Joining the Navy from school he had served for 22 years by June 1939 then within two months, August 1939, was recalled for WWII.

In May 1920 Albert married Margart Mary (Merrigan) who was to predecease him. After their marriage the couple moved to Kent, first to Old Brompton and then to Gillingham. They had two sons and two daughters Alfred, Ann, Vincent and Daphne.

Alfred standing with his daughter Ann (Nancy) aged about 22, his wife Margaret and Daphne in about 1946.

Daphne with Alfred in Santa's Grotto in about 1951.

Alfred as a fine proud but humble man with his stunning array of medals. He is aged 80.
All photos courtesy Daphne and Mary Stubbersfield

Alfred, like Mahoney earlier in this book, took part in the relief of Dunkirk. While in the Navy in order to earn some extra money he became the unofficial ship's tailor and on his Singer sewing machine made and repaired uniforms for his fellow crew members. His machine is still a treasured possession in his family. After the accident in which he lost all the fingers of his right hand he was fitted with a prosthesis and a special glove. His daughter Daphne remembers that the fingers were always breaking though he is also remembered for having made good use of his plastic fist when hammering down carpet tacks with it at his daughter's house!

HMS Saltash in 1940.
Courtesy Mike Thomsett

Once he had recovered from the accident the Navy found him a job in the Admiral's garden until he was discharged. Alfred's last job was at Chatham Dockyard from where he finally retired in 1966.

Always a Londoner at heart he liked to go up to town to the theatre until late in life. After his wife died he was never short of company as his wife's family came to stay. With courage and will-power he overcame two separate cancers and it was only after a fall that he decided to move into the Naval Association Home.

Citation: *25th April 1941*
29th April 1941
His Majesty has also been graciously pleased to approve the following Awards:
For gallantry in saving life at sea:
The Albert Medal.
Able Seaman Alfred Miles, P/23965.

On 1st December, 1940, when H.M.S. *Saltash* was passing from one dock basin to another, a wire was run out from the starboard bow to the weather corner of the gate so as to hold the bow up to the wind. The wire was taken to the windlass, but this was too slow, and men were picking up the slack by hand, leaving some loose turns on the deck. As the ship drew level the order was passed to turn up. The wire was taken from the windlass to the bollards. Able Seaman Miles saw Able Seaman Thompson standing in a bight of wire and called out to him to get clear, but he failed to do so and the wire drew taut round his ankles. Miles knew that Thompson might be hauled through the bull-ring and that if he himself were caught in the wire he would be in the same danger; yet he tried to force the bight open with his hands. His right hand was jammed between the wire and Thompson's foot. He said nothing and still tried to free his shipmate.

The hurt which caused the loss of his hand was not known till later. Thompson was dragged along the deck to the bull-ring but way (*sic*) was taken off the ship just in time to save him.

Presented by the King to Able Seaman Alfred Miles For Gallantry
in risking his life and losing his right hand to save a shipmate on HMS *Saltash* on 1st December 1940.
©National Maritime Museum

©National Maritime Museum

Other awards: AM (Bronze Sea) – GC exchange. The AM was presented on 29th July 1941. The reverse of his GC is inscribed *Able Seaman Alfred Miles, 1940* and will appear in the last book of the series.

1914–15 Star, British War Medal, Victory Medal, 1939–45 Star, Atlantic Star, Defence Medal, War Medal 1939–45, 1977 Queen's Silver Jubilee Medal and Royal Naval Long Service and Good Conduct Medal. Miles' GC and Albert Medals are in the National Maritime Museum at Greenwich.

The story

Illustration of how it may have been.
©*L White*

For most of us unfamiliar with nautical terms it is worth explaining some of them in order fully to understand the citation.

starboard bow — right-hand side of the boat when facing forward, the bow being the front of the boat

weather corner — the side or corner from which the wind is blowing

windlass — a large and more elaborate type of winch used for operating the anchor

bight of wire — the centre part of the wire rolled up

bull-ring — rings for lashing the cargo in containers

Methil docks was opened in 1887 and by the the mid-1920s was Scotland's chief coal port exporting in excess of 3 million tons of coal. The coal trucks can be seen in the foreground of this picture.
Author's collection

Background: *HMS Saltash*

There is an interesting aside to this ship as this was the name Nicholas Montsarrat gave to his ship in *The Cruel Sea*.

HMS *Saltash* (J62) was a Royal Navy Hunt class minesweeper which was launched 25th June 1918 and served through the latter part of the World War I as well as through all of World War II. She was involved in the evacuation of Dunkirk, during which, on 1st June 1940 she sank HMS *Havant* (H32) after *Havant* had been heavily damaged by German aircraft. *Saltash* would later return to northern France as part of the Normandy landings in 1944. She was decommissioned on 13th March 1947.

Sources: National Maritime Museum, Greenwich
Chatham Naval Base in Pictures by the Chatham Dockyard Historical Society
Daphne and Mary Stubbersfield — daughter and granddaughter
Sailing small cruisers by Guy Pennant
Nancy Wilson — daughter

Leonard James MILES, GC

Self-sacrifice in bomb disposal, 21st–22nd September 1940, Ilford, Essex

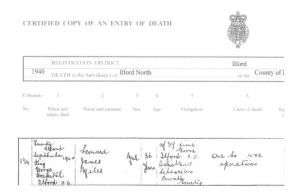

Extract from Leonard's death certificate confirming his second name as James.

Status: Warden, ARP

Life dates: 27th September 1904, West Ham, London – 22nd September 1940, Hainault, Ilford. Leonard died in St George's Hospital after his GC action.

Biography: Leonard James Miles was the son of John Ruston and Elizabeth (Jopnathan) Miles. His father was working as a journeyman gas meter maker at the time of his birth. The family were living in Upton Park. **Author's note:** There has long been confusion over Leonard's middle name, it can now be confirmed from both his birth and death certificates that it is James and that the Citation is incorrect.

Leonard's wife's name was Constance and they had a son Colin Roston. Leonard was a painter and decorator by trade and signed up for the ARP soon after war broke out.

Citation: *14th January 1941*

17th January 1941

The KING has been graciously pleased to approve the award of the GEORGE CROSS to:-

Leonard John (*sic*) Miles (deceased), A.R.P. Warden, Ilford.

Volunteer warden, Mr. L. J. Miles, was on duty when he was warned of imminent danger of an explosion nearby. He could have taken a few paces and gone to a public shelter only a few yards away, but instead his sense of duty forced him to run towards the scene to warn members of the public he knew to be in their houses. He had succeeded in warning certain of the residents when the explosion occurred, inflicting serious injuries which proved fatal.

Whilst lying awaiting the ambulance to remove him to hospital, he was conscious and obviously suffering; this did not reduce his sense of duty and when a fellow warden approached him to render whatever aid he could, Miles instructed him to attend first to the fire which had been caused by a fractured gas main.

Warden Miles showed magnificent courage and devotion to duty.

Other awards: Miles' medal is presently being held by the Worshipful Company of Skinners where a replica is on display at Skinner's Hall.

Courtesy of Tom Miles and the Worshipful Company of Skinners

Memorials: Leonard Miles is one of the names recorded in the Book of Remembrance containing the names of Ilford citizens who gave their lives during the Second World War. This book is on display in a case on the ground floor of Redbridge Central Library in Clements Road, Ilford. Warden Leonard Miles is commemorated on page 75 in the Civil Defence WW2 Book of Remembrance at the Millennium Chapel, National Memorial Arboretum, Alrewas, Staffs.

Leonard Miles also appears in the Roll of Honour of citizens killed in the United Kingdom during the War which was produced by the Imperial War Graves Commission. The Ilford section of which includes the entry:

Miles, Leonard James aged 36; GC; Air Raid Warden; of Lime Grove, Hainault. Son of Elizabeth Miles; husband of Constance Miles. Injured 21 September 1940 at Lime Grove; died 22 September 1940 at King George Hospital.

Background: *Worshipful Company of Skinners and Leonard Miles*

The Skinners' Company is one of the "Great Twelve" livery companies with a history going back some 700 years. It is one of the most ancient of the City Guilds and in times gone by governed the use, production and sale of furs used for trimming garments for people of exalted rank. It also controlled the conditions of apprenticeship in the craft. Skinners' Hall occupies the site at 8 Dowgate Hill in the City of London, which it has owned since the 13th Century.

Leonard was not a member of the Skinners' Company. His son Colin Roston Miles was apprenticed into the Company in 1966 and became a Freeman of the Company in 1973. He took his son Thomas on as an Apprentice in 1986 and Tom became a Freeman in 1993. His daughter Katie was also apprenticed in 1986 and took her Freedom with Tom in 1993.

We are now holding the George Cross medal for safekeeping on behalf of Tom and Katie, at their request, because they have their Freedom of The Worshipful Company of Skinners.

Courtesy Paul Richards who is the custodian of the Medal.

Sources: Tom Miles — grandson
Paul Richards of Worshipful Company of Skinners
Tudor Allen of Redbridge Central Library
More Gallant Deeds of the War by Stanley Rogers

Henry James (Dusty) MILLER, GC

Self-sacrifice, 29th April 1940, North Sea

Henry's mother Lilian Miller.

Henry and Vida's wedding 7th May 1927.

The carefree, happy sailor.
All Courtesy M French

Status: P/J 55387 Able Seaman, H.M. Submarine *Unity*, Royal Navy
Life dates: 28th November 1900, Poole, Dorset – 29th April 1940, North Sea
Biography: Henry was the younger son of Albert and Lilian Maud (Giles) Miller and he had two brothers Albert and Thomas and two sisters Ethel and Rose. Albert Snr was a blacksmith.

He married Vida Maude Woodward in Church Hanborough church in May 1927 and they had a daughter Mary. The couple met when Henry, who lived in Basingstoke, came to visit a cousin who owned the Hand and Shears pub next door to the Woodward family home in Church Hanborough.

Henry as Captain of the Water Polo team on HMS *Vanessa* in 1925.

P/J.55387 AB. HJ Miller
Service Record:
H J Miller enlisted in the Royal Navy c.1918
joined RN 28.11.1918
promoted AB 2.3.1920
passed Education Cert (Part I) 7.9.20
volunteered for Sub Service 5.3.34
joined HM Sub *L26* 9.10.35
ashore, ready for foreign service 15.10.37
joined HM Sub *Clyde* (Mediterranean)19.11.37
ashore for a course 14.8.39
joined HM Sub *Unity* 19.1.40

Mary remembered: "I was sitting in the classroom in school opposite our home (in picture below) when the postman come up and knocked on our door and handed in the telegram."
Jane Kelley wrote to me. "We have not found anywhere the telegram that my Grandmother received, and indeed my Mother does not recall ever being shown one. Now whether it was at some time destroyed or is still somewhere that we have not thought of looking I don't know, and the fact that Mum does not recall seeing one may be due to the fact that at the time it was probably not felt to be the right thing for a young child to see. What we did find however was a letter sent to my Grandmother from the Commodore on 30th April 1940", see below.

The proud young parents, Henry and Vida with Mary.
©M French

Henry's granddaughter Jane and daughter Mary French.

The home to which Henry came in Church Hanborough in 2006, it has barely changed at all.
©M Hebblethwaite

Citation: *16th August 1940*

The KING has been graciously pleased to approve of the following posthumous Awards for gallantry in one of H.M. Submarines: —

The Medal of the Military Division of the Most Excellent Order of the British Empire, for Gallantry.

The late Lieutenant John Niven Angus Low, Royal Navy, H.M. Submarines.

The late Able Seaman Henry James Miller.

Other awards: EGM (Military) – GC exchange named 'P/J-55387, H.M. Submarines'. War Medal 1914–18, Victory Medal, 1939–45 Star, Atlantic Star and War Medal 1939–45, Royal Navy Long Service and Good Conduct Medal — George V 2nd Type (coinage head), post 1932 (to 1936).

©All J Kelley and Mary French

Vida with Henry's GC.

The story

HM Submarine *Unity* had been laid down on the 19th February 1937, launched 16th February 1938 and commissioned the following August. Just nine days before her final voyage, Lt Francis Brooks had taken over command. HMS *Unity* had put to sea from Blyth at 1730 hrs on the 29th April 1940.

Sailing on the surface, by 1830 visibility was down to 100 yards due to a heavy mist closing in. At 1907 a prolonged blast of a ship's siren at 50 yards was heard on *Unity's* bridge. Neither vessel was aware of the other until the submarine spotted the Norwegian freighter *Atle Jarl* sailing from Methil in Fife for Tyne. There was just time to shut the bulkhead doors and order the engines astern before the freighter, sailing at a speed of 4 knots on a collision course, smashed into the submarine in the area of the port forward hydroplane.

HMSub *Unity*.

HMSub *Clyde*.

124

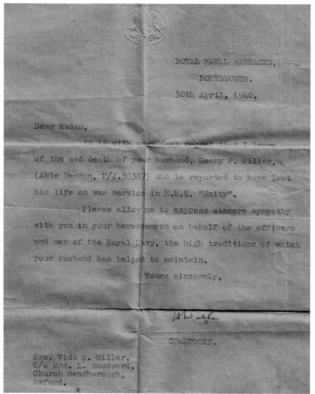

The order to abandon the submarine was given at 1910 Lieutenant Low and Able Seaman Miller were the two men on duty in the submarine control room. They were instrumental in helping every member of the submarine to escape except themselves. The crew made their way topside and were crowded on the bridge awaiting rescue.

Memorials: There are, fittingly, many memorials to Henry Miller remembering that he is one of the only 4 posthumous EGMs to be awarded the GC — with Low, **Jolly** and McCabe.

Portsmouth Naval Memorial, Southsea, Hampshire Panel 39, Column 1. Plaque in the Memorial Chapel, Church Hanborough Parish Church, and on the War Memorial in Long Hanborough, Oxfordshire. Note that here the GC appears to have been added on to the memorial later than the rest of the inscriptions. The memorial has been cleaned up in 2006.

Letter from the Commodore to Vida Miller.
Courtesy M French

The inscription at Portsmouth, compare this with Mahoney where there is no post-nominal.

The sinking of HM Submarine *Unity* by the Alte *Jarl*.

The inscription in the church in Church Hanborough.
©*M Hebblethwaite*

The War Memorial in Long Hanborough, Oxfordshire.

Sources: Jane Kelley — granddaughter
Mary French — daughter

John Bryan Peter MILLER, GC, known later as DUPPA-MILLER, is to be found in Volume 3 under D

Thomas Frank (Tom) MILLER, GC

Putting down disturbance, 24th September 1921, Nilambur, Malabar, India

Status: 5718907 Private, 2nd Battalion, The Dorsetshire Regiment
Life dates: 7th October 1890, Portland, Dorset – 13th December 1974, Birmingham. Tom was cremated at Robin Hood Crematorium and his ashes were scattered in Lawn D where his wife Elsie's ashes had been strewn before him.
Biography: Thomas was the son of Thomas and Louisa Miller. His father was a Portland Prison Warden and he was their sixth child. In the 1901 Census he is described as a General Labourer but his position is described as 'Pauper' which seems rather harsh as he was working and presumably contributing to his family's income. He was still living in the prison along with 164 others.

Tom and Elsie Miller in about 1972.

Tom attested in the Dorsetshire Regiment on 2nd December 1907 as No 8417 and served in the 2nd Bn in Mesopotamia and Palestine. He was wounded twice. The first time on 14th April 1915 at the Battle of Shaiba and the second on 25th March 1917 during the Battle of Tebel-Hamrin.

He re-enlisted for four years at Damascus in 1919 and went out to India with the 2nd Dorsets from Portland in September 1919. Based at Belgaum, the Bn became embroiled in the Moplah Rebellion of 1921–22. He later served with the Battalion in Sudan and Egypt and after leaving the Army with 18 years' service, Miller became a jobbing Gardener and later moved from Portland to Birmingham.

Citation: *1st June 1923*
2nd June, 1923, St. James's Palace, S. W. 1
The KING has been graciously pleased to approve of the award of the Medal of the Military Division of the Most Excellent Order of the British Empire to the undermentioned, for services rendered in connection with military operations in Malabar, 1921–1922: —
For Gallantry.
No. 5718784 Private Frederick Chant, 2nd Bn., The Dorsetshire Regiment.
No. 5718234 Sergeant William George Hand, M.M., 2nd Bn., The Dorsetshire Regiment.
No. 5718907 Private Thomas Miller, 2nd Bn., The Dorsetshire Regiment.
No. 5719290 Private Frederick Henry Troake, 2nd Bn., The Dorsetshire Regiment.
Assistant Surgeon, 3rd Class, George David Rodriques, Indian Medical Department.
Other awards: EGM (Military) – GC exchange 1914–15 Star, British War Medal, Victory Medal, India General Service Medal 1908–35 with clasp 'Malabar 1921–22' and 1953 Coronation Medal. The investiture for the GC took place on 29th July 1947.

The story
At Nilambur, Malabar, India on the 24th September 1921, Private Miller displayed great gallantry by going forward towards a rebel ambush and firing on it at close range. He was instrumental in dislodging several snipers who were causing casualties to the British troops. He and Sergeant Hand subsequently showed great courage in clearing up the situation. All three other men lived to become GCs.

Portland Prison in 1903. Could one of these men be Miller's father?

Background: *Portland Prison*
Portland Prison opened in 1848 and held convicted adults until 1921 when it was converted into a Borstal, a place of detention for boys between 15 and 21. As the word Borstal and all it stood for became controversial it changed and is now a Young Offender Institution holding young men aged between 18 to 21. Inmates in the past were employed in such useful public works as building breakwaters or improving dockyards and such features as Nothe Fort which stands on the promontory overlooking Weymouth Bay.

Sources: *The Dorsetshire Regiment* by Terry Bishop   *Dorsetshire Regimental Journal*
Keep Museum   Oliver Pepys at Spink

Ahmed Muhammad MIRGHANY, GC

Life-saving, 18th September 1932, River Nile, Khartoum, Sudan

Life dates: – 25th August 1951
Biography: Mirghany was Sudanese.
Citation: *30th December 1932*
2nd January 1933
The KING has been graciously pleased to approve of the Award of the Medal of the Civil Division of the Most Excellent Order of the British Empire to the undermentioned:—
For Gallantry.
Mirghany Ahmed Mohammed.
On September 18th, 1932, at the height of the Nile flood, and at a point where the stream is particularly dangerous even for the strongest swimmer, Mirghany Ahmed rescued three girls, the eldest fifteen years of age, from certain death by drowning.
Other awards: EGM (Civilian) – GC exchange 1953 Coronation Medal
Background: *Spelling variants*
The OED lists the following variants — on advice from a Sudanese friend I use the first of these.
Muhammad — Arab, Sudanese
Mohammed — Turkish and the usual spelling in English
Mahomed — Sudanese
Mahommed, Mohamed, Muhammed, Mahumed

John Henry MITCHELL, GC, BEM

Sea rescue, 27th September 1940, Iceland

From the *Police Review*
Courtesy Alan Moss

Status: LT/JX 173154 Acting Second Hand, Royal Naval Volunteer Reserve but see *The London Gazette* change below

Life dates: 1st January 1917, Grimsby – 12th April 1972, Wandsworth

Biography: John was the son of John Henry and Minnie Selina (Parrot) Mitchell. The family moved to Fleetwood when he was young. John's father had been a well-known trawler skipper and son John trained and worked with him as a radio operator and mate for six years after elementary education. He married Evelyn (Edith?) Sparks on 29th May 1941 and they had a son, Ian and a daughter.

When war broke out John joined the RNVR. He served on aircraft carriers and cruisers from 3rd December 1939 to 13th April 1946 retiring as a Lieutenant Gunnery Officer. However, according to *The London Gazette* of 29th April 1941 he was by then serving in the Royal Navy.

After demob John Mitchell joined the Metropolitan Police on 1st April 1946 (the overlap was probably an administrative simplification) as Probationer No 12844. On 9th April 1948 his appointment as a Constable was confirmed and moving up the ranks he finally became a Detective Inspector on 3rd December 1965. At that time he was also appointed to the Stolen Motor Vehicle Investigation Branch in which he served until his early death.

While with the Met Mitchell was commended three times, first in 1957 for "ability and initiative in a case of shopbreaking", second for "valuable assistance in a murder investigation in 1965 in Antigua". This was a brutal murder of a cattle dealer, and third in 1970 his BEM. His certificate of conduct is marked as Exemplary. In the *Police Review* of 1970 there is the additional information that John was a "first-class swimmer" born out by the rescue he effected in 1940.

Citation: *25th April 1941*

29th April 1941

His Majesty has also been graciously pleased to approve the following Awards:

For gallantry in saving life at sea:

The Albert Medal.

Acting Second Hand John Henry Mitchell, LT/JX.173154, R.N.R.

On 27th September, 1940, Chief Engineman Wedderburn fell into the sea between two trawlers in harbour. He could not swim, and was soon unconscious. An unknown seaman, who jumped in to save him was soon in difficulties. Mitchell, hearing his shouts, clambered over a vessel to the quay, ran 100 yards, climbed across two other ships and jumped into the water. He seized Wedderburn, who was sinking, by the hair, and held up the other man until a rope was passed down from the trawler. This he secured with a bowline round the now helpless seaman, using one hand, while he supported both men and himself by gripping the rope with his teeth. The seaman was then hauled out of the water by the men in the trawler. Mitchell, although fully clad, and wearing sea boots, supported Wedderburn by treading water until a pilot ladder could be lowered. He made the rope fast round Wedderburn, and steadied him as he was hauled out. He had been in very cold water for 35 minutes, and was unconscious when rescued.

John Mitchell's Albert Medal was deposited with the IWM at his request when he exchanged for the GC.

In the New Year's Honours of 1970, BEM Citation

Her Majesty The Queen has been graciously pleased to make the following appointments and awards:

Detective Inspector JH Mitchell, AM, C Department

(*London Gazette* 17th June 1941)

The following corrections are made:-

In *The London Gazette Supplement* Number 35147 of 29th April, 1941:-

For Acting Second Hand John Henry Mitchell, LT/JX. 173154, R.N.R.

Read Acting Second Hand John Henry Mitchell, LT/JX. 173154, Royal Navy.

Other awards: AM (Bronze Sea) – GC exchange, British Empire Medal (Civil 1.1.70), 1939–45 Star, Atlantic Star and War Medal 1939–45. The AM was presented on 21st October 1941. Police Long Service & Good Conduct Medal which was dated 21st June 1968.

Background: *Difference between BEM, EGM and OBE briefly — see Index for further information*
There is so much confusion about these three awards. See John McCabe who even had OBE on his headstone when in fact he was awarded the much rarer and greater honour of the Empire Gallantry Medal. The reason for the confusion is that the names are rather cumbersome and ambiguous.

Officer of the Most Excellent Order of the British Empire — OBE — with which we are familiar, an Order of Merit of which many are awarded each year in the New Year Honours in particular. This is not a Gallantry award.

The BEM awarded to Douglas Farr, brother of John Farr GC and as John Mitchell was honoured.
©M Hebblethwaite

Medal of the Most Excellent Order of the British Empire for Meritorious Service (British Empire Medal) — BEM — while this medal until 1940 was for Meritorious Service only and the medal is so inscribed this was not so *after* 1940 (when the EGM ceased) when it could be awarded for Gallantry until the introduction of the Queen's Gallantry Medal.

Medal of the Military Division of the Most Excellent Order of the British Empire OR *Medal of the Order of the British Empire for Gallantry* (Empire Gallantry Medal) — EGM — the crucial word here is Gallantry whereas the BEM was initially for Meritorious Service. However, *after* 1940 when the living holders of the EGM exchanged their medals for the GC the BEM could be awarded for Gallantry (confusing isn't it). Again there are anomalies and a thorough reading of the literature such as Peter Ducker's *British Gallantry Awards* is worth reading as is the *Medal Yearbook*.

In the case of Commander Richard Jolly GC (Exchange) there is considerable correspondence in the National Archives from the Fifth Sea Lord about his EGM which was first noted in the newspapers as an OBE.

in the 9 o'clock news that evening. This statement explained the nature and meaning of the Empire Gallantry Medal, and specifically referred to its award to the late Commander Jolly.

I have answered a number of queries, in writing and on the telephone, about this same question. The trouble of course is that the Empire Gallantry Medal (Military) has been so rarely given that it is, though a very honourable award, at present hardly known. It is difficult to say what more can be done.

Letter from the Fifth Sea Lord.

Police Long Service and Good Conduct Medal
To qualify for the Long Service and Good Conduct Medal police officers must have served at least 22 years, while Special Constables are honoured for 9 years 'willing and competent' voluntary service. For each additional 10 years Specials receive a bar which is added to their medal.

Sources: Alan Moss
British Gallantry Awards by Peter Ducker
Medal Yearbook
Police Review
National Archives
M Jolly

Police Long Service and Good Conduct Medal.

Richard Valentine (Dick) MOORE, GC, CBE, FIEE, FIMechE

Bomb/Mine disposal, 1940–1944, England

Status: Temporary Sub-Lieutenant, Royal Naval Volunteer Reserve
Life dates: 14th February 1916, Lambeth, London – 25th April 2003, Warrington, Lancashire. He was cremated at Walton Lea and his ashes were scattered in the Autumn Section where there is no memorial to him. **Obit:** *The Daily Telegraph*, 29th April 2003, *Nuclear Energy Journal*, December 2003
Biography: Richard, known always as Dick, was the only son of Randall and Ellen (Keny) Moore. He was educated at the Strand School and at London University, where he took a degree in Mechanical Engineering.

Dick started work with the County of London Electricity Supply Company from 1936 until the outbreak of the Second World War.

Moore's promotions were announced in *The London Gazette* as follows:
RV Moore to be T/SubLt 1.12.39 (seniority 15.10.39) (*LG* 2.4.40)
T/Elect Sub Lt R V Moore GC to be T/Elect Lt 14.2.41 (*LG* 4.4.41)
Commissioned into the Royal Naval Volunteer Reserve in 1939, Moore joined the Naval Unexploded Bomb Department from the cruiser *Effingham*, aboard which he had been serving as an assistant torpedo officer. The *Effingham* was later sunk off Norway on 18th May 1940 during the Norwegian Campaign. Moore served with the mines counter-measures section at the Admiralty until appointed Torpedo Officer of the light cruiser *Dido* in the Mediterranean in 1942. He saw action in support of the Eighth Army in the coastal waters of North Africa and during *Operation Vigorous*, when Rear-Admiral Sir Philip Vian tried to fight a relief convoy through to Malta. After being involved in the Navy's support for the Allied landings in Sicily, Salerno and Anzio, Moore served as Deputy Director of Torpedoes and Mining on the Admiralty delegation in Washington DC for the last year of the war.

In 1944 he married Ruby Edith Pair. She predeceased him with one of their three sons.

Dick Moore was a quiet, modest man, and devoted himself to golf and gardening in retirement.

A trubute and appreciation of RV Moore
Abridged from *The Journal of the British Nuclear Energy Society* with permission. I am particularly grateful for this as the debate over the building of new nuclear power stations is pertinent and of importance to all of us.
The appreciation was written by David Fishlock and colleagues.

RV Moore was the initiator and driving force behind Britain's Gas-Cooled Nuclear Power Programme.

After the War he joined Harwell and supervised the construction and maintenance of the first heat-producing UK reactor — British Experimental Pile '0' (BEPO). He quickly recognised the potential of a gas-cooled graphite moderated reactor system to become a source of steam for electrical power generation and in 1950 put forward a detailed cost analysis showing it to be a viable alternative to coal. A design team under his direction was commissioned to produce a design for a reactor producing both power and plutonium for weapons. In 1952 the design known as PIPPA (pressurised Pile for producing Power and Plutonium), which was to become Calder Hall emerged. Dick and his team moved to Risley to take charge of design and construction, and the first of four reactors at Calder Hall was opened by the Queen in 1956. A further four were subsequently built at Chapelcross. A national nuclear power programme was authorised and eventually five industrial consortia were formed which between them built 10 Magnox stations (20 reactors) all based on the Calder Hall design and with a total output of 5260 MW(e) But Dick was concerned that Magnox as cladding material limited the gas outlet temperature and consequently resulted in a lower efficiency than in modern steam plants. Low enriched uranium had become available from the Capenhurst Diffusion plant and this as fuel enabled stainless steel to be used as cladding and hence higher temperatures to be achieved.

Dick initiated the appropriate metallurgical and chemical studies and the design of the Windscale Advanced Gas-Cooled Reactor (WAGR), which was commissioned in 1962. The design principle was again adopted for the national programme and industry subsequently built 6 stations (12 reactors) with a total output of 7500 MW(e). In addition, as Managing Director of UKAEA Reactor Group, Dick was closely involved in the development and construction of the Prototype Fast Reactor (PFR) at Dounreay and the Steam Generating Heavy Water Reactor (SGHWR) at Winfrith.

Thus, although many others have contributed alternative reactor systems, it was Dick Moore's original concept, foresight and determination that gave us a very successful nuclear industry, which will surely yet again become a vital part of our national energy supply system.

Further detail

Dick was an engineer; one of a small band of pioneers drawn by the immense challenges of harnessing the atom's energy after the Second World War ... In 1944 — the year he was appointed Lieutenant Commander —he accompanied the British Admiralty delegation to Washington DC. The following year he read the Smythe Report on Atomic Energy, the official US account of the atom bomb's development. Britain announced that it was proceeding down the same road in August 1945.

Dick's nuclear career began in 1946 at the age of 30 when the tall, handsome ex-naval officer joined the newly-established Atomic Energy Establishment at Harwell, initially to set up a maintenance group for a 6 MW research reactor the industrial group at Risley had designed to Harwell specifications. He is said to have been a congenial leader. Another colleague recalls him as "pleasant, well-built and well-dressed (compared to the rest of us), usually in a smart blazer with an air of quiet competence".

Harwell, under the direction of John Cockroft from Cambridge, was modelled on Cockroft's laboratory; the (old) Cavendish Laboratory. It had a very broad brief relating to nuclear matters and a university's breadth of purview, yet worked closely with industry to produce new technology. Dick, with prior experience of electric power and naval electro-technology, immediately became involved in the control and instrumentation of BEPO and began to recruit his maintenance team for the experimental pile.

BEPO was the forerunner of the air-cooled plutonium piles at Sellafield, designed by Christopher Hinton's Industrial Group. Such was the pace postwar, BEPO took shape as the two piles were being designed. In was an air-cooled, graphite-moderated unpressurised system with an air outlet temperature of 100°C.

Dick drew on his earlier experience to suggest that such a system could be developed into a nuclear boiler that would raise steam of a quality that could drive an electricity turbo-generator. In 1950, together with Jack Diamond's Enriched Reactor Group (ERG) at Harwell, he developed his idea in a short but closely argued paper, dated 11th August 1950. This showed how a gas-cooled, graphite-moderated reactor using natural uranium fuel could generate the steam for a 30 MWe turbo-alternator at a cost comparable to a conventional fossil fuel boiler, and would also produce significant quantities of plutonium for a weapons programme.

The initial study was of a 40 MW CO_2-cooled reactor and this study began to tackle all the generic material problems of such a system. A Harwell conference that autumn, on natural uranium power reactors, attended by the Ministry of Fuel and Power, the British Electricity Authority and C.A. Parsons, decided that natural uranium reactors for combined production of power and plutonium might well be a sound way of starting a national nuclear power programme. Sir Leonard Owen, Hinton's deputy, later wrote: 'One paper was of exceptional interest because it presented new estimates of the cost of generating electrical power using the heat from a gas-cooled reactor.' Harwell set up the Natural Uranium Reactor Group (NURG) under the leadership of Dick Moore, with a steering group chaired by Brian Goodlet, Deputy Chief Engineer.

Enter PIPPA

However, early in 1952 it became clear that a 40 MW design would need enrichment. By this time the demand for plutonium had increased and it was agreed that the concept should be modified to achieve both power and plutonium production. Project PIPPA (pressurised Pile for producing Power and Plutonium) was born and a design was developed for a reactor of about 145 MW providing steam for a 35 MWe generator.

Dick produced the design study in January 1953 ... Project PIPPA was developed with help from the Ministry of Supply and Ministry of Works at Risley, and industry ...

Dick and his small design team transferred to the Ministry of Supply at Risley in April 1953 and he headed the enlarged design team. By then the British Electricity Authority and several industrial companies were already participating, and PIPPA had grown into a 150 MW (heat) reactor. A design team of 70 now took over the project — to build what was to become the first of eight Calder Hall reactors ...

By 1955 the Government was sufficiently confident of progress to announce a £300 million programme of civil nuclear power based on the reactor, aiming for 1500–2000 MW of electricity by 1965.

Faraday Lecture

In 1966 it fell to Dick to deliver the premier annual public lecture of the Institution of Electrical Engineers, the Faraday Lecture, commemorating Michael Faraday. By then he had earned Fellowship of two major engineering institutions, the Electricals and the Mechanicals. The Faraday is a major production, presented at several venues across the nation, culminating in London, over the course of a year.

Dick, as Managing Director of the UKAEA's Reactor Group, Risley, addressed the topic *Nuclear power, today and tomorrow*, assisted by the full resources of the UKAEA's public relations department providing film clips and reactor models ...

He began: "*I want to tell you the story of how we first demonstrated nuclear power was practicable, then how we made it economic, and finally how we plan to make it abundant for centuries.*" Dick introduced his audiences to the basic physics of reactors, leading to the three essential ingredients of any reactor: fuel, coolant and moderator. A lot of development was needed to produce steam this way of a quality that would drive a turbine, he observed. "*A team of engineers and scientists (of which I was fortunate to be one) started serious study of these problems in 1951, and by 1953 we had established the major features of the first power reactor which was to be constructed later at Calder Hall in Cumberland.*" It required the biggest pressure vessel built at that time, and a heat exchanger 70 ft tall and 18 ft in diameter.

"*Calder Hall was the first nuclear power plant,*" stressed Dick. "*You can imagine our feelings of excitement mixed with a little anxiety as the plant took shape in steel and concrete. Anxiety as to whether it really would produce the power we had designed it to do. But all went extremely well and full power was achieved with scarcely a hitch.*"

...

Dick continued, "*While the first Calder reactor was still under construction we felt sure enough of the design to formulate plans for a series of reactors of bigger output, to operate as part of the UK electricity system.*" The Government encapsulated these plans in a White Paper in February 1955. "*It was a programme formulated with vision and courage, of which we, as a nation, can be justly proud.*"

...

Continuing, with the first of Britain's commercial AGRs still on the drawing board, Dick was optimistic of the future.

"*The more efficient and compact design of the AGR has cut capital costs per installed kilowatt by more than half, and this, together with reduced costs from the better fuel, has brought generating costs down from over a penny a unit to less than a halfpenny. In economic terms imports of uranium to support a large nuclear programme will be very small, while refuelling costs will be very low, since the reactors are forming more fuel than they consume,*" he enthused. (We can in 2006 wonder at the ever-rising prices we pay for our energy. What happened to the hlafpenny unit?)

Without question, Dick Moore was the visionary who saw in Britain's earliest efforts to produce plutonium on an industrial scale the possibilities of a new electricity-generating system — the nuclear boiler — and pursued his vision through to a world-beating demonstration.

Citation: *27th December 1940*

The King has been graciously pleased to approve the award of the GEORGE CROSS for great gallantry and undaunted devotion to duty, to:-

Temporary Lieutenant Robert Selby Armitage, R.N.V.R.

Temporary Sub-Lieutenant (Sp.) Richard Valentine Moore, R.N.V.R.

Probationary Temporary Sub-Lieutenant (Sp.) John Herbert Babington, R.N.V.R.

Citation for the CBE *31st May 1963*

8th June 1963

To be Ordinary Knights Commanders of the Civil Division of the said Most Excellent Order :

Richard Valentine Moore, Esq., G.C., Managing Director, Reactor Group, United Kingdom Atomic Energy Authority.

Other awards: CBE, 1939–45 Star, Atlantic Star, Africa Star, Italy Star, Defence Medal, War Medal 1939–45, 1953 Coronation Medal, 1977 Queen's Silver Jubilee Medal and 2002 Queen's Golden Jubilee Medal. The investiture took place on 17th June 1941.

The story

Although from the Citation it appears that Moore's action was concurrent with that of **Babington** and **Armitage** in fact it took place with **Ryan** and **Ellingworth** who both received GCs.

It is important to understand why naval men worked on land. This was because the Germans had started to drop magnetic mines, usually expected only in water, on land by parachute. These German non-contact mines were attracted by a ship's magnetic field which then triggered them with devastating results. In **Newgass GC's** entry you will find many pictures of mines.

On the night of 16th September 1940, the Luftwaffe parachuted 25 mines on to London, where they caused widespread damage at roof-top or ground level. Moore and Ryan volunteered to render the 17 that did not explode safe. Four nights later in Dagenham of the four mines that were dropped only one exploded. Moore, carefully examining one, found that the fuze ring had become distorted and resorting to a method practised by many bomb and mine disposal men, using whatever tool was to hand (sometimes a hammer or screwdriver though not made of iron for magnetic mines could thus be set off) borrowed a drill from the now empty factory outside which the mine lay, drilled two gaps on opposite sides of the ring so that it broke enabling him to remove the fuze aware that at any time the mine could explode. As he was in the process of removing the mine's magnetic trigger Ryan arrived from neutralising the third mine. They had a short conversation and Ryan moved off to deal with the last of the four mines with Ellingworth. This was hanging from its parachute in a warehouse 200 yards away. Without warning it exploded and killed both men.

Courtesy Sue McDonald of British Nuclear Group

Memorials: There is a memorial to Ryan and Ellingworth in Dagenham. The RV Moore Memorial Lectures are held annually in his memory. A tribute to Dick Moore appeared in the British Nuclear Energy Society Journal in 2004. Plaque in the Visitors' Centre at Sellafield.

Background: *Strand School*

The Strand School originated in the Evening Department of King's College, London. In 1848 evening classes were taught and over the next 40 years a range of subjects was taught mainly of a non-academic nature. In 1875 William Braginton had set up private classes for those wishing to enter the Civil Service in response to changes in the requirements thereof. The relationship with King's College changed somewhat when it's own academic school, King's College School, moved to Wimbledon in 1897. Strand then moved into the basement of King's College and continued to offer commercial exams such as those necessary for telegraph learners, excise and customs appointments, and assistant surveyorships. Until 1910 Braginton jointly administered the two Colleges, resigning the Headmastership of the Strand School to be replaced by R B Henderson in 1910. Henderson supervised the school's move to Brixton in 1913. Strand School flourished for a number of years as a boys' grammar school and later merged with a nearby girls' school.

The Nuclear Debate

The debate rages on as more countries in the world acquire the technology to enrich Uranium and wish to build their own nuclear power stations. Depending on the country concerned this is sometimes seen as a first step towards developing a nuclear bomb with the subsequent outrage and threat of sanctions or worse still military action by those countries which already have their own weapons.

The International Atomic Energy Agency (IAEA) is the overseeing body. It provides a forum for scientific and technical co-operation in the nuclear field. As part of its remit it examines the nuclear installations on the ground and significantly found no WMD (weapons of mass destruction) in the run-up to the Iraq War.

For those who wish to know more it is worth reading the *Statement to the Sixty-First Regular Session of the United Nations General Assembly by* IAEA Director General Dr. Mohamed El Baradei.

Sources: King's College London

UKAEA, Harwell

Sue McDonald of British Nuclear Energy Society

Danger over Dagenham 1939–1945 by the Borough of Dagenham

On the Home Front, Barking and Dagenham in World War II compiled by Tony Clifford, Kathryn Abnett and Peter Grisby. This publication contains many contemporary pictures as well as lists of bombs, with maps showing where they fell.

www.iaea.org/

Alfred Ernest MORRIS, GC

Mine rescue, 29th May 1923, Ashanti Gold Mine, Obuasi, Gold Coast (now Ghana)

	Nineteenth August 1881	Alfred		Walter	Ann
1	6 Church Street S. Paul U.S.D.	Ernest	Boy	John MORRIS	Elizabeth MORRIS formerly THURSTON

Extract from Morris' birth certificate.

Status: Mill Foreman, Ashanti Goldfields Corporation
Life dates: 19th August 1881, Norwich – 24th November 1973, Bulawayo, Zimbabwe
Biography: Alfred was the son of Walter John and Ann Elizabeth (Thurston) Morris. His father was a compositor and the family lived in Church Street, Norwich. In all there were thirteen children.

Of all the George Cross recipients Alfred Morris is one of the least well-known and yet had one of the most fascinating lives. Both his work and his interests span a huge range of accomplishments.

Apart from the cars the Cape Town City Hall home of the Orchestra has hardly changed at all since Morris' time playing there.
©B Greene

Stanistreet states that Morris served in the Life Guards in 1910 and led the funeral procession of King Edward VII on the Drum Horse on 20th May 1910. He also mentions that during WWI he was in East Africa with the African Pioneer Corps and the Rhodesia Mounted Rifles in Umtali. No record of any medals for this service have so far been uncovered.

Alfred went to Norwich Grammar School and was an accomplished musician, playing in both the London and Cape Town Symphony Orchestras. He served in the Boer War, as well as in both WWI and WWII being demobbed in 1945.

Citation: *4th July 1924*
His Majesty The KING has been graciously pleased to award the Edward Medal in recognition of the gallantry of Mr. Geoffrey Walter Chardin, late engineer of the Ashanti Goldfields Corporation Limited, who lost his life in endeavouring to save life in a mine accident at Obuasi, Ashanti, on the 29th May, 1923, and to Mr. Ernest Alfred Morris (*sic*), a mill foreman of the Company, for the bravery displayed by him on the same occasion : —

On May 29th, 1923, at Obuasi, Ashanti, while a cyanide solution was being prepared in a vat on the premises of the Ashanti Goldfields Corporation a native, named Robert, who was working in the vat contrary to orders was overcome by the fumes. Two other natives Sikeyena and Guruba attempted to rescue him but were themselves overcome. Mr. Chardin, who was on the spot realised the danger and the need for immediate action if the men were to be saved. Without hesitation he entered the vat by a ladder but was himself overpowered by the fumes. Mr. Morris, and Mr. Skinner, the shift engineer, arrived and between them managed to drag Mr. Chardin out of the vat. Skinner then collapsed but Morris tied a rope round himself, re-entered the vat and eventually succeeded in bringing out the three natives alive. Unfortunately Mr. Chardin and the two natives Sikeyena and Robert succumbed, but the conduct of Mr. Chardin and Mr. Morris was extremely gallant and Mr. Morris undoubtedly risked his life in entering the vat no less than three times in his work of rescue.

Queen's South Africa Medal with three clasps: Cape Colony October 1899 – May 1902 Orange Free State – July 1900 Transvaal May 1900 – May 1902. Morris did not have the OFS clasp but the Wittebergen one.

King's South Africa Medal with 1901 and 1902 clasps.
©*M Hebblethwaite*

Other awards: EM (Bronze Mine) – GC exchange. At the time of the exchanges Morris was 90. Queen's South Africa Medal with clasps 'Wittebergen', 'Transvaal' & 'Cape Colony', King's South Africa Medal with clasps 'South Africa 1901' & 'South Africa 1902', 1939–45 Star, Africa Star & War Medal 1939–45. The Edward Medal is in the British Museum, it had been presented to Morris in Gaberone in Botswana.

Disc shaped pectoral suspended from fibre cords.
Photos by Pierre-Alain Ferrazzini

Necklace of small beads showing fine workmanship, may date from 19th century.
All ©AngloGold Ashanti

Background: *Ashanti Gold*
The archives for the company pre-1950 were placed with the Guildhall University (now London Metropolitan) and they have thrown them all away as not being relevant to present-day students, future students not being considered.

The gold operation at Obuasi, 200km north west of Accra in Ghana, was the major asset of Ashanti Goldfields Company (AGC), established in London in 1897. AGC started underground mining in 1907.

The company has come in for some criticism connected with labour conditions and pollution in recent times. However, programmes of both social and environmental responsibility are undertaken and international protocols adhered to.

Gold ornaments and jewellery have long been fashioned in Ghana and date back hundreds of years, they can be exceptionally beautiful.

The official history of the Ashanti goldfields
In late 1897, the principals of the newly formed Ashanti Goldfields Corporation led a team which dragged and carried 40 tonnes of equipment nearly 200 km from the coast to begin exploitation of their new property at Obuasi, in Ghana (formerly known as the Gold Coast). On New Year's Eve of that year they made their first mark on the land. It was the birth of an enterprise which, over 100 years on, is a flagship African Company and Ghana's foremost earner of foreign exchange.

Over the years, 25 million ounces of gold have derived from its efforts — $10 billion dollars' worth if it were all valued at today's price. Gold had long been panned and mined from the quartz reefs of Ashanti by local gold seekers, the galamsey.

But it was not until toward the end of the 19th century that the idea of an orderly commercial approach to gold mining in the Gold Coast began to gather momentum. Europeans had rarely ventured peaceably into the region — the powerful Ashanti dynasty had terrorised intruders and dominated neighbours for centuries — but travellers knew of this "neglected Eldorado", as Sir Richard Burton called it. British soldiers returned from the Ashanti wars with nuggets of ore bearing glittering streaks of the precious metal. One intrepid traveller told the Liverpool Chamber of Commerce that he had passed through districts where "you could pick up gold as you would potatoes". During the 1870s, a Frenchman, Marie Joseph Bonnat signed leases and exploited concessions on the River Ankobra at Awuda and later at Tarkwa, but his rights died with him in 1882. Thus it was two Fante merchants from Cape Coast, Joseph E. Ellis and Chief Joseph E. Biney, and their accountant, Joseph P. Brown, who opened the modern story of Ashanti gold.

Lured by travellers' tales, they crossed the River Pra into the kingdom of Adansi and saw the outcrops being worked for the king of Bekwai by local prospectors. In March 1890, the partners negotiated the mining concessions for 25,900 hectares (100 sq miles) of land in the Obuasi District. Among the foothills of the Moinsi and Kwisa ranges, between the rivers Oda and Offin, they laid claim to what was, and still is, one of the world's richest goldfields.

galamsey — a local artisanal gold miner in Ghana, West Africa. Galamseys are people who do gold mining independent of mining companies, digging small workings (pits, tunnels and sluices) by hand. Generally they can only dig to a limited depth, far shallower and smaller than commercial mining companies. Under current Ghana law, it is illegal for galamseys to dig on land granted to mining companies as concessions or licenses. Most galamseys find gold in free metallic dust form or they process oxide or sulphide gold ore using liquid mercury. The number of galamseys in Ghana is unknown, but it is believed to be from 20,000 to 50,000. As a group, they are economically disadvantaged; galamsey settlements are usually poorer than neighboring agricultural villages. They have high rates of accidents and are exposed to mercury poisoning. In some cases, galamseys are the first to discover and work extensive gold deposits before mining companies find out and take over, and galamsey workings are an indicator of the presence of gold.
From Wikipedia

Drum horse
These are horses that carry a rider and 2 silver kettledrums during various State and Royal processions. The horse needs to be large and strong but docile for not only does it carry a heavy weight but has to be able to cope with crowds of people. The rider will have his hands free and guide the horse through his feet as the reins are attached to the stirrups. The horses colouring is typically pinto and they have thick silky tails and are the favoured horse of the Romany Gipsy.
Sources: *'Gainst all Disaster* by Allan Stanistreet
The Boer War by Thomas Pakenham
B Greene
AngloGold Ashanti
John Lang of the Household Cavalry
Gold of Africa Museum, Cape Town
Wikipedia
London Metropolitan University

Francis Austin (Frank) MORTESHED, GC

Apprehending robber, March 1924, Belfast, N. Ireland

Status: 3234 Police Constable, Royal Ulster Constabulary
Life dates: 21st April 1897, Nenagh, Co Tipperary, Ireland – 14th April 1948, Belfast **Obit:** *Ulster Post*, 22nd April 1948. The death certificate states that at the time of his death Frank was working as a Head Ward's Master — what exactly that means is still to be found out. His brother-in-law Ian Gibson registered the death. At the time of Frank's death in hospital his wife was living at 12 Lower Windsor Avenue. The house is no longer there. In the funeral announcement Frank is credited with both the GC and the OBE.

Biography: Frank's father Francis Morteshed worked as an auctioneer. Frank served in WWI as a Driver in the Royal Corps of Signals from 15.11.1915 until 17th September 1922. On 17th December 1922 he joined the Ulster Special Constabulary as a B Special. Shortly afterwards on the 7th December it became the Royal Ulster Constabulary. During his time he had, in addition to his EGM (noted as a BEM) three favourable records, *for pursuing and capturing a murderer, stopping a runaway horse and tracing a person in a motor accident.*

Constable Morteshed served in Belfast throughout his RUC service and was elected to the Men's Representative Body in the years 1929–30 and 1930–31. He left the RUC due to ill health on 31st May 1931 and moved to England, his discharge records show his "Character as Very Good". During the Second World War he served as Sergeant No 1498263 in the RAF Security Control Police, he had joined in April 1941 but only served until February 1942 with no reason given for this short appointment on his record card.

Frank married Evelyn May Neely on 7th January 1925 and their only son Samuel Ronald was born on 26th March 1926.

Cliftonville FC in 1926. Winners of the Antrim Shield and Runners-up Gold Cup.
Frnk Morteshed is first player on the right sitting.
While his name is spelt Mortished in this picture on his death certificate and funeral notice it is spelt with an e.

F. A. Mortished,

©Cliftonville FC and courtesy Hugh McCantor, Chairman

A TRIBUTE TO LATE FRANK MORTESHED

A Very Gallant Gentleman: Kings Honoured Him

A VERY GALLANT MAN — he did not know the meaning of the word "fear" — and a great amateur sportsman, has passed on.

Frank Mortished, O.B.E. (*sic*) G.C., with whom I spent some of the happiest days of my life, unfortunately contracted T.B. at a stage when most people are thought to be immune from its dread clutches and in his early fifties passed away in a Belfast hospital. If ever a man lived dangerously that man was Big Frank Mortished. What thrills fell to the lot of former Irish amateur and Cliftonville centre-forward. A giant of a man — he stood 6ft. 4in. — he not only won renown in many branches of sport; he made the dramatic arrest of a gunman who was executed at Belfast. Born at Downpatrick (*sic*) Mortished started his football career as a wing three-quater for King's Hospital, Dublin. On forsaking Rugger for Soccer while in his teens, he became general utility man of the Brantwood Club. When the call came in World War I, Frank joined the 36th (Ulster) Division.

Hugh McCantor chairman of Cliftonville FC in front of the clubhouse which is soon to be demolished. This is the oldest club in Ireland almost 130 years old.

As football colleagues in the Army he had Tucker Croft (Glentoran), Jimmy Murdoch (Queen's Island) and Hal Burnison (Distillery). On the one occasion, when playing for Cairo against Alexandria one of his team mates was Jimmy McMenemy, of Scottish International and Glasgow Celtic fame. Following his Army career, which extended four years after the war, and found him serving in Syria, Egypt, Palestine and Western Europe. Mortished joined the Royal Ulster Constabulary.

He became the Cliftonville centre-forward, gaining a Co. Antrim Shield medal and one awarded to the unsuccessful finalists in the Irish Cup. Frank's most vivid soccer memory was at Blackpool where, following eight successive defeats in amateur internationals by England, Ireland succeeded in holding the Saxons to a draw of one goal each. That was 21 years ago.

The most thrilling incident of Frank Mortished's adventurous and varied life was in March, 1924. Mr. Henry Leech, a well-known Belfast man, was making up the pay packets in an office close to the city centre.

Three masked and armed men entered and there was a command: *"Hands Up!"*

It was obeyed by two terrified women assistants. Mr. Leech bravely walked towards the telephone, but before he could notify the police, was shot through the back and died a couple of hours later. One of the woman assistants ran after the retreating gunmen, screaming that Mr. Leech had been shot. Constable Mortished, on orderly duty in the nearby police barracks, heard the alarm.

Then followed an exciting chase and capture. One of the fugitives, seeing that escape was impossible, turned at bay. Producing an automatic pistol, he pushed it practically against the body of Mortished. Luckily for Frank, the safety catch was still in position and there was no explosion. The hero of the drama wrenched the deadly weapon from the grasp of the gunman and marched him to the barracks.

During the inquest on Mr. Leech, the Coroner, in a high tribute to Mortished's gallantry, said:-

"You are a very brave man. What I most admire is your humanity. Instead of shooting down the misguided man, you risked your own life and yet succeeded in arresting him."

The gunman was hanged and Frank received the O.B.E. (*sic*) from the late King George V. He moved to England and joined the police department of the RAF.

In 1941, when in the RAF police he was decorated by the present King George VI with the George Cross in recognition of a very gallant action, and Frank who had invited me to accompany him to London for the ceremony, remarked *"I can now claim that I have been decorated by three Kings."* As the winner of a 120yards hurdle event he was handed his medal by the Prince of Wales — King Edward VIII.

Frank Mortished was a most versatile sportsman and won numerous prizes for athletics, and in addition to being a footballer, was a cricketer, a swimmer and a rider at point-to-point races.

He was the best type of amateur and a Cliftonville man to the core. One of several officials of that club for whom he had the greatest admiration, was Jimmy Lunnebach, one of the most gentlemanly and most sincere friends he ever had.

As handsome a man as ever wore the King's uniform Frank, who, as I have stated, stood 6ft 4ins, enjoyed a joke at the expense of his great height on his first appearance as a recruit on the parade ground at Ballykinlar. A pert little sergeant-major eyed him from head to foot and then cutely remarked: *"Blimey, if you had been any longer I would have marked you absent."*

Big-hearted Frank has answered the last roll-call and Ulster has said good-bye to one of its bravest sons.

To his wife and family I tender the heartfelt sympathy of his many pals.

©*John Parker*

As Morteshed is usually described as having been in the Signals it now looks like he was a driver in the Royal Engineers and when in 1920 the Corps of Signals was formed moved over. He enlisted in the Royal Engineers on 3rd October 1915 with number 57933 which was later changed to 343693.

Frank's medal card.

Citation: *30th May 1924*

3rd June 1924

The King has been graciously pleased, on the occasion of His Majesty's Birthday, to approve the Award of the Medal of the Civil Division of the Most Excellent Order of the British Empire to the undermentioned:-

For Gallantry

3234 Constable Francis Austin Morteshed. Royal Ulster Constabulary

S1466 Constable Samuel Orr. Ulster Special Constabulary.

Other awards: EGM (civilian) – GC exchange. 1914–18 British War Medal, 1914-15 Star and Victory Medal.

The story

Nelson Leech was a book-keeper with Messrs Purdy and Millards. He was preparing the pay packets for his staff when he was suddenly disturbed by 3 masked men armed with handguns. Fortunately for Morteshed when Michael Pratley fired his gun the second time it failed and he was arrested. He was a married man from Moira Street. Nelson Leech died at 10pm from shock and abdominal haemorrhaging.

Background: *Michael Pratley*

Pratley had a history of crime and had indeed been due to stand trial for another murder committed nearly two years previously. He was alleged to have been involved in the murder of the Northern Ireland M.P. Councillor William Twaddell at 10.30am on the 22nd of May 1922.

The following has been provided by **Eamonn Andrews** and is printed with permission.

This letter was produced at Pratley's trial as evidence against him.

To My Dearest Joe, (his wife Josephine)

I want to say a few things, which are best, said now. When I stand on my trial it is not unlikely that I may be sentence to death, and it is best to know it now, instead of coming as a shock later on. The letter is being slipped out and it would be better to burn it in case it comes into the hands of the police. No matter how the case goes, I hope the two men who were with me will do their best for you. When the trial comes I am going to say that after the shooting I changed guns with one of the others, as his gun was too big to go in his pocket. That was how I had that particular gun.

The letter had been given to a person sharing a cell with Pratley who in turn gave it to the head warder. The attorney general then asked him if he had changed guns with anyone and he replied, "I never exchanged weapons at all". On conclusion of the case the jury retired at seventeen minutes past one in the afternoon. After twenty-eight minutes they returned with a guilty verdict. Pratley did not show any emotion when the verdict was made known to the court but he looked deadly pale. When the judge asked him if he had anything to say he replied, "I have no more to say than I have already said".

His Lordship then spoke to Pratley. *"Michael Pratley, you have received a fair trial in open court before a jury of your fellow townsmen. You have had every opportunity of vindicating yourself that was possible. The jury has convicted you and in my opinion rightly so, for it is clear that you have been guilty of a cowardly murder. Nothing remains for me but to pass sentence upon you".* The judge then assumed the black cap and the death sentence was fixed for the 8th May 1924. Pratley was then removed from the dock and returned to Belfast prison to become prisoner 298/24.

The attorney general and the trial judge commended Constable Morteshed for his actions in apprehending Pratley. The judge told the constable that he had behaved in a manner worthy of the best traditions of the RIC (Royal Irish Constabulary) and of the new RUC of which he was a member.

Sources: *Ulster Post*, 1948
The Thin Green Line by Richard Doherty
http://executions.mysite.wanadoo-members.co.uk/page7.html
John Parker
Eamonn Andrews
Northern Ireland Statistics & Research
Frank McMenamin
Hugh McCantor, of Cliftonville FC

Behind the Garden Wall — A History of Capital Punishment in Belfast by Steven Moore
Roy Black and Frances Orr of the RUC George Cross Foundation
www.royalulsterconstabulary.org/history3.htm on the B Specials
From the Inside Out, An account of all the prisoners hanged at H.M.P. Belfast by Johnston J. Fitzgerald
Medals. A Researcher's Guide by William Spencer

William Radenhurst (Bill) MOSEDALE, GC

Blitz rescue, 12th December 1940, Birmingham

**This painting by an unknown artist bears the note
Too dark, more detail necessary.
©*National Archives***

Status: Station Officer & Rescue Officer, Birmingham Fire Brigade
Life dates: 28th March 1894, Birmingham – 27th March 1971, Nailsea, Somerset. Bill was cremated at Arnos Vale Crematorium, Bristol **Obit:** *The Times*, 3rd April 1971
Biography: William was the son of Richard and Ellen Mosedale. In 1901 his father was working as a railway porter at New Street Station. William had a sister Nellie and a brother Albert at that time and the family lived in Balsall Heath, in all he was to be one of six children. When he left Sherborne Road School at the age of 14 he joined the 5th Bn of the Royal Warwickshire Regiment (TA) as a private while working as a tinsmith. However, in 1910 he joined the 5th Royal Irish Lancers and reached the rank of Corporal after three years. Due to the early death of his parents Bill was released by the Army after the intervention of the Relief Officer to look after his widowed grandmother and his younger brothers and sisters. He became a railway porter but by 1914 had applied to and been accepted by the Birmingham Fire Brigade, joining them on 19th August 1914. Bill's military training had stood him in good stead. In late 1914 he married Louisa Brown and they had two sons.

In September 1929 he was appointed Acting Officer in Charge of Rescue Department. In 1930 he became Station Officer and became an expert in breathing apparatus and special fire rescue appliances a skill for which he would be much in demand when in 1939 war broke out. Bill's service in the Birmingham Fire Brigade was of the highest order and the first acknowledgement of this was in 1931 when he received the Professional Fire Brigades Long Service and Good Conduct Medal. 1935 saw Bill, still as Station Officer, receive the Birmingham Fire Brigade Long Service Medal presented to him by HRH The Duke of Kent KG at the opening of the new HQ on 2nd December. In 1937 he was further rewarded, this time he received the First Star of Merit and the sum of £2/10/0 for work in connection with rescue breathing apparatus. In 1939 he was awarded his 5-year bar to his Birmingham Fire Brigade Medal after 25 years service.

In September 1941 he was further appointed as Column Officer. Bill was known throughout the district and his bravery was legendary.

Bill retired from the Fire Brigade on 28th September 1944 after 30 years' service to become a fire prevention consultant in South Yardley where his expertise was sought after by businesses of all types and sizes. He was now able to spend more time on his hobby — breeding bull terriers — a long way from those terrifying days and nights during the war.

He was a Freemason and was initiated in the Lodge of Security No 5650 in Birmingham in 1942.

There is a letter in Bill's records at the IWM from The Gramophone Company in 1941 offering all GCs a free copy of King George VI's speech announcing the institution of the George Cross. **Author's note:** You can hear this on my website *www.gc-database.co.uk* and read **Holloway GC** for more information.
Fred Benbow recollects his father's friendship with Bill.

"I was born in 1930 and in the 30's and 40's my father George Benbow was the village Police Constable at Severn Stoke, near Worcester. He was a great friend of Bill Mosedale.

He was a frequent visitor to fish in Knightshill Pool in Severn Stoke and in the nearby Croome River and Pirton Pool. Indeed my father was instrumental in Lord Coventry issuing William Mosedale with a permit to fish at any time in any waters owned by the Croome Estate.

Lord Coventry was killed in action in France in 1940. I well remember Bill Mosedale fishing in these waters in the early days of the war and I well remember hearing on the Wireless that he had been awarded the George Cross for rescuing people from damaged buildings.

He and my father remained friends until the 1950's.

My hope is this provides some background information about a very brave gentleman and one whom I am proud to have known in my childhood."

©FGA Benbow

Citation: *25th March 1941*

28th March 1941

The KING has been graciously pleased to award the GEORGE CROSS to: -

William Mosedale, Station Officer and Rescue Officer, Birmingham Fire Brigade.

An Auxiliary Fire Station was completely demolished by a very large high explosive bomb. A number of Auxiliary Firemen were trapped in the station and civilians were buried in an adjoining house which had also been demolished.

Station Officer Mosedale immediately began tunnelling and propping operations. Hundreds of tons of debris covered the site and Mosedale fully realised that at any moment he might be buried by a further collapse.

When the first tunnel was completed and the Control Room reached, he found that there were still men whom he could not extricate. He carried out another tunnelling operation from a different direction and again entered the Control Room. Five men were found, one dead, the others injured.

The Station Officer crawled through and administered oxygen to the injured men and they were then taken out through the tunnel.

The entrance to the cellar of the private house was full of debris. Station Officer Mosedale directed operations for removing this, only to find that the cellar itself had collapsed. He nevertheless persevered and, after a time, reached seven people who were trapped. Three had been killed outright when the roof collapsed. He gave oxygen to the remaining four and succeeded in extricating them.

To reach other victims it was again necessary to tunnel, and Mosedale immediately commenced this work. The dangers to be faced were similar to those which he had found in reaching the Control Room. He nevertheless completed the tunnel and entered the cellar under the Fire Station. Four men who were alive were given oxygen and, despite their injuries, were safely removed.

Road named in his memory at the Fire Service College.
©M Kernan

Tunnelling through such difficult material had necessarily been extremely hazardous, and the cellar collapsed completely, shortly after the removal of the last victim.

These operations, which lasted more than twelve hours, were carried out under a most intense bombardment. Twelve lives were saved by Station Officer Mosedale who showed outstanding gallantry and resource. In effecting the rescues he repeatedly risked his own life.

Other awards: Defence Medal, War Medal 1939–45, 1953 Coronation Medal. The George Cross and other medals were acquired by Birmingham City Museum. Association of Professional Fire Brigades Officers Long Service Medal, Birmingham Fire Service Long Service with Bars 5 years and 20 years. One newspaper stated that the announcement of the GC was made on his 46th birthday, another on his 47th, while another headline was *Birmingham's First VC*. As they say "never believe anything you read in the papers".

Birmingham Fire Officer Wins G.C.

SAVED 12 LIVES

Headline in the *Birmingham Gazette*, 29th March 1941.

The story

The 11th December 1940 saw the most gallant action of Mosedale's career in the Fire Service but it was not the first nor the last. However, it was the night of the 11th–12th December 1940 that remained in the memory of all who knew him. He had already pulled three people from the wreckage of a house when he was called out again, this time to the Auxiliary Fire Station, Grantham Road, Sparkbrook, Birmingham.

Time and again he went in to save first people in the Control Room, next in the cellar which had itself collapsed and no sooner had he aided the survivors in reaching daylight and ambulances than he heard there were more men trapped in another cellar and again he donned his breathing apparatus and started tunnelling again and found four men alive. No sooner had operations ceased than the whole structure collapsed.

©*Evening Mail*

26th March, 1941.

Dear Mr. Mosedale,

The Officer Commanding the Birmingham Fire Brigade recently drew my attention to your gallant conduct on 11th December 1940 when you took the lead in the rescue of persons trapped in the demolished Auxiliary Fire Station at Grantham Road Sparkbrook and in an adjoining house, tunnelling three times in very hazardous circumstances under tons of debris.

I have had the honour to bring your heriosm to the notice of His Majesty the King who greatly appreciated the initiative and courage you displayed throughout this difficult and dangerous operation. In recognition of your devoted services on this occasion His Majesty has been graciously pleased to award you the George Cross.

The notice of your award will be included in a list appearing in a Supplement to the London Gazette on the evening of Friday, 28th March, 1941.

Yours sincerely,

Station Officer
William Mosedale.

Letter from the Home Secretary, Herbert Morrison.

When interviewed by the *Evening Mail* in 1968 Bill commented.

"The sight of the dead men and the looks on the faces of the living in that cellar!"

Bill expostulated to the interviewer, "Don't for God's sake write about me as a hero. I wasn't. Just a fireman doing his duty. Dammit I was in the rescue department wasn't I?"

"Talk about the bull terriers shall we.

"There is just one thing though. I thnk I echo many an old trooper who feels he is stagnating, when I say I miss the old days when life was a matter of chance."

...

"The George Cross makes one feel good but it's only a fraction of a lifetime."

Memorials: Road at the Fire Service College where there was also a plaque which was unveiled in 1970 on an accommodation block. Painting in the National Archives. A road in Attwood Green, Birmingham is to be named after William Mosedale GC.

Sources: Michael Kernan of the Fire Service College
Birmingham Post
Birmingham Mail
Birmingham Gazette
Evening Mail

For Gallantry by K Hare-Scott
Birmingham Heroes by JP Lethbridge
Georgette Wright and Chris Sutton of Optima Community Association
FGA Benbow

Brandon MOSS, GC

Bomb rescue work, 20th October 1940, Coventry

Status: Special Constable, Coventry Special Constabulary
Life dates: 5th June 1909, Badingham, Suffolk – 9th August 1999, Coventry. Some books state that Brandon was born in Brandon, Norfolk, this is not born out by his birth certificate. He was cremated at Canley Crematorium and his ashes were taken away.
Biography: Brandon was the son of Harold Kenneth and Clara Elizabeth Jane (Woolmington) Moss. He had five brothers and sisters and at the time of his birth his father is noted as being a poultry farmer though later he is known to have worked for a firm of Sugar Refiners. Brandon was educated at Coventry Elementary and Stratford-on-Avon Grammar Schools which is indeed some way from Norfolk so it is most likely that the family moved while he was still quite young. On leaving school he entered the building trade but during the war took employment as a fitter at the Armstrong Siddeley Ltd plant in Coventry where he joined the Coventry Special Constabulary in 1932. He married Vera Watson in 1935 in Coventry and they had two daughters. He retired from the Specials in 1948 and returned to the building industry.

Citation: *10th December 1940*
13th December 1940
The KING has been graciously pleased to approve the award of the GEORGE CROSS to:-
Brandon Moss, Special Constable, Coventry Special Constabulary.

Special Constable Moss was engaged on duty when a house was struck by an H. E. bomb and completely demolished, burying the three occupants. He led a rescue party in clearing an entry to the trapped victims under extremely dangerous conditions owing to collapsing debris and leaking gas. When conditions became critically dangerous he alone worked his way through a space he cleared and was responsible for the saving of the three persons alive.

It was then learned that other persons were buried in the adjoining premises and Moss at once again led the rescue. The workers became exhausted after many hours of work but Moss laboured unceasingly and inspiringly throughout the complete night, again with falling beams and debris around him, and as a result of his superhuman efforts and utter disregard for personal injury one person was rescued alive and four other bodies recovered. During the whole of the time of the rescue, bombs were dropping around and it was known that there was a delayed action bomb in the doorway of a tavern only 20 yards away. Moss was working from 11 p.m. until 6.30 a.m. without pause.

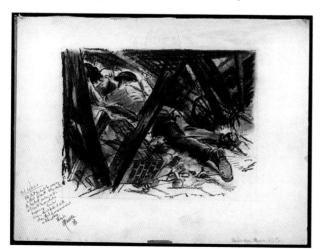

Brandon Moss by O'Connell.

At bottom left there is the following note.

Note to Artist.
OK, but he should be wearing a steel helmet. Also clarify the top left portion as it is difficult to see what is happening. Finished drawing should make it quite clear that a rescue incident is taking place. Thanks.

©*National Archives*

Other awards: Defence Medal, 1953 Coronation Medal, 1977 Queen's Silver Jubilee Medal and Special Constabulary Long Service Medal (GVIR). This last medal is awarded for a service of 9 years or more during peacetime or three years of service during wartime without pay.

RECOMMENDATION ORIGINATED BY Deputy Chief Warden and Chief Constable of Coventry.

NO. 9 (Midland) REGION: REGIONAL COMMISSIONER'S RECOMMENDATION G.M.

Brandon Moss was first recommended for the George Medal. This was upgraded to the GC.

Special Constabulary Long Service Medal.

Another story

We have seen in 2006 what devastation aerial bombardment can cause and to have been in Coventry in 1940 must have been a frightening experience. Being the centre of the aircraft industry the Germans had good reason to bomb the factories but did not stop there. They bombed indiscriminately, flattening houses as well as industrial buildings, the cathedral and the hospital. On the night of the 14–15th** November 1940 Brandon was on duty in Clay Lane at 11pm when the first bomb fell. He and three of his colleagues dodged as a bomb flew by. As Brandon dropped to the ground his colleagues had run for cover into a passageway only for the house beside them to be the destination of the bomb. The walls collapsed on them. Assuming them to be dead Brandon immediately went to search for the occupants of the house and found them safe though shocked under a piano. Then he and other members of the rescue team found the dead bodies of his colleagues but he was not finished yet. Bombs were still falling and unstable ruins and debris fell around him. He found one more survivor before he stopped, exhausted 7 hours later.

** Some books say 14–15th but the Watch Committee minutes confirm 20th October 1940.

CONTROLLER'S OBSERVATIONS.

I recommend MOSS in the highest possible terms for the award of the George Medal. He risked his life again and again for several hours and went on in spite of the exhaustion of the others whom he led. His was an outstanding example of courage and self denial and all members of the rescue party who were present speak highly of his bravery.

Chief Constable and
A.R.P. Controller, Coventry.

Extract from the Recommendation for a Gallantry award.

Background: *Another author*

Kenneth Hare-Scott in his book *For Gallantry* tells the stories of 16 GCs. He puts each into context in a particular way that is now rather old-fashioned and not very PC. He describes the life of the inhabitants of the Midlands and also rather oddly compares it with what life was like for him in the Officer's Mess in Hampshire. I personally find his style rather patronising and paternalistic with such comments as "it is well and hopeful to remember that behind this poorer facade, where beats the big heart of Britain, live the Freds and their families" (**F Davies GC**) and of Brandon Moss he quotes the Chief Constable as saying "he was a good type".

These days such remarks are reminiscent of the prevailing class system which talked of the "little man" for the carpenter or electrician. Hare-Scott describes how the new University in Bristol was "to the country dweller, inspiring beyond words", or how Father Arbuthnott visited **Ted Heming GC** at his "little house in Holly Grove". Meanwhile he interspersed these stories with his own middle class life of public school and motor cars. I don't like it at all but no doubt in years to come my books will come up for criticism too for society is changing and so is the language we use to describe it.

Armstrong-Siddeley Ltd in Coventry — see also Volume 2

In 1938 the Hawker Aircraft Company merged with Armstrong Siddeley Ltd to form Hawker Siddeley Aircraft which was based at Bagington Airport, Coventry where between 1942 and 1945 the company built Lancaster Bombers.

Sources: Sandra Hoskin   National Archives   *For Gallantry* by K Hare-Scott
The Bravest of the Brave by Anthony Rae in *Police Review, 1987*

Joseph Edward (Joe) MOTT, GC

Action to prevent bomb explosion, 25th December 1937, Haifa, Palestine

Status: 6009084 Private, 1st Battalion, The Essex Regiment
Life dates: 30th March 1914, Stepney – 12th January 1983, Basildon, Essex. Joseph was cremated at South Essex Crematorium and his ashes were scattered on Lawn 28, Area 4. There is an entry in the Book of Remembrance. **Obit:** *The Times*, 20th January 1983
Biography: Joseph Mott was the son of Joseph Robert and Ada (Champ) Mott. His father was a postman. He was educated at Stevens Road School, Becontree.

Joe joined the Army in 1930 and served in both the 1st and 2nd Battalions of the Essex Regiment first in India then in Egypt and Palestine. He originally enlisted in the 4th Bn (TA) on 14th July 1930 and then, obviously enjoying the life which would have guaranteed regular pay and resonable living conditions during the Depression, he signed on as a Regular on 18th January 1932 for 7 years' Full Time. He went on the Reserve on 19th March 1939 and, following recall in 1939, was discharged to the Z Reserve on 15th February 1946. Joe's service medals give a good indication of at least some of the theatres of war in which he served.

Citation: *25th February 1938*
The KING has been graciously pleased to approve of the Award of the Medal of the Military Division of the Most Excellent Order of the British Empire to the undermentioned: —
For Gallantry.
No. 6009084 Private Joseph Edward Mott, 1st Battalion, The Essex Regiment.

At about 8.20 p.m. on the 25th December, 1937, a bomb was thrown into the Jordania Cafe, Haifa. The Cafe was crowded with soldiers and civilians at the time. The bomb fell at the feet of Private Mott who was seated at a table with some other men of the Battalion. With the utmost coolness and presence of mind, Private Mott picked it up and hurled it through the window into the street, where it exploded with great violence. This highly courageous act undoubtedly saved several lives, and injuries to many.

Other awards: EGM (Military) – GC exchange (6009084 Pte. Joseph Edward Mott, The Essex Regt, 25th February 1938), General Service Medal 1918–62 (KGVI, with clasp 'Palestine', named '6009084 Pte. J E Mott, Essex R.' with Mention in Despatches 23.12.38), 1939–45 Star, Africa Star, Burma Star, Defence Medal, War Medal 1939–45, Coronation 1953, 1977 Queen's Silver Jubilee Medal. Pte J E Mott's George Cross group was sold by Glendining on 15th December 1966. The group was, for a while, on display in the Essex Regiment's Museum.

The story
Joseph who was 24 at the time saved nearly sixty British soldiers and policemen from serious injury. Fortunately no one was in the street outside or if there were there is no mention of any injuries.

Background: *The Essex Regiment in Palestine 1936–1939*
During the summer of 1936 the 1st Bn received orders to move to Palestine and Mott along with his fellow soldiers were in Haifa by Christmas under Brigadier JF Evetts, CBE, MC, but under the overall command of General Wavell, see **Durrani GC**. The Battalion's role "was that of internal security, preventing Arabs from murdering Jews, protecting transport and keeping the main roads open for traffic". The situation is familiar though some would see it the other way round.

They were not successful, again we have heard these reasons before. Insufficient numbers of personnel, poor overall organisation, intimidation of the local police and poor intelligence.

In January 1938 (after barely a year) the Battalion moved to Cairo having been told that they were "thoroughly efficient and well-disciplined" by Wavell.

In Egypt training began for desert warfare and mechanisation but within six months they were ordered back to Palestine for more of what they had been doing before. A re-organisation plan was put into place and this produced more 'successes' than previously, ie more Arabs killed. However, their stay was not for long as they were ordered to return once more to Cairo in September 1938 to dig trenches and building defences. But once again their stay was not long and Christmas 1938 saw the Bn split up between Cyprus and Egypt. A far more serious conflict was fast approaching for which the Bn was trained and no doubt prepared, though the endless moving about must have had an unsettling effect on the men.

Sources: Ian Hook of the Essex Regimental Museum
www.marxists.de/middleast/palquest/britpol.htm
The Essex Regiment 1929–1950 by Col TA Martin
The Sphere 13th July 1946

John Stuart (Mouldy) MOULD, GC, GM

Mine disposal, 14th November 1941 – 30th June 1942, UK

John and his wife Margaret.
Courtesy P Brooks

©Len Traynor

Status: Lieutenant, Royal Australian Navy Volunteer Reserve, attached Royal Navy (Mine Clearance Specialist)

Life dates: 21st March 1910, Gosforth, Newcastle-upon-Tyne, Northumberland – 9th August 1957, Sydney, New South Wales, Australia. John was cremated and there is a plaque at Northern Suburbs Crematorium Sydney, RSL Section, Niche 443JD. **Obit:** *The Times,* 10th August 1957

Biography: John was the son of Stuart Mill and Ethel Kate (Robinson) Mould. Stuart was an architect and surveyor. The family emigrated to Australia when John was two years old and he was educated at Sydney Grammar School. His father established himself as an architect in Sydney. John studied part-time at the Sydney Technical College while working in his father's office from 1927–1932 when he left for London.

In his nomination papers to become as an Associate of the Royal Institute of British Architects he rather naively stated, "I have been touring three countries and have seen many fine examples of architecture". In July 1933 he passed the required exams and was registered to become an Associate on 7th November 1933 which was approved on 5th February 1934. He then returned home.

On his return to Sydney John joined his father in a practice in Hunter Street, Sydney which became Mould and Mould, Architects. On 29th April 1935 he married Phyllis Sarah Palmer and they had one child.

On 14th June 1940 John enlisted in the Australian Imperial Force. However, he fell ill but made good of his time recuperating and qualified through the Yachtsmen Scheme for appointment as Sub-Lieutenant, Royal Australian Naval Volunteer Reserve in which he enlisted on 14th (Staunton says 1st) September 1940 and was soon to return once more to England where, in March 1941, he joined HMS *Vernon* for enemy mining work. As part of the Rendering Mines Safe (RMS) section of the RN he worked mainly on bombs and mines dropped in the sea or which had been washed ashore. Amongst the particular German mines was the Type G. As for all the men who were involved in RMS the work was hazardous and he was commended three times culminating in the GC in November 1942.

John's cap on a mine rendered safe.
Courtesy P Brooks

Promoted A/Lt Cdr in January 1943, John worked with the team developing a diving-suit with an independent air supply. Later that year Mould, **Goldsworthy**, and Lt Cdr J. L. Harries, Royal Canadian Navy, trained groups of men known as 'P' parties in preparation for the invasion of Western Europe. These units were to be dispatched to newly captured harbours to clear them of booby traps, mines and other obstructions. Declining the opportunity to command one of the parties, Mould chose instead to continue training men who would serve in them. It was a notable tribute to him that no one lost their life during these operations, their training had been faultless. Following the German surrender in May 1945, he was sent to Ceylon (Sri Lanka) and Australia to assess the requirement for 'P' parties in the Far East and Pacific theatres.

When peace came he returned to his professional career first serving with the Allies in Germany on reconstruction projects before finally returning home in 1948. In 1947 he had married Margaret Agnes Massey (Heeps) and together they had two sons and a daughter.

There is an interesting note in *Reserve News* that the Mould's applied for passage to Australia but it was refused and the couple were required to go as assisted immigrants. Honours and Awards did not cut any ice with the authorities in 1948.

Back in Sydney John worked for the Department of Public Works and was appointed Chief Architect to the Housing Commission of New South Wales in 1950. The amount of construction increased dramatically during his tenure, and he was responsible for the design of housing estates and shopping centres. His most conspicuous buildings are the Greenway apartment blocks in Ennis Road, Milsons Point, immediately east of the northern approach to Sydney Harbour Bridge.

This contemplative picture of John Mould was taken by Harold Newgass GC.
©Newgass family

Firkins in *Of Nautilus and Eagles* describes Mould as possessing a "brilliant mind and at the same time the personification of the legendary tough, lanky, hard-living, hard-drinking, devil-may-care Australian".

Felix Tavener knew Stuart in Germany after the war. He recalled this story.

"One night a retired colonel upset by the noise emanating from the crew's room, knocked on the door and demanded to see the commanding officer whereupon a crew member looked under the bed and said "*Hey Mouldy there's a bloke wants to speak to you!*"

Of such apocryphal stories are lives remembered — often they are the only memories of a person's whole life. Fortunately Ivan Southall recorded John Mould's life and describes in incredible detail his Mine Disposal exploits.

Citation: *30th October 1942*
3rd November 1942

The KING has been graciously pleased to approve the award of the GEORGE CROSS for great gallantry and undaunted devotion to duty to:-

Lieutenant John Stuart Mould, G.M., R.A.N.V.R.

Lieutenant Mould has shown the highest form of personal courage combined with exceptional skill in planning and executing the many difficult and dangerous operations he has been charged with. He joined HMS *Vernon* for enemy mining work in March 1941, and since then has been almost continuously employed on most dangerous work. His outstanding work in dock clearance operations and those resulting in the stripping of the early German mine Type G, has been the subject of a previous recommendation for which he was ultimately awarded the George Medal. Since that time he has carried out the most important recovery, rendering safe and investigation of the first German magnetic acoustic unit and moored magnetic mine.

Inscription on the George Medal.
Courtesy P Brooks

Citation for the George Medal *24th April 1942*

St. James's Palace, S.W. I.
28th April, 1942

The KING has been graciously pleased to approve the following awards for gallantry and undaunted devotion to duty: —...

The George Medal.

Temporary Lieutenant-Commander Charles Walter Albert Chappie, D.S.C., R.N.V.R.

Temporary Lieutenant Hugh Verschoyle Cronyn, R.N.V.R.

Temporary Lieutenant David Law, R.N.V.R.

Lieutenant John Stuart Mould, R.A.N.V.R.

Other awards: GM, 1939–45 Star, France and Germany Star, Defence Medal, War Medal 1939–45 with King's Commendation oak leaf (HMS *Vernon*, *LG* 27.6.41), Australia Service Medal 1939–45 & 1953 Coronation Medal. The group was sold by his family soon after his death in 1957. The GM was presented on 28th July 1942 and the GC on 23rd March 1943.

Courtesy Peter Brooks

The story

John Mould was one of four Australian volunteers to join HMS *Vernon* in 1940. All four were to be awarded the George Medal, they were Mould, **Syme GC, GM**, Lieutenant James Henry Hyndman Kessack GM, R.A.N.V.R. and Lieutenant Howard Dudley Reid, GM, R.A.N.V.R.

John was the first to render safe the German magnetic acoustic unit and the moored magnetic mine — Type T. Like Martin GC his George Cross was a recognition of a series of dangerous operations culminating in the recovery of a German mine in May 1942. He perfected techniques for stripping the mines and one might suggest that his hand/eye co-ordination, a talent and skill used to advantage in his civilian occupation, was here invaluable.

Memorials: There is a tribute to Mould and **Syme** at HMAS *Waterhen*, Sydney, plaque in Canberra.

Background: *Francis Greenway*

The building for which Mould is best known is named after Francis Greenway who is sometimes referred to as the convict architect. He was born in 1777 near Bristol of a family of stonemasons, builders and architects. He himelf practised as an architect until being found guilty of forging a document which carried the death penalty. Fortunately for Australia this was commuted to transportation and he arrived in Sydney in 1814 with his family following behind. It did not take long for his skills to be recognised and he set up practice and designed many early Sydney buildings.

Greenway Apartments, Sydney. The small square bits sticking out of the brick work are air vents. The building was built in 1951.

©*Paul Murphy*

HMAS Waterhen

This is a shore establishment of the Royal Australian Navy and is the parent establishment for the RAN's mine countermeasures forces, and forms part of Fleet Base East. First commissioned in 1962, it was used for a variety of minor warfare vessels, including patrol forces. Then in the 1990s it was rebuilt to house Fleet Intermediate Maintenance Authority (FIMA) — *Waterhen* and the Mine Warfare Faculty. Altogether the complex comprises three main buildings, two new wharves, a small boat jetty and boat ramp, a four-level car park (196 car spaces), an oil fuel installation (OFI), a gatehouse and a magazine.

Rendering a bomb safe.

Sources: *Softly Tread the Brave* by Ian Southall
RIBA Information Centre
Australian Dictionary of Biography
Reserve News, 2001
Felix Tavener
Of Nautilus and Eagles. History of the Royal Australian Navy by P Firkins
Royal Australian Navy
Len Traynor

PO Andrew Campbell
Peter J Brooks
Australian Sunday Telegraph, Men of Valour, May 1962
Richard Yielding
Victoria Cross. Australia's Finest and the Battles they Fought by Anthony Staunton

Eric Lawrence MOXEY, GC

Bomb disposal, 27th August 1940, Biggin Hill Aerodrome, Kent

Eric and his brother Nigel when Nigel was at Dartmouth Naval College.

Eric and May Moxey lie together.
Happily united
© *Tim Hatwell*

All other photos © *W Moxey*

Eric and May.

Douglas, Nigel and twins Jack and Bill.

Douglas, May, Jack, Eric, Bill, Nigel and Eric's secretary Betty in November 1939.

DOG 7, Eric and May in his Wolseley, the envy of Winston Churchill.

Status: 73498 Acting Squadron Leader, Royal Air Force Volunteer Reserve

Life dates: 14th April 1894, Sao Paulo, Brazil – 27th August 1940, Biggin Hill Aerodrome, Kent. Eric is buried in the churchyard of St. Peter & St. Paul, Cudham, Orpington, Kent, Grave Reference Section NN. Grave No. 26. Although this is a war grave maintained by the CWGC, the records show that the ashes of Mary Arthur Moxey were interred in the grave on 5th January 1982. **Obit:** *The Times*, 13th September 1940 and 19th September 1940.

Biography: Eric was the son of William Hall and Margaret Lawrence (Christie) Moxey. He was born in Brazil because his father was a founder and Secretary of the Sao Paulo Railways. Like so many expat children he was sent home to school to Malvern College and then Sheffield University, where he read engineering. He had one brother and two sisters.

Eric second from the right in the Zenith team.

Eric was a talented bike rider and won the gold medal in the Isle of Man TT as the winning amateur while still at school when he was 17. In order not to alert his parents to his fame he called himself by his second name hence the medal is inscribed L Moxey. While at school he helped a boy called Morgan to build the first three-wheel Morgan motor car. He was also a talented musician, playing, in particular, the violin, taking lessons with Yehudi Menuhin's sister Hepsibar when, for a while, the family lived in Brighton. Years later together with his sons playing different instruments the family formed a small band though Douglas preferred the gramophone which he thought superior. On the day that Eric was killed he was bringing home a new drum kit for his young son Jack.

Eric in his Bristol Bulldog aeroplane mounted on his propellor tip.

More medals for motor bike sports dated 13.05.1912 and 12.07.1912.

When Eric left University he went to work for Vickers Steel and it was there that he and his fellow apprentice Paul Stanley first met the MD's daughter Mary Arthur Clark of Whiteley Wood Hall, Sheffield, and vied for her hand. Eric won and he and May, as she was always called, were married on 10th January 1917 at Christ Church, Fulwood, Sheffield. They had four sons, Douglas, Nigel and twins Jack and William (Bill). After Eric was killed May was left with little money and had to remove her youngest two from Malvern to which they had followed their father. "*She was the true hero of the family*" says Bill. "*She had four sons and two years to the day after losing Dad she lost her second son Nigel*". Nigel died aged 21, killed in a motorbike accident.

But back to his early life.

Paul Oldfield summed up:

I wrote the history of the Sheffield City Battalion (12th York & Lancaster) in 1988 and Eric was one of the original members of that famous battalion.

1. He commanded No. 7 Platoon in B Company, SCB.

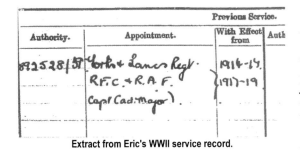

Authority.	Appointment.	Previous Service.	
		With Effect from	Auth
8925528/51	orks & Lancs Regt.	1914-14.	
	R.F.C. & R.A.F.	(1917)-19	
	Capt (Cad Major)		

Extract from Eric's WWII service record.

2. Commissioned 2Lt on 23rd September 1914, Lt 5th December 1914, Acting Capt 7th September 1916, took command of B Coy in October 1916 and promoted to Capt 23rd February 1917.

3. Went to Egypt with the Battalion arriving in January 1916. By then he was the Machine-gun officer. The Bn moved to France in March and he was one of very few officers left standing after the abortive attack on 1st July at Serre, where over 500 casualties were suffered in less than half an hour.

4. Left the Bn on 21st July 1917 to join RFC.

Eric was demobbed in 1918, though his record of service states 1919, and he returned to engineering.

The family moved to Birmingham and Eric worked for New Conveyors which manufactured conveyors for the mines and factories. In 1934 he set up his own company Moxey Conveyors whose largest contract was to build the longest conveyor belt in the country at the Longbridge works for The Austin Motor Car Company.

Churchill in Moxey's Wolseley on VE Day.

It was during this time that Eric designed and had built a unique Wolseley. After his death it was abandoned at Biggin Hill with no son around to drive it. How Churchill subsequently came to be driven in it through the VE Day crowds down Whitehall has never been satisfactorily explained!

In time when Douglas was demobbed he too joined Moxey Conveyors as did Bill.

However, war was to beckon Eric again and this time he joined the RAFVR as an Intelligence Officer. He was commissioned as 'P/O on probation Admin & Spec Duties Branch RAFVR' on 14.3.39 with confirmation of appointment on 21.5.39 as listed in *The London Gazette*:

P/O E L Moxey (73498) promoted Flying Officer (Admin & Spec Duties Branch) RAF Reserve. His term of service was to be cut short by his untimely death.

Eric was a committed Freemason though May was unimpressed when there was no offer of aid after his death. She worked as a VAD and nursed German PoWs during the war.

Eric Moxey in the middle with Air Intelligence colleagues.
Lepraic is on his right.

Above is another photo showing *Freddie* in a simulated operation on a German 1000KG Bomb, the fuze is under the vertical column. The system is operated by a small compressed air cartridge, it has a built-in delay to allow the operator to get to a safe point. The compressed air cartridge is in the silver/aluminium container level with the man's head. It is located at the RAF Bomb Disposal display at Eden Camp, Malton.

©*F Knox*

Bill Moxey with the Rev Raye Follis DFC with Eric's invention
Freddie, now held at RAF Hendon.

Bill Moxey writes of his father:

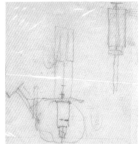

This is Eric Moxey's original sketch of the *Freddie* fuze
extractor.

"Dad invented a device for extracting fuses from German bombs which he nicknamed *Freddie*. After the war my mother received a letter from the Air Council saying that Dad was to have been awarded £500 for his invention and that she would receive it but that Dr Arthur Douglas Merriman GC claimed it for himself though they knew it had been his invention." (see Merriman GC earlier in this book).

Like many other GCs Eric had previously performed acts of courage. One Bill remembered was when his father and brother Nigel were driving across Walton Bridge only to witness a Blenheim Bomber crashing into a small lake. Eric did not hesitate to dive into the water and clamber on to the now burning plane. A doctor on the bank desperately called him to return and came out in a punt to get him. Meanwhile Eric had found all the crew dead inside.

The Legacy. Bill Moxey's wife Patricia, her sister Jill Skeet and
the five Moxey children and many grandchildren.

Amanda, Patricia and Bill Moxey in 2006.

Eric captioned this 'My Bus'.

Night bombing.
These taken by Eric Moxey

Citation: *13th December 1940*
17th December 1940

The KING has been graciously pleased to approve of the posthumous award of the GEORGE CROSS to:-
Acting Squadron Leader Eric Lawrence Moxey (73498), Royal Air Force Volunteer Reserve.

On the 27th August, 1940, it was reported that two unexploded bombs were embedded in an aerodrome. Squadron Leader Moxey, a technical intelligence officer employed at the Air Ministry, immediately volunteered to proceed to the site and remove them, though from the nature of his duties he was very fully aware of the risk entailed in such an operation. One of the bombs exploded causing his death. On many occasions Squadron Leader Moxey has exhibited similar complete disregard for his personal safety.

Other awards: 1914–15 Star, British War Medal, Victory Medal, 1939–45 Star, War Medal 1939–45, France & Germany Star, Defence Medal. The picture is not absolutely correct as the War Medal and Defence Medal have been replaced by Stars.

War Memorial in Malvern College Chapel.
©Mike Eglington, The Malvernian Society

Memorials: Name on the Honours Boards at RAF Wittering and in the Church of St Clement Danes. A road in a new development at Biggin Hill will be named in Eric's memory, Moxey Close. The full name of which will be

Moxey Close
Squadron Leader Eric Lawrence Moxey, GC
Bomb disposal officer
Killed in action
27th April 1940, aged 46.

The RAF Church, St Clement Danes.
©M Hebblethwaite

Background: *Sheffield City Battalion (12th York & Lancaster)*
The Duke of Norfolk and Sir George Franklin approached the War Office on 4th April 1914 with the intention of forming a Pals battalion in the Sheffield area. Within a short time men from all walks of life signed up. The Battalion's story is told in *History of the 12th (Service) Battalion, York & Lancaster Regiment* by Richard A. Sparling.

Pals battalion and a bit more on sizes — one drawn from an area where the recruits knew and trusted each other. They were established all over the country.

Note that a Bn during WWI and WWII was larger than one today (see Volume 5). This from **George Hendry** on previous sizes.

"If I recall correctly, approx 35 all ranks in an infantry platoon (3 sections of 10 + Pl HQ); there were three platoons in a company for approx. 137 all ranks, and there were four rifle companies plus HQ company plus Support Company in an Inf Bn. Support was large because it included the Bren Carrier Pl, 3" mortar platoon, and other specialists. Something over 800 I think when at full strength — which was seldom to last after the first wipeouts in action.

The above are after the reorganization following Dunkirk evacuation. The British Expeditionary Force went into France with the same organization as in WWI, marching in fours and with six rifle companies per Bn, four batteries of

Artillery per Field Regiment, etc, which organization proved so unwieldy that I doubt, for example, if they ever got all the batteries in a Field Regiment "zeroed in" in time to be of any use before they had to move again."

SQUADRON LEADER E.L. MOXEY, R.A.F.V.R.

Sir,

I have the honour to refer to the lamented death of the above named Officer in the execution of his duties. Since the announcement of his death I have been expecting to see his name gazetted as the recipient of some posthumous award, but as it has not appeared I feel it my duty to forward the following recommendation from my own personal knowledge of him.

Following the mass German bomb raid on Paris early in June, 1940, when delay-action bombs were dropped there, Flight Lieutenant Moxey, as he then was, was sent out to arrange through me for permission to dismantle some of these bombs in order to discover what form of fuse or other device was incorporated in them to produce the delay action.

He attacked the problem of obtaining this permission from the French authorities, who, as usual, were thoroughly obstructive, with great enthusiasm. Days went by and the danger of explosion became greater, but Flight Lieutenant Moxey's determination to dismantle the bombs never flagged. Finally, with the help of Major General E.L. Spears, we obtained permission from M. Dautry, the Minister of Armaments, for Moxey to have access to the bombs and he finally dealt with them.

Later he arrived back in France again, and as French organisation by that time had entirely broken up and H.M. Embassy had moved to Bordeaux, he had an adventurous time in rejoining me after he had looked at more bombs. He finally arrived in Bordeaux on a motor bicycle and was despatched by me to England in one of H.M. destroyers.

In my opinion Squadron Leader E.L. Moxey was the bravest man that I have ever met. His enthusiasm for his extremely dangerous task was supreme, and I consider that he is a fit recipient for the George Cross which, I understand, like the Victoria Cross, can be awarded posthumously.

As I understand that he has left a widow and two sons, both of whom are serving in H.M. Forces, I consider that such a posthumous award would be extremely appropriate.

The Under-Secretary
of State,
Air Ministry,
Whitehall,
LONDON. S.W.1.

I am, Sir,
Your obedient Servant,

Douglas Colyer.

Group Captain,
R.A.F.

The Recommendation for the GC.

Royal Flying Corps (RFC)

Founded in May 1912 by the end of the year it included 1 squadron of airships and 3 of aircraft, each consisting of 12 machines. However, with the appointment of Hugh Trenchard in August 1915 came many changes. He believed in putting many more planes over enemy territory, though lost many with their valuable crew, partly of course because the planes were not fast enough. Technological and structural improvements resulted in the building of thousands of planes so that by late 1918, now amalgamated with the Royal Navy Air Service to become the RAF, over 4000 aircraft were in operation employing over 100,000 personnel. The RAF came under the control of the new Air Ministry.

Sources: William Moxey — son
Amanda Moxey — granddaughter
The Times
Sheffield City Battalion by Ralph Gibson and Paul Oldfield
UXB Volume II by Jim Jenkinson for stories of RAF Bomb Disposals

Taylor Woodrow Developments
The Battle of Britain by Ed Bishop
Designed to Kill by A Hogben for a photo of Moxey's fuze extractor
The Malvernian Society
Tom Johnson
Fred Knox

Muhammad Abdulla MUHAMMAD, GC

Action during mutiny, 27th and 28th November 1924, Khartoum, Sudan

This photograph of three Sudanese GCs is a puzzle as no annotation has to date been found. The man in the middle is Jak Taha and the GCs at either end are Muhammad and Negib but I do not know which is which.
Courtesy of the Sudan Studies Centre

Status: Nafar, Khartoum Police Force
Life dates: – 23rd June 1978, Khartoum, Sudan
Biography: Note that the correct spelling is Muhammad with a U — from Jaafar Abdelhalim in Sudan.
Citation: *12th December 1924*
The KING has been graciously pleased to approve of the Award of the Medal of the Civil Division of the Most Excellent Order of the British Empire to the undermentioned: —
For Gallantry.

Sol Ibrahim Negib, Khartoum Police Force.

Shawish Jak Taha, Khartoum Police Force.

Nafar Mohammed Abdulla Mohammed, Khartoum Police Force.

Other awards: EGM (Civilian) – GC exchange. 1953 Coronation Medal and 1977 Queen's Silver Jubilee Medal. Muhammad may well have held other medals of which we are not aware.

The story

On 27th and 28th November 1924 two platoons of the 11th Sudanese Regiment mutinied and ran amok at Khartoum. Three British officers and two Syrian medical officers were killed by the mutineers and some nine other ranks were wounded. Nafar Muhammad Abdulla Muhammad and two other members of the Khartoum Police were recommended for great gallantry displayed during the disturbances.

Background: *Sudan in 2006*

Although the actions for which Muhammad was awarded the George Cross are now more than 80 years since it seems appropriate to write something about the country as it is now and there will be more in a later book in the series. It is not just a country of sand and ethnic cleansing with vicious rebels on horseback with swords or guns in their hands.

Safety — apart from the more remote western and southern areas where there is political instability the major towns and Khartoum in particular are safe for tourism though acquiring a visa is not simple.

BUT

Darfur — the desperate situation for hundreds of thousands of displaced people in this dry, dessicated land is one of the world's most intransigent problems. Without the political will of the Sudanese Government there does not seem to be a solution to the rape, killing, starvation and helplessness of the refugees.

YET

Historic sites abound in the north. The cuisine is wonderful and the markets colourful and have been operating for centuries.

Sources: *Sudan* by Paul Clammer
Shu Shu Wageialla
Sudan Studies Society of the United Kingdom based at Durham University

Michael Joseph MUNNELLY, GC

Self-sacrifice to save a friend, 24th December 1964, Regents Park Road, London

Status: Journalist for *The People*

Life dates: 17th April 1941, St Helens – 25th December 1964, Regent's Park, London.

Biography: Michael was the son of John and Theresa (Mulligan) Munnelly and he had at least one brother, James. His father was an Auxiliary Fireman in St Helen's AFS while working as a contracting plasterer.

Although based in Cardiff, Michael had come to London to spend Christmas with his brother.

Citation: *25th June 1965*
29th June 1965
The QUEEN has been graciously pleased to make the undermentioned award:-
GEORGE CROSS
Michael Joseph Munnelly (deceased), Journalist, London S.E.24.

Fourteen youths had been drinking at Kentish Town and had travelled in a van to Regent's Park Road to a flat where two of them had been invited. They were in an extremely rowdy mood shouting and swearing. The fourteen were refused entry to the flat and some of them immediately attacked the occupier. Others went to a dairy opposite and from crates left outside began to bombard the flat with milk bottles, resulting in all the windows being broken, also the window of the shop next door. Some of the youths were attacking the occupier of the flat, some were throwing dozens of bottles and all were shouting, swearing and milling about. Although there were several onlookers, it appears they were all too frightened to interfere.

In an endeavour to protect his property, the dairyman went into the street where he was immediately attacked by being butted, kicked and knifed in the groin. Michael Joseph Munnelly, his brother and a friend were the occupants of a third floor flat and hearing the noise of breaking glass and shouting, looked out of the window and saw the dairyman was on the ground being kicked. All three men decided they must go and help him and ran to the street. They detained two men but Munnelly was hit on the head by some person and released the man he was holding. The van, which had left the scene, then returned and was followed into the next turning by Munnelly's friend who in an attempt to stop the van banged on the side. The van stopped and he grabbed a youth who was sitting next to the driver.

This resulted in a cry for help, the rear door of the van opened and several of the youths attacked him until they had kicked him senseless. Munnelly immediately went to his rescue. Bottles were thrown at him, he was kicked and received a fatal stab wound in his lower left abdomen. The youths then fled. Munnelly and the others were mere onlookers who could have stayed in the safety of the flat but without thought for themselves they went to the assistance of the dairyman. Munnelly saw his friend being attacked with knives and immediately went to his rescue. Within a few minutes he was dead. He had given his life to save that of his friend.

Other awards: Awarded the Binney Memorial Medal in April 1965 which was presented to his family. Almost uniquely, Donald Smith also received this Medal. Michael is believed to be the only GC to have received this award.

©and courtesy Worshipful Company of Goldsmiths

156

The story

At about 12.30am on Christmas Day 1964 the gang tried to gatecrash a party and on being refused entry they hurled the milk bottles from the nearby dairy at the flat. The Citation for Donald Smith and William Griffiths is included as, although it is similar to that for Munnelly, it includes additional details of the story.

Citation for the George Medal to Smith and BEM to Griffiths

Awarded the George Medal:
Donald Smith, Writer, London N.W.I.
Awarded the British Empire Medal for Gallantry (Civil Division):
William Eirwyn Thomas Griffiths, Dairyman London N.W.I.

Fourteen youths had been drinking at Kentish Town and had travelled in a van to Regents Park Road to a flat where two of them had been invited. They were in an extremely rowdy mood shouting and swearing. The fourteen were refused entry to the flat and some of them immediately attacked the occupier. Others went to a dairy opposite, and from crates left outside, began to bombard the flat with milk bottles, resulting in all the windows being broken, also the window of the shop next door. Some of the youths were attacking the occupier of the flat, some were throwing dozens of bottles and all were shouting, swearing and milling about. Although there were several onlookers, it appears they were all too frightened to interfere. In an endeavour to protect his property, the dairyman, Mr. Griffiths, went into the street where he was immediately attacked by being butted, kicked and knifed in the groin. Mr. Smith and his friend were the occupants of a third floor flat and hearing the noise of breaking glass and shouting, looked out of the window and saw Mr. Griffiths was on the ground being kicked. Smith decided they must go and help him and ran to the street The van, which had left the scene, then returned and was followed into the next turning by Smith. In an attempt to stop the van, Smith banged on the side and the van stopped. He grabbed a youth who was sitting next to the driver. This resulted in a cry for help, the rear door of the van opened and several of the youths attacked Smith until they had kicked him senseless. Smith was a mere onlooker who could have stayed in the safety of his home, but without thought for himself went to the assistance of Griffiths who exposed himself to great danger in an attempt to prevent further trouble.

Further information

The Times and other newspapers carried the story and its consequences for many weeks.

Frederick Charles Bishop (18) was charged with the murder of Michael Munnelly and sentenced to life imprisonment. There were additional charges of having "in a public place an offensive weapon, a knife, without lawful authority and of wounding William Griffiths with intent to do him grievous bodily harm". Twelve other youths were remanded in custody being accused of "causing an affray", one of whom was the twin brother of Fred Bishop. The oldest was 21. The prosecution described the scene as "one man being killed, one gravely wounded, two others beaten up and a battlefield of broken bottles". Not to mention the mess from hundreds of pints of spilt milk.

It is mentioned in the Citation to Munnelly that he went to the aid of his friend while in fact he also went to the aid of a stranger, the dairyman. The dairy was called St George's Dairy.

Background: *The People*

This tabloid newspaper appears to have sunk somewhat in the quality of its articles being now mainly stories of TV soaps, gossip about little-known 'celebrities' and sport.

Binney Memorial Medal

Captain Ralph Binney CBE, RN acted in a way not dissimilar to Munnelly when he saw robbers in Birchin Lane in 1944 when he was 56 years old. He jumped on to the running-board of the get-away car but lost his foothold and ended up being dragged along under the car. He died soon after. Binney had had a distinguished Naval career as well as being a man of literary talents. The response to a suggestion that there be a memorial fund in his memory was eagerly taken up. The fund was to be administered by the Goldsmith's Company and a committee — comprising the Chief Metropolitan Stipendiary Magistrate, acting as Chairman, the Commissioners of the Metropolitan and City Police, the Chief of Fleet Support and the Clerk of the Goldsmith's Company — makes the awards of the Binney Memorial Medal and the lesser, Certificate of Merit, on an annual basis. The qualifications for the awards are precise and nominees who are not selected for the Medal, of which only one (very rarely two as in the case above) is awarded each year, are presented with certificates. It is thus extremely rare and is by definition often awarded posthumously. The Binney Memorial Medal was designed by Gilbert Bayes in 1948 and is made of bronze.

The Medal is awarded "*to the British citizen, not being a member of the police force or any other force maintaining order, who performs the bravest act in each year in support of law and order within the Metropolitan and City police areas*".

Sources: Worshipful Company of Goldsmiths   *This England* Summer 1985
Victor Knight in *Medal News*

Index

This Index DOES NOT include entries for all previous Volumes containing recipients from A–K due to the page constraint. However, a complete Index will appear in the final Volume. The number prefixes L & M refer to pages within this book. GCs are written in CAPS thus, MORRIS followed by the first names with no comma while all other people are listed conventionally, eg Greenway, Francis

Marion Hebblethwaite continues this series with further in-depth accounts of the George Cross recipients. She records with sensitivity and understanding the effects that extreme bravery may have on many people. The true stories are often shrouded in mystery through time, bureaucracy or sheer lack of information. She does not embellish for embellishment's sake. The years are passing and with them the lives of some of our senior GCs. These books are a fitting memorial to them all.

All previous books are available in limited editions of 500.
When complete the set will be available in a slipcase.